Big Data Analytics and Its Impact on Basin Water Agreements and International Water Law

International Water Law

Volumes published in this Brill Research Perspective are listed at *brill.com/rpwls*

Big Data Analytics and Its Impact on Basin Water Agreements and International Water Law

A Study of the Ramotswa Aquifer

By

Imad Antoine Ibrahim
Rafael Dean Brown
Jon Truby

BRILL

LEIDEN | BOSTON

Library Congress Control Number: 2021951481

Typeface for the Latin, Greek, and Cyrillic scripts: "Brill". See and download: brill.com/brill-typeface.

ISBN 978-90-04-50761-6 (paperback)
ISBN 978-90-04-50762-3 (e-book)

This book is printed on acid-free paper and produced in a sustainable manner.

Contents

Acknowledgments IX
Notes on Contributors X
Abstract 1
Keywords 1
Introduction 1
1 An Overview of Big Data Analytics from a Technical and Legal Perspective 9
1.1 *What Is Big Data and BDA?* 9
1.1.1 Defining Big Data and BDA 9
1.1.2 The Advent of BDA 11
1.1.3 BDA and the End of Theory 13
1.1.4 BDA in International Private Law and the Private Sphere 15
1.1.5 In Summary 16
1.2 *BDA in International Environmental Law and Environmental Governance* 17
1.2.1 Historical and Current Appraisal 17
1.2.2 Challenges Surrounding the Use of BDA in the Environmental Sphere 19
1.2.3 BDA and International Environmental Law 20
1.2.4 BDA in Transboundary Water Governance 23
1.3 *Legal Frameworks That May Play a Role* 25
1.3.1 International Space Law 25
1.3.2 International Climate Change Law 28
1.3.3 In Summary 32
1.4 *Open Water Data Law as a Framework* 32
1.4.1 Background 32
1.4.2 Open Data in the Water Sector 34
1.4.3 Open Data and the Law 36
1.4.4 Open Data and Water Law 39
1.4.5 In Summary 44
2 Case Study 44
2.1 *Project Description* 44
2.1.1 Shared Fresh Water in Southern Africa 45
2.1.2 The State of Transboundary Aquifers 47
2.1.3 The Importance of Transboundary Groundwater Data Sharing in Southern Africa 49

2.2 *Legal Framework Applicable to the Region* 51
2.2.1 The SADC Protocol 52
2.2.2 Other Important Documents 55
2.2.3 Shortcomings of the SADC Protocol 57
2.2.4 In Summary 58
2.3 *The Ramotswa Aquifer as a Case Study* 59
2.3.1 The Limpopo River Basin 59
2.3.2 The Aquifer 61
2.3.3 Legal and Institutional Developments in the Limpopo River Basin 62
2.3.4 Harmonizing National Laws of the Limpopo Basin Countries 65
2.3.5 The Application of BDA to the Ramotswa Aquifer 66
2.3.6 Improving the Legal and Institutional Governance of TBAS in the SADC Region 69
2.3.7 Improving the Legal and Institutional Governance of the Ramotswa Aquifer 70
3 Data and Information Exchange in IWL 71
3.1 *Data and Information Exchange in the Transboundary Water Context* 71
3.1.1 History of Water Information and Data Exchange 71
3.1.2 Importance of Data and Information Exchange 73
3.1.3 Factors and Obstacles Affecting Data and Information Exchange 76
3.2 *Data and Information Exchange within International Water Conventions and Instruments* 78
3.2.1 Regular Exchange of Data and Information 80
3.2.2 Notice of Natural and Human Triggered Emergencies 84
3.2.3 Notice of Planned Measures 87
3.3 *Data and Information Exchange within the SADC Revised Water Protocol* 91
3.3.1 Regular Exchange of Data and Information 92
3.3.2 Notification of Natural Emergencies and Those Caused by Human Activity 92
3.3.3 Notification of Planned Measures 93
4 Establishing an Open Data Regulation for the Ramotswa Aquifer 95
4.1 *Current Suggestions for Addressing Water and Information Exchange in the Ramotswa Aquifer* 95
4.2 *Effectiveness of Transboundary Water Agreements and Protocols* 98

4.3 *Addressing Data and Information Sharing between States in the Context of BDA and Other Emerging Disruptive Technologies* 101
4.4 *Practical Implementation in the Ramotswa Aquifer* 105
4.4.1 Data and Information Exchange Provisions within the SADC Protocol and Relevant Water Provisions 105
4.4.2 The Protocol or Protocols Must Consider Data and Information Exchange Provisions within the Draft Articles on the Law of Transboundary Aquifers 107
4.4.3 The Protocol or Protocols Must Include Provisions Replicating the Ones in the Open and Transparent Water Data Act and the Water Data Act 108
5 Implications of Establishing an Open Data Regulation on IWL 125
5.1 *Addressing Data and Information Sharing in the Context of BDA and Other Emerging Disruptive Technologies in the General Framework of IWL* 125
5.2 *Should IWL Replicate Provisions of the Transparent and Open Data Act and the Data Water Act?* 130
5.3 *Limitations of the Findings* 134
Conclusion 135
Bibliography 137

Acknowledgments

This monograph is an output of the Big Data and Transboundary Water Collaboration in Southern Africa initiative, https://tfcaportal.org/big-data-analytics-and-transboundary-water-collaboration-call-research-proposals. The Big Data Analytics and Transboundary Water Collaboration is jointly funded by USAID, the South African Department of Science and Technology, and the SADC Groundwater Management Institute, and managed primarily by the Water Research Commission, with technical support from the US Geological Survey and the IBM Research Africa Lab in South Africa. The initiative aims to address the consolidation of data and application of big data tools to enhance national and transboundary data sets in Southern Africa that support water resources security decision-making. The program explores how enhanced big data capabilities potentially can improve the robustness of data, analysis and decision-making of transboundary ground and surface water. The authors are conducting research related to the legal implications of big data in the transboundary water context in the framework of projects funded by the initiative. The authors are grateful to the Water Research Commission and Winrock International for their support and the provision of the documents and reports related to the project and initiative. The authors are especially grateful to Clara Bocchino and John Dini for their support. The authors would like to thank reviewers for their constructive comments and suggestions.

This publication was made possible by the NPRP award NPRP 11S-1119-170016 from the Qatar National Research Fund (a member of The Qatar Foundation). The statements made herein are solely the responsibility of the author.

Notes on Contributors

Imad Antoine Ibrahim
is a Research Assistant Professor at the Center for Law and Development, College of Law, Qatar University, Doha, Qatar and a Research Associate at gLAWcal – Global Law Initiative for Sustainable Development, Essex, United Kingdom. He has been working on global environmental issues and their interplay with other fields such as emerging technologies. He is currently involved in several projects related to natural resources management in South Africa, Middle East and North Africa region, Central Asia, and China.

Rafael Dean Brown
is a Clinical Assistant Professor at the College of Law, Qatar University, Doha, Qatar. He is Vice Chair of Faculty Affairs in the QU Faculty Senate, and an Affiliate Member of the Center for Law and Development. His research focuses on AI, cybersecurity, data protection, arbitration, and legal skills. He is licensed to practice law in Ohio, where he previously taught in the LLM Program at the School of Law, Case Western Reserve University. He has been teaching for over 15 years.

Jon Truby
is Associate Professor of Law and Director of the Centre for Law & Development at the College of Law, Qatar University, where he works on major research grants delivering solution in legal fields related to financial and technological innovation. A lawyer and legal academic, he specialises in law and policy related to digital and financial innovation, and the application of legal and fiscal tools in sustainable development policy. He joined Qatar University in 2010 from Newcastle Law School at Newcastle University, where he both taught and completed his doctorate in environmental taxation law. He is an avid publisher and is currently researching legal fields in blockchain, artificial intelligence, cybersecurity and financial technology. He recently spoke at the United Nations on Blockchain's energy consumption problem. He was Founding Editor-in-Chief of the *International Review of Law*.

Big Data Analytics and Its Impact on Basin Water Agreements and International Water Law: A Study of the Ramotswa Aquifer

Imad Antoine Ibrahim, Rafael Dean Brown and Jon Truby

Abstract

Big data analytics is transforming the water sector at the national and international levels. Its potential impact on transboundary water resource governance is being assessed, for example, in the context of selected basins, including the Ramotswa aquifer shared between South Africa and Botswana. However, international water law and transboundary water agreements have yet to address its emergence. This monograph examines the impact of big data analytics on transboundary water governance from a legal perspective, using the Ramotswa aquifer as a case study. The authors argue that several features of the California Open and Transparent Water Data Act of 2016 and the New Mexico Water Data Act of 2019 can be applied in the context of transboundary water agreements.

Keywords

big data analytics – open data – transboundary water agreements – transboundary water governance – Ramotswa aquifer – disruptive technology

Introduction

In the last decade, Big Data Analytics (BDA) has become a mainstream term that divides experts and scholars. Some see it as a new opportunity for gaining value from existing data that cannot be processed by humans, while others see it as a threat given the many risks that have been noticed when it is used.[1]

1 V. Mayer-Schönberger & K. Cukier, *Big Data: A Revolution That Will Transform How We Live, Work, and Think* (Boston: Houghton Mifflin Harcourt, 2013); J. J. Berman, *Principles of Big Data: Preparing, Sharing, and Analyzing Complex Information* (Walthham: Morgan Kaufman, 2013); M. Deng & L. Di, *'Building Open Environments to Meet Big Data Challenges in Earth Sciences'*, in H. A. Karimi (ed.), *Big Data: Techniques and Technologies in Geoinformatics* (Boca Raton: CRC, 2014) 69–90; A. E. Hassanien, *Machine Learning and Big Data Analytics*

 | DOI:10.1163/9789004507623_002

BDA is seen as a new means to support decision-making processes and provide further clarity and information on the basis of which decision-makers can draw policies and strategies.[2] Among the many definitions provided to the term, 'big data' can be described as any data related to extremely large sets that cannot be processed by a given user[3] requiring the use of sophisticated technologies and analysis to gain added value from it.[4] Examples of big data include the data being incorporated in the databases of social media sites. For instance, it is estimated that 500+ terabytes of new data is added to Facebook every day.[5] In that sense, BDA is being used to process big data. Many other definitions have been proposed for BDA, but the term remains poorly defined.[6] BDA has been applied in the public and private sphere, prompting public and private lawyers to address its impact.[7] Nonetheless, the literature on this topic from an international legal perspective is only emerging, especially in public international law.[8] This is the case as well for international environmental law and International Water Law (IWL) where very few studies have so far

Paradigms: Analysis (Dordrecht: Springer, 2021). The term emerged and developed over the several decades of the twentieth century. See B. Marr, *'A Brief History of Big Data Everyone Should Read'*, 25 February 2015, at https://www.weforum.org/agenda/2015/02/a-brief-history-of-big-data-everyone-should-read/, last accessed 14 June 2021.

2 Z. Milosevic et al., *'Real-Time Analytics'*, in R. Buyya, R. N. Calheiros & A. V. Dastjerdi (eds), *Big Data: Principles and Paradigms* (Cambridge: Morgan Kaufman, 2015) 53.

3 R. Olendorf & Y. Wang, *'Big Data in Libraries'*, in S. C. Suh & T. Anthony (eds), *Big Data and Visual Analytics* (Dordrecht: Springer, 2017) 191.

4 A. Weiss, *Big Data Shocks: An Introduction to Big Data for Librarians and Information Professionals* (London: Rowman & Littlefield Publishing Group, 2018) 27; D. Leslie et al., *Artificial Intelligence, Human Rights, Democracy, and the Rule of Law: A Primer* (The Council of Europe, 2021).

5 Guru 99, *'What is BIG DATA? Introduction, Types, Characteristics, Example'*, at https://www.guru99.com/what-is-big-data.html#1 last accessed 14 June 2021.

6 T. Pellegrin, *'Economics of Big Data: A Value Perspective on State of the Art and Future Trends'*, in R. Akerkar (ed.), *Big Data Computing* (Boca Raton: CRC Press, 2014) 345.

7 A. Završnik (ed.), *Big Data, Crime and Social Control* (Abingdon: Routledge, 2018); G. Peruginelli & S. Faro, *Knowledge of the Law in the Big Data Age* (Amersterdam: IOS Press, 2019); J. Cannataci, V. Falce & O. Pollicino (eds), *Legal Challenges of Big Data* (Cheltenham: Edward Elgar Publishing, 2020); V. Mak, *Legal Pluralism in European Contract Law* (Oxford: Oxford University Press, 2020).

8 S. Puig, J. Pauwelyn & W. Alschner, *'The Data-Driven Future of International Law'*, at https://www.ejiltalk.org/the-data-driven-future-of-international-law/, last accessed 20 January 2020; F. Johns & L. Grolman, *Big Data and International Law* (Oxford: Oxford University Press, 2019); G. Sarfaty, *'Can Big Data Revolutionize International Human Rights Law?'*, 39:1, University of Pennsylvania Journal of International Law (2017) 73–101.

addressed the impact of BDA on transboundary environmental issues such as shared water resources.[9]

BDA is one of the many disruptive technologies that have emerged recently. Others include Artificial Intelligence (AI), internet of things, blockchain, 3D printers, bioinformatics, medical innovations, and space colonisation.[10] The term disruptive technology falls in the general framework of the theory of 'disruptive innovation' coined in the 1990s by Clayton Christensen.[11] He used the theory to describe the emergence of new technologies that can reshape business models and form new markets where the above-mentioned technologies are a consequence of the digital disruptive revolution. Emerging technologies have a great potential in the development field,[12] especially in the natural resources sector where companies and governments are forced to rethink the entire governance and business models.[13] Disruptive technologies

9 See generally, J. Xu & H. Zhang, *'Environmental Activism and Big Data: Building Green Social Capital in China'*, 12: 8, Sustainability (2020) 3386; G. Beier, J. Kiefer & J. Knopf, *'Potentials of Big Data for Corporate Environmental Management: A Case Study from the German Automotive Industry'*, Journal of Industrial Ecology (2020) 1–14; I. A. Ibrahim, *'Legal Implications of the Use of Big Data in the Transboundary Water Context'*, 34, Water Resources Management (2020) 1139–1153; R. Lokers et al., *'Analysis of Big Data Technologies for Use in Agro-Environmental Science'*, 84 Environmental Modelling & Software (2016) 494–504.

10 E. Harris, *'9 Amazing Examples of Disruptive Technology (Inspired by the WTIA)'*, at https://www.resultist.com/blog/9-amazing-examples-of-disruptive-technology-inspired-by-the-wtia, last accessed 20 January 2020; D. Cag, *'11 Amazing Examples of Disruptive Technology'*, 4 September 2020, at https://richtopia.com/emerging-technologies/11-disruptive-technology-examples, last accessed 20 January 2020.

11 The term 'describes a process by which a product or service initially takes root in simple applications at the bottom of a market – typically by being less expensive and more accessible – and then relentlessly moves upmarket, eventually displacing established competitors'. Not all products are disruptive despite being a breakthrough as many unable to compete with existing technologies. See, The Christensen Institute, *'Disruptive Innovation'*, at https://www.christenseninstitute.org/disruptive-innovations/, last accessed 20 January 2020; C. M. Christensen, M. E. Raynor & R. McDonald, *'What Is Disruptive Innovation?'*, 2015, at https://hbr.org/2015/12/what-is-disruptive-innovation, last accessed 20 January 2020; C. M. Christensen et al., *'Disruptive Innovation: An Intellectual History and Directions for Future Research'*, 55:7, Journal of Management Studies (2018) 1043–1078.

12 S. Cairns, A. von Richthofen & A. Stokols, *Disruptive Technology for Development* (World Bank Group (WBG); Future Cities Laboratory (FCL), 25–27 June 2018) 7–8.

13 T. C. Ling, *'Disruptive Innovation and the Natural Resource Revolution'*, 7 June 2017, at https://www.lexology.com/library/detail.aspx?g=a8034b69-3c1d-4bb3-9ccb-950f947ff7e2, last accessed 20 January 2020.

such as AI and BDA are affecting the way natural resources such as oil, gas and water are produced and consumed.[14]

Disruptive technologies like BDA are changing the way information and knowledge can be accessed in every field, including the environmental field and environmental law. Already BDA is being used to 'process the large volumes of data collected by sensors and create visualizations of air quality from that data' and to improve migratory bird conservation.[15] Other examples include its potential for improving resource management, forecasting climate change problems and reducing carbon footprints.[16] As a result, governments are already looking at the potential use and regulation of BDA in the environmental field given its prospects of improving environmental management and sustainability through the push towards environmental friendly business models and structures.[17] Still, few articles and studies have addressed the impact of BDA on environmental law despite its recorded impact on the environment.[18] The impact of BDA on law in general has been addressed in the last decade and currently is being debated among legal scholars.[19]

In the water sector, innovation in the information technology field is being used to strengthen water supply and sanitation services. The ubiquity of constant data emerging from the installation of technologies, such as sensors that monitor activities, have resulted in an enhanced capacity to control daily operations and track potential incidents, such as leakage, to avoid trillions of gallons of water loss. The enhanced monitoring allows for quick repair and prevents the disruption of activities. Sensors can also measure water quality more

14 J. Woetzel et al., *'How Technology is Reshaping Supply and Demand for Natural Resources'*, 15 February 2017, at https://www.mckinsey.com/business-functions/sustainability/our-insights/how-technology-is-reshaping-supply-and-demand-for-natural-resources, last accessed 20 January 2020; S. Andrews et al., *Reinventing Business Through Disruptive Technologies: Sector Trends and Investment Opportunities for Firms in Emerging Markets* (International Finance Corporation, World Bank, March 2019).

15 J. Tsui, *'Using Big Data Technology for Environmental Protection'*, 25 March 2020, at https://eponline.com/articles/2020/03/25/using-big-data-technology-for-environmental-protection.aspx, last accessed 14 June 2021.

16 R. Kh, *'Can Big Data Help Save The Environment?'*, at https://www.smartdatacollective.com/can-big-data-help-save-environment/, last accessed 14 June 2021.

17 F. Calza, A. Parmentola & I. Tutore, *'Big Data and Natural Environment. How Does Different Data Support Different Green Strategies?'*, 2: Sustainable Futures (2020) 100029; L. K. Breggin & J. Amsalem, *Big Data and Environmental Protection: An Initial Survey of Public and Private Initiatives* (Washington, DC: Environmental Law Institute, 2014).

18 Beier, Kiefer & Knopf, *supra* note 9, at 1–14.

19 See, for instance, R. Kitchin, *'New Epistemologies and Paradigm Shifts'*, Big Data & Society (2014) 1–12; G. Sivinski, A. Okuliar & L. Kjolbye, *'Is Big Data a Big Deal? A Competition Law Approach to Big Data'*, 13:2/3, European Competition Journal (2017) 199–227.

rapidly than lab tests, while users can be notified of water pollution incidents immediately, preventing health crises as a result. Using in-situ measurements, water quantity and quality currently is being collected in remote and inaccessible places, which is then sent to central control points. This data is converted and used for various purposes such as warning or flood forecasting systems. The combination of field-based data and satellite data, as well as images and historic data, also support the management of water resources. This strategy is being used at the basin level and in the transboundary context.[20] These are just some examples of the benefits of disruptive technologies in the water sector.

The emergence of disruptive technologies affecting all types of sectors in the water industry led to calls for new ways to manage water resources, mainly through Smart Water Management (SWM).[21] SWM is defined as 'the use of integrated, real-time information and communication technology solutions – such as sensors, monitors, geographic information systems and satellite mapping, and other data-sharing tools – in water management'.[22] In other words, it is a technology driven innovative strategy to address the economic, social, and environmental challenges in diverse locations, while enhancing the use and management of water resources.[23] The main fields in the water sector where SWM already has been applied are 'efficient water and wastewater management by industries and utilities in urban contexts at regional or city scales'.[24] SWM has also been applied on a small scale, for instance in the universities of Pumagua, Unam, Mexico City[25] as well as in big cities such as the Greater Paris region.[26]

20 C. Leb, *'Data Innovations for Transboundary Freshwater Resources Management: Are Obligations Related to Information Exchange Still Needed?'*, 4:4, International Water Law (2020) 3–78, 3–6.

21 N. S. Grigg, *'Smart Water Management: Can It Improve Accessibility and Affordability of Water for Everyone?'*, 45:6, Water International (2020) 608–620, 608; K. Hartley & G. Kuecker, *'The Moral Hazards of Smart Water Management'*, 45:6 Water International (2020) 693–701, 693.

22 S. Kuisma et al., *'The Report that Sparked this Special Issue'*, 45:6, Water International (2020) 520–525, 520.

23 *Id.*, at 521.

24 H. Bjornlund et al., *'Institutional Innovation and Smart Water Management Technologies in Small-Scale Irrigation Schemes in Southern Africa'*, 45:6, Water International (2020) 621–650, 621.

25 F. G. Villarreal et al., *'SWM Technology for Efficient Water Management in Universities: The Case of PUMAGUA, UNAM, Mexico City'*, 45:6, Water International (2020) 526–551, 526.

26 J. P. Tabuchi, B. Blanchet & V. Rocher, *'Integrated Smart Water Management of the Sanitation System of the Greater Paris Region'*, 45:6, Water International (2020) 574–603, 574; P. F. Moniz et al., *'A GIS-Based Solution for Urban Water Management'*, 45:6, Water International (2020) 660–677, 660.

This reality has led to targeted investments by international organisations and agencies attempting to use disruptive technologies for improving and enhancing transboundary water management, such as in Southern Africa,[27] as transboundary water resources data include various types of data, is voluminous and has great velocity.[28] The experimental use of AI and BDA in the Southern African transboundary water context is particularly driven by its heavy reliance on surface and groundwater resources for agriculture and mining.[29] The Big Data Analytics and Transboundary Water Collaboration in Southern Africa Initiative is one of these investments.[30] The Initiative's main objective is to 'address the consolidation of data and application of big data tools to enhance national and transboundary data sets in Southern Africa that support water resources security decision-making'.[31]

Several projects have been conducted in the context of this Initiative,[32] including the Ramotswa aquifer shared between South Africa and Botswana, where a pilot project was carried out by both countries. The project was considered to be in an ideal location, with AI techniques having the potential to improve the existing databases for enhancing water management and policy.[33] The project is seeking to 'apply big data tools to enhance national and

27 A. Gemmell et al., *'Big Data Analytics and Transboundary Water Collaboration: Theme 1: Consolidation of Data and Application of Big Data Tools to Enhance National and Transboundary Data Sets in Southern Africa that Support Decision-Making for Security of Water; Resources'* (Deliverable 1: Inception Report 4; Version 1.1; UMVOTO Africa (Pty) Ltd, 28 March 2019).

28 *Id.*, at 9.

29 C. Bocchino & K. Adkisson, *'Using Big Data Analytics for Transboundary Water Management'*, 28 July 2020, at https://www.preventionweb.net/news/view/72968, last accessed 20 January 2020.

30 Gemmell et al., *supra* note 27, at 15. The Initiative is funded by the 'United States Agency for International Development (USAID), the South African Department of Science and Technology (DST), and the SADC Groundwater Management Institute (GMI), managed primarily by the Water Research Commission (WRC), and with technical support from the US Geological Survey (USGS) and the IBM Research Africa Lab in South Africa'.

31 *Id.*, at 4.

32 K. Pietersen, T. Kanyerere & G. J. Wanangwa, *Big Data Analytics and Modelling: Localising Transboundary Data Sets in Southern Africa: A Case Study Approach. Deliverable 2a: Workshop with Key Stakeholders to Understand the Status Quo* (Report to the Water Research Commission, WRC Project 2878, September 2019) 6.

33 T. Chiwewe & C. Bocchino, *'AI Pilot to Address Transboundary Water Challenges in Southern Africa Launches'*, 11 November 2019, at https://www.ibm.com/blogs/research/2019/11/ai-pilot-to-address-transboundary-water-challenges/, last accessed 20 January 2020; C. Bocchino, *'Exploring Big Data Solutions for Southern Africa (USAID from the American People)'*, at https://www.swpwater.org/exploring-big-data-solutions-for-southern-africa/, last accessed 20 January 2020.

transboundary datasets in Southern Africa that support water resources security decision-making'.[34] Topics such as 'data standardization, data availability, and data sharing between countries that share water resources, and the application of big data analytics to the resulting data sets' are being examined.[35] The Ramotswa aquifer suffers from numerous water governance problems due to increasing population, urbanisation, water pollution, and economic growth.[36] Governance is further worsened by climate change.[37] The use of BDA in this context aims to ensure the sustainable management of groundwater resources.[38]

In a previous article, Ibrahim highlighted from a theoretical perspective the legal implications of the use of BDA in the transboundary water context.[39] He stated that BDA is most likely going to cause new legal challenges to nations sharing freshwater resources, identifying four scenarios: (1) all nations decide to use BDA; (2) some states choose to use BDA; (3) only one country makes use of BDA; and (4) no parties use BDA. He then suggested the need to include new provisions addressing big data within IWL and within transboundary water agreements.[40] This monograph takes this argument further by providing a detailed analysis of the practical impact of BDA on transboundary water resources, and by applying BDA to the Ramotswa aquifer shared between South Africa and Botswana.

Several provisions of the California Open and Transparent Water Data Act of 2016[41] and the New Mexico Water Data Act of 2019[42] can apply in the

34 International Groundwater Resources Assessment Center (IGRAC), *'Big Data for Groundwater Management'*, at https://www.un-igrac.org/special-project/big-data-groundwater-management, last accessed 20 January 2020.

35 Bocchino & Adkisson, *supra* note 29.

36 G. J. Nijsten et al., *'Transboundary Aquifers of Africa: Review of the Current State of Knowledge and Progress Towards Sustainable Development and Management'*, 20, Journal of Hydrology: Regional Studies (2018) 21–34.

37 B. M. McGill et al., *'Complex Interactions between Climate Change, Sanitation, and Groundwater Quality: A Case Study from Ramotswa, Botswana'*, 27, Hydrogeology Journal (2019) 997–1015.

38 Z. Gaffoor et al., *'Big Data Analytics and Its Role to Support Groundwater Management in the Southern African Development Community'*, 12:10, Water (2020) 2796, 2797.

39 Ibrahim, *supra* note 9, at 1139–1153.

40 *Id.*

41 State of California, Assembly Bill No. 1755; Chapter 506: An act to add Part 4.9 (commencing with Section 12400) to Division 6 of the Water Code, relating to water data. [Approved by Governor September 23, 2016. Filed with Secretary of State September 23, 2016.] Legislative Counsel's Digest. AB 1755, Dodd [Open and Transparent Water Data Act].

42 State of New Mexico, House Bill 651; 54th Legislature, First Session, 2019; Introduced by Melanie A. Stansbury and Gail Armstrong and Antoinette Sedillo Lopez [House Bill 651].

transboundary water context. 'Open' in this context refers to 'information collected, produced or paid for by the public bodies and made freely available for re-use for any purpose'.[43] To prove this claim, the Ramotswa aquifer was selected as a case study to highlight the practical implementation of the suggestion made, given that both Botswana and South Africa are seeking to establish a protocol on groundwater data sharing. Such a protocol must consider data and information exchange provisions within the Revised Southern African Development Community (SADC) protocol, other relevant water provisions, and data and information exchange provisions within the International Law Commission (ILC) Draft Articles on the Law of Transboundary Aquifers. This monograph then examines specific provisions within the Open and Transparent Water Data Act and the Water Data Act that can be replicated. Adoption of four measures are proposed: (1) developing an integrated water data platform within transboundary water agreements, in this case the future protocol between South Africa and Botswana on groundwater data sharing in the Ramotswa aquifer; (2) integrating existing water and ecological data information from multiple databases; (3) developing protocols and standards for data sharing further to the planned; and (4) financing the operations through a 'water data administration fund' or a 'water data account'. After noting the application of some of the provisions of the Open and Transparent Water Data Act and the Water Data Act to transboundary water agreements, the discussion here turns to the application of specific provisions to IWL. A model provision to be included within IWL is proposed while considering the provisions of this global regulatory framework. This model provision can either be included within existing instruments that have not yet become water conventions through amendment, within new international water agreements or as a follow-up to existing water conventions.

Section 1.1 of this monograph introduces the concept of BDA, its development and role within international law. Section 1.2 focuses on the interplay between BDA and international environmental law and governance as well as transboundary water governance. Section 1.3 examines regulatory frameworks that were suggested for the regulation of BDA in the transboundary water context, including international space law and international climate change law. Section 1.4 discusses national open data laws, mainly the California Open and Transparent Water Data Act and the New Mexico Water Data Act. Sections 2.1 and 2.2, provide an overview of the shared water resources in Southern Africa

---

43 Data.Europe.eu, *'What is Open Data'*, at https://data.europa.eu/en/trening/what-open-data, last accessed 14 June 2021.

and the legal framework applicable to the region, mainly the revised SADC[44] Protocol. Section 2.3 examines a selected as a case study, the Ramotswa aquifer, in the general context of the legal and institutional developments in the Limpopo river basin. Section 3 provides an overview of data and information exchange in the transboundary water context, within international water conventions and instruments and within the SADC Water Protocol. Section 4 examines how to establish a data and information exchange regulation for the Ramotswa aquifer, while Section 5 investigates the implications of establishing such a regulation on IWL.

It is worth noting that the legal analysis here focuses on the application of water law to BDA and not to big data. Rather, big data is used to highlight the need for BDA or to push for the use of open data and the inclusion of specific open data provisions in legislation to provide a solution to legal dilemmas.

1 An Overview of Big Data Analytics from a Technical and Legal Perspective

1.1 *What Is Big Data and BDA?*

This section provides a brief overview of big data and BDA that have affected public and private international law where it has been discussed mainly only within international private law.[45] Yet, the impact of BDA on public law is emerging with scholars debating the best regulatory approach.

1.1.1 Defining Big Data and BDA

Numerous studies have attempted to define and provide an explanation of the concept of big data. Adamala defined it as a 'term used to describe data that is high volume, velocity, and variety; requires new technologies and techniques to capture, store, and analyse it; and is used to enhance decision making, provide insight and discovery, and support and optimize processes'.[46] In simple terms, big data 'refers to large sets of complex data, both structured and unstructured,

44 Revised Protocol on Shared Watercourses in the Southern African Development Community, 7 August 2000, at https://www.sadc.int/files/3413/6698/6218/Revised_Protocol_on_Shared_Watercourses_-_2000_-_English.pdf, last accessed 14 June 2021.

45 See, for instance, M. Ebers & S. Navas (eds), *Algorithms and Law* (Cambridge: Cambridge University Press, 2020); M. C. Compagnucci, *Big Data, Databases and "Ownership" Rights in the Cloud* (Dordrecht: Springer, 2020); V. Mak, E. T. T. Tai & A. Berlee (eds) *Research Handbook in Data Science and Law* (Cheltenham: Edward Elgar Publishing, 2018).

46 S. Adamala, *'An Overview of Big Data Applications in Water Resources Engineering'*, 2:1, Machine Learning Research (2017) 10–18, 9.

that traditional processing techniques and algorithms are unable to operate on'.[47] Another explanation is that it aims at gathering 'enough details about the past, apply the right analytical tools, [such that] you can find unexpected connections and correlations, which can help you make unusually accurate predictions about the future'.[48]

Big data is described as 'a collection of data that is so large that it exceeds one's capacity to process it in an acceptable amount of time with available tools'.[49] In the context of the big data initiative, big data has been defined as a 'term applied to data sets whose size or type is beyond the ability of traditional relational databases to capture, manage, and process the data with low-latency (lag). And it has one or more of the following characteristics – high volume, high velocity, or high variety'.[50]

In contrast, BDA is defined as the 'process of collecting, organizing, analyzing large data sets to discover different patterns and other useful information'. It represents a 'set of technologies and techniques that require new forms of integration to disclose large hidden values from large datasets that are different from the usual ones, more complex, and of a large enormous scale'.[51] A more detailed description of this term considers BDA as

> the complex process of analysing and developing innovative platforms of applications that provides benefits in handling large and varied data streams, often referred to as big data, with the objective of uncovering the information contained in the data streams that might otherwise be invisible yet carrying valuable insights that could help organizations make informed business decisions. The information carried include hidden patterns, unknown correlations, market trends, customer preferences and any other information that could be useful for decision making. It uses advanced analytical tools that include, structured query language

47 L. Ndlhovu et al., *Imagining Solutions for Extracting Further Value from Existing Datasets on Surface and Groundwater Resources in Southern Africa: Deliverable 2 – Collection of Existing Surface and Groundwater Analytical Data and Conducting Preliminary Data Analytics* (Water Research Commission, July 2019) 9.

48 J. Lerman, *'Big Data and Its Exclusions'*, 66: Stanford Law Review Online (2013) 55–63, 57.

49 S. Fahey, *'The Democratization of Big Data'*, 7, Journal of National Security Law & Policy (2014) 325–331, 325.

50 Gemmell et al., *supra* note 27, at 9.

51 Y. Riahi & S. Riahi, *'Big Data and Big Data Analytics: Concepts, Types and Technologies'*, 5:9, International Journal of Research and Engineering (2018) 524–528, 525.

(SQL), not only SQL (NoSQL), data mining, statistical analysis, data visualisation, artificial intelligence and natural language processing.[52]

The definitions adopted despite their importance do not include all the characteristics related to BDA, which are constantly evolving.[53] For the purpose of this monograph, this text will use the definition adopted in the context of the big data initiative to describe BDA, given the focus of this study on addressing the use of BDA to the management of the Ramotswa aquifer. In this context, it is worth mentioning that beyond big data and BDA, the term 'open data' is also used here to refer to data 'free to use, re-use or redistribute, subject at most to measures that preserve provenance and openness'.[54]

1.1.2 The Advent of BDA

Big data is considered as the new oil. Like oil, data is a valuable element that society relies and can also have negative consequences requiring comprehensive regulation.[55] It is almost impossible not to read a new article or headline on a daily basis discussing the big data revolution and how it is reshaping aspects of modern life ranging from medicine to national security. Legal debates between proponents and opponents have only started with opponents warning of 'potential government abuses of civil liberties, erosion of long-held privacy norms, and even environmental damage'.[56] For instance, there are concerns that the personal privacy of individuals can be breached through big data, potentially resulting in 'unwanted personal disclosures, identity theft, and discrimination in contexts such as employment, housing, and financial services'.[57]

Data has very little value without analysis, which turns such data into new information through the use of a combination of tools, mainly advanced techniques of data science and traditional tools. This data-based information is vital for decision-making, which is why access to data and information

52 Z. Gaffoor et al., *Big Data Analytics and Modelling: Localising Transboundary Data Sets in Southern Africa: A Case Study Approach: Deliverable 1: Project Scoping and Overview Report* (Report to the Water Research Commission; WRC Project No 2878); Pietersen, Kanyerere & Wanangwa, *supra* note 32, at 1.

53 Gemmell et al., *supra* note 27, at 9.

54 World Bank, *'Open Data Essentials'*, at http://opendatatoolkit.worldbank.org/en/essentials.html, last accessed 14 June 2021.

55 D. D. Hirsch & J. H. King, *'Big Data Sustainability: An Environmental Management Systems Analogy'*, 72:3 Washington and Lee Law Review Online (2016) 406–419, 407–408.

56 Lerman, *supra* note 48, at 55–56.

57 A. L. Allen, *'Protecting One's Own Privacy in a Big Data Economy'*, 130, Harvard Law Review (2016) 71–78, 71–72.

has become a valuable and strategic asset.[58] This reality can be seen with the 'number of acquisitions of data sources and the prices paid for them, the vast investments in data gathering, and in the creation of better machine-learning tools'.[59] The scale of the data collected and analysed is fairly new in contrast to the challenge of finding new methods for the analysis of large datasets, which has been ongoing for the last century. Data processing was initiated by 1890 in the United States (US) with the decennial census being completed in one year following the invention of the electric tabulating machine and the introduction of large-scale data processing. State practice in collecting and analysing data further evolved during World War II through code breaking and target tracking computers, while the Cold War and commercial interests pushed for the development of high-performance computers. New companies emerged in the 1990s and 2000s because of the internet, such as Google, Amazon, Yahoo and Facebook. These tech companies collect and analyse data on a massive scale, basing and driving their business models and strategies on the use of data to understand consumer behaviour. The scale of data processing needed led to the emergence of BDA.[60]

The emergence of BDA created a new opportunity for all sectors of the economy as the data collected in sectors such as engineering, health and robotics can be processed in an efficient manner, leading to new outcomes that have important values. The term 'big' in this context not only reflects the amount of data, but also that this data is very complex and compiled from various sources. BDA has a few metrics, namely, volume (data is being collected every second from a wide range of sources); variety (data acquired can have a wide range of properties due to current technologies); veracity (the accuracy and integrity of data and its sources is very important if one wants to have a value after processing it); velocity (data collection, management and processing is being done at a very rapid speed), and value (data has to make sense after the entire process so that it can be used for decision-making purposes).[61]

Other characteristics are added depending on the definition provided. Those are verification and value, where information professionals are positioned to

---

58 D. L. Rubinfeld & M. S. Gal, *'Access Barriers to Big Data'*, 59, Arizona Law Review (2017) 339–381, 342.

59 *Id.*, at 343.

60 Fahey, *supra* note 49, at 326–327; T. Widmer, *'How the Census Changed America'*, 1 May 2019, at https://www.newyorker.com/culture/culture-desk/how-the-census-changed-america, last accessed 14 June 2021.

61 Y. Nuapia et al., *Imagining Solutions for Extracting Further Value from Existing Datasets on Surface and Groundwater Resources in Southern Africa: Deliverable 1 – Project Approach and Workplan* (Water Research Commission, Project No. K5/2881, February 2019) 1.

determine which data is useful and has value. Value is the most important characteristic given that it is challenging to determine, track, and use the data; and it is risky and expensive as such activities require substantial investments that may not yield results. Still, BDA represents a big opportunity for industries and governments,[62] as it may lead to more informed decision-making resulting in more efficient decisions.[63] Governments, international institutions, corporations, consultancies and Non-Governmental Organisations (NGOs) have identified barriers that are currently preventing the full deployment of BDA.[64] These barriers include, *inter alia*, 'financial constraints and lacking a business case for the environment; lack of skills and training; lack of equality; the nature of conservation and cultural legacies and confidentiality, security, and disclosure'.[65] To tackle these barriers, the same stakeholders mentioned the following solutions: 'partnerships; demonstrating powerful examples and healthy competition; personalising the environment; emerging and accessible technology and emerging sources of funding for innovation'.[66] Still, this debate is in its infancy and requires further development and studies to address all the topics and matters associated with BDA.

1.1.3 BDA and the End of Theory

The literature is full of articles examining the role of BDA in global governance in fields such as privacy, administrative law, constitutional law and human rights.[67] Legal scholars are realising the regulatory risks associated with the use of BDA in global governance and are seeking to address these risks.[68] Data protection requires a different broader approach given the current use of

62 A. Affelt, *'Big Data, Big Opportunity'*, 21:2, Australian Law Librarian (2013) 78, 78–85.

63 Rubinfeld & Gal, *supra* note 58, at 347.

64 A. Keeso, *'Big Data and Environmental Sustainability: A Conversation Starter'* (Smith School Working Paper Series No 14–04, December 2014) 17.

65 *Id.*, at 18–20. On the issue of professionalizing programmers to ensure bias training is included their education, see the Agency for Digital Italy, *'Artificial Intelligence at the Service of Citizens'*, https://ia.italia.it/assets/whitepaper.pdf, last accessed 14 June 2021.

66 Keeso, *supra* note 64, at 22–24.

67 F. Johns, *'The Turn to Data Analytics and International Law'*, 3:4, ESIL Reflections (2014) 1–7, 2; Council of Europe, Recommendation CM/Rec(2020)1 of the Committee of Ministers to Member States on the human rights impacts of algorithmic systems (Adopted by the Committee of Ministers on 8 April 2020 at the 1373rd meeting of the Ministers' Deputies), https://www.coe.int/en/web/freedom-expression/committee-of-ministers-adopted-texts/-/asset publisher/aDXmrolovvsU/content/recommendation-cm-rec-2020-1-of-the-committee-of-ministers-to-member-states-on-the-human-rights-impacts-of-algorithmic-systems?_101_INSTANCE_aDXmrolovvsU_viewMode=view/, last accessed 14 June 2021.

68 *Id.*, at 5.

algorithms and data-intensive technologies.[69] The main concern is that algorithmic regulations are the future on which decisions concerning individuals and society will be made by software based on a multitude of variables that are incomprehensible for humans and even experts.[70] This potential future led its advocates, especially technology writers, to declare the 'end of theory'.[71] One of the assumptions made as a result of the rise of BDA is that theory is no longer needed to make decisions as the basis of policies will be applied using mathematical and statistical techniques on the basis of algorithms. In that sense, it would be possible to 'engineer mistakes and errors out of decision-making, and usher in a form of omniscience and rationality in legal decision-making'.[72] Yet, this assumption has been criticised as flawed.[73]

Claims are being made that the combination of computers, algorithms and BDA will provide outcomes that are more accurate and useful than specialists relying on hypotheses, models and theories.[74] This is because the aim of BDA is ensuring objectivity through evidence-based law as new rules and legal decisions will be adopted on the basis of an analysis of past and current data, making decisions and legal reasoning more objective and scientific. In fact, BDA has already affected law firms by providing them with the means for predicting costs and outcomes, among other things. For instance, data analytics can highlight patterns of courts activity and even judicial decisions. It can also provide information about the experience of the opposing counsel. BDA has affected

---

69 A. Mantelero, *'AI and Big Data: A Blueprint for a Human Rights, Social and Ethical Impact Assessment'*, 34:4, Computer Law & Security Review (2018) 754–772, 754; J. Truby & R. Brown, *'Human Digital Thought Clones: The Holy Grail of Artificial Intelligence for Big Data, Information & Communications Technology Law'*, 30:2, Information and Communications Technology Law (2020) 140–168.

70 J. Truby, *'Governing Artificial Intelligence to Benefit the UN Sustainable Development Goals'*, 28:4, Sustainable Development (2020) 946–959.

71 S. Grafanaki, *'Autonomy Challenges in the Age of Big Data'*, 27:4, Fordham Intellectual Property, Media & Entertainment Law Journal (2017) 803–868, 805. The term 'algorithmic regulations' refers to 'standard-setting, monitoring and behaviour modification by means of computational algorithms'. They may be self-executing where 'standard-setting integrates with behaviour modification' or may 'provide decisional support or advice, based on predictive algorithms that basically infer standards to better monitor, predict and influence behaviour'. M. Hildebrandt, *'Algorithmic Regulation and the Rule of Law'*, 376: Philosophical Transactions of the Royal Society A (2018) 1–11.

72 C. Devins et al., *'The Law and Big Data'*, 27:2, Cornell Journal of Law and Public Policy (2017) 357413, 362–364.

73 *Id.*, at 363.

74 *Id.*, at 365.

different legal fields, such as financial regulation and criminal law.[75] Yet, the assumption that BDA is objective and can predict precisely the outcomes has been criticised, especially when applied in the context of the legal system. In that sense, there is a need to interpret data that requires theory and human judgment. Moreover, BDA cannot consider the non-algorithmic evolution of the legal system and suffer from limitations in predictive power.[76] In fact, it has been stated that BDA is subjective and incomplete, as theory is needed to interpret the data to make sense of the correlations.[77] This is yet another discussion that is taking place and one which certainly will affect water law when BDA is applied. The use of BDA depends on the approach chosen concerning the role of BDA in drawing policies and the role of theory in the same context.

1.1.4 BDA in International Private Law and the Private Sphere

Discussions concerning the challenges and opportunities for the use of BDA in the private sphere have been ongoing for a few years,[78] where such data is being generated by humans, machines or a human-machine combination, from any place 'where any information is generated and stored in structured or unstructured formats' such as industry, the military, and the internet.[79] BDA has limitations in the private sphere. It is expected that the behaviour of individuals will change once they figure out how data is being collected and used. In fact, there are concerns related to the protection of the privacy of individuals, problems affecting consumers potentially resulting in exclusion or discrimination, while consumers also may change their conduct.[80] BDA will affect individual autonomy, especially given the rapid developments occurring that affects the lives of citizens, their work and daily interactions.[81] For instance, citizen medical data are being analysed along with medical history

75 *Id.*, at 365–371; R. Conley, *'How Data Analysis is Disrupting the Legal Industry'*, 20 March 2019, at https://www.biggerlawfirm.com/how-data-analysis-is-disrupting-the-legal-industry/ last accessed 14 June 2021.

76 Council of Europe, Declaration by the Committee of Ministers on the manipulative capabilities of algorithmic processes (Adopted by the Committee of Ministers on 13 February 2019 at the 1337th meeting of the Ministers' Deputies). at https://search.coe.int/cm/pages/result_details.aspx?ObjectId=090000168092dd4b, last accessed 14 June 2021.

77 Devins et al., *supra* note 72, at 371–372.

78 Cannataci, Falce & Pollicino, *supra* note 7; B. L. Garrett, *'Big Data and Due Process'*, 99, Cornell Law Review Online (2014) 101–110.

79 M. Ghotkar & P. Rokde, *'Big Data: How it is Generated and its Importance'*, IOSR Journal of Computer Engineering (2016) 1–5, 2.

80 Rubinfeld & Gal, *supra* note 58, at 348–349; Truby & Brown, *supra* note 69, at 140–168.

81 Grafanaki, *supra* note 71, at 810–814.

to facilitate the tracking of diseases and to assess a treatment's efficacy. This work can also occur through data and information analysis applications on a phone or wearable device.[82] The more information technologies are available to the population, the more challenges to privacy and autonomy are witnessed.[83] Access of companies and governments to such information technology and data about an individual could create more problems. Companies are using this information to affect human behaviour, especially to encourage the consumer to make further purchases. Access to data on individuals by governments can lead to an Orwellian nightmare in the form of thought police where people's ideas are surveyed online affecting individual autonomy and self-determination. As a result, people may change their behaviour to conform, while at the same time feeling vulnerable and powerless.[84] Barocas and Selbst noted that BDA has the potential of discriminating against populations, especially vulnerable ones, depending for instance on the type of data fed to the algorithms.[85] These were some of the concerns mentioned. Further analysis on the impact of BDA in the private sphere is beyond the scope of this monograph. Yet, it is important to acknowledge that the legal developments taking place in the private sphere may be replicated in the context of public international law. These developments may affect the private use of water resources, for instance in the context of water distribution and allocation in a smart city, or in the identification of water consumption patterns, especially through smart water metering systems.[86]

1.1.5 In Summary

The potential use of BDA for changing the world led to debates about its possible impact on policies,[87] and resulted in the emergence of numerous books, articles and studies discussing all the aspects related to it,[88] and whether

---

82 Michigan Tech, *'Eight Ways Big Data Affects Your Personal Life'*, 30 April 2020, https://onlinedegrees.mtu.edu/news/ways-big-data-affects-your-personal-life, last accessed 14 June 2021.

83 Grafanaki, *supra* note 71, at 810–814.

84 *Id.*, at 820–825.

85 S. Barocas & A. D. Selbst, *'Big Data's Disparate Impact'*, 104:3, California Law Review (2016) 671–732.

86 A. Y. Sun & B. R. Scanlon, *'How Can Big Data and Machine Learning Benefit Environment and Water Management: A Survey of Methods, Applications, and Future Directions'*, 14, Environmental Research Letters (2019).

87 S. Williams, *'More Than Data: Working with Big Data for Civics'*, 11:1, I/S: A Journal of Law and Policy (2015) 181–199, 182–183.

88 M. C. Caldarola & J. Schrey, *Big Data and Law* (Oxford: Beck/Hart, 2020); B. Mäihäniemi, *Competition Law and Big Data: Imposing Access to Information in Digital Markets*

it is considered the greatest innovation or the greatest danger of this era.[89] The coverage of BDA can be characterised as being optimistic and dystopian simultaneously given its great potential, but also its great risks.[90]

1.2 *BDA in International Environmental Law and Environmental Governance*

This section examines the use of BDA in the environmental field from a historical perspective, and environmental law's response to such use. It analyses the existing challenges, the response of international environmental law and the application of big data to transboundary water resources.

1.2.1 Historical and Current Appraisal

The emergence of big data took place after decades of technological breakthroughs. The 1960s and 1970s witnessed great advances in analytical techniques and detection capabilities affecting, among others, environmental regulation. For instance, the developments in analytical techniques and detection capabilities resulted in finding substances such as chemical residues in food, water and air, as well as other existing living tissues, at 'far lower concentration than was possible in previous decades'.[91] Between the 1980s to the 2010s, models and simulation tools for environmental decision-making were developed. The period from the 2010s to 2030s is considered as the age of BDA due to the significant developments occurring in data science and information technology, which led to the creation of the new buzzword 'big data' as a cornerstone of environmental regulation.[92]

Environmental law since the 1970s has been based on risk assessment with the focus on the adoption of environmental regulations based on acceptable risks. The main objective is the identification and reduction of risks to a point deemed acceptable.[93] This approach seemed very sophisticated and complex at the time as it was based on 'a range of extrapolative techniques and models, which included within them various default assumptions and inference choices intended to deal with data limits and gaps to manage uncertainty'.[94]

(Cheltenham: Edward Elgar Publishing, 2020); M. C. Corrales, M. Fenwick & M. Forgó, *New Technology, Big Data and the Law* (Dordrecht: Springer, 2017).

89 Devins et al., *supra* note 72, at 358.

90 K. E. C. Levy, *'Relational Big Data'*, 66, Stanford Law Review Online (2013) 73–79, 73.

91 W. Boyd, *'Environmental Law, Big Data, and the Torrent of Singularities'*, 64, UCLA Law Review Discourse (2016) 544–570, 549–551.

92 *Id.*

93 *Id.*, at 558.

94 *Id.*, at 559.

Shortcomings to this approach arose in the 2000s, especially concerning knowledge delivery, regulatory relevance, and the emergence of new and complex environmental harms. The main problem was uncertainty, which affected the decision-making process as the process of determining the relevance of a risk and its potential for causing environmental harm was very challenging while the outcome was uncertain. By 2010, it was clear that this approach needed to be changed.[95] BDA promised a 'more experience-based approach to environmental decision-making' where data is the cornerstone providing the capacity to identify environmental harm and reducing the amount of resources needed to do so through a risk-based approach.[96]

International organisations such as the United Nations (UN) see BDA as a new means for the realisation of the common good and the Sustainable Development Goals (SDGs).[97] The importance of BDA for sustainable development led the UN to appoint an Independent Expert Advisory Group on a Data Revolution for Sustainable Development to examine how BDA can help realise the SDGs. A report adopted in 2014 highlighted how policy-makers can benefit from the BDA revolution.[98] For instance, according to the report, the 'clean and affordable energy goal can be achieved by reducing waste thanks to electricity, gas and water consumption data collected by smart sensors'.[99] BDA is perceived as a new solution to meet environmental challenges that involves big tech industries and the private sector. BDA allows the government to understand what needs to be done to realise sustainable development, to adopt policies, to monitor them for reaching this objective, and to provide transparency and accountability. The importance of such data stems from it being generated daily from various sources and activities. In this regard, the digital universe has grown at a rapid pace since 2005.[100]

BDA will shift the knowledge practices of environmental law in the coming decades, which will have important implications.[101] For instance, environmental law is already facing questions related to the responsibility for protecting against certain environmental damage related to BDA. The developments of

95 *Id.*, at 559–560.

96 *Id.*, at 560.

97 C. Lajaunie, B. Schafer & P. Mazzega, *'Big Data Enters Environmental Law'*, 8:3, Transnational Environmental Law (2019) 523–545, 523–524; Truby, *supra* note 70, at 946–959; United Nations, *'Big Data for Sustainable Development'*, at https://www.un.org/en/sections/issues-depth/big-data-sustainable-development/ last accessed 20 January 2020.

98 F. Lucivero, *'Big Data, Big Waste? A Reflection on the Environmental Sustainability of Big Data Initiatives'*, 26, Social and Engineering Ethics (2020) 1009–1030, 1009.

99 *Id.*, at 1010.

100 *Id.*, at 1012.

101 Boyd, *supra* note 91, at 547.

BDA has led mainly to the 'unprecedented ability to track sources, concentrations, and receptors (human and environmental) over time and space using geographic information technologies, ubiquitous sensing for individual and ecological exposure assessment, cheap and widespread biomonitoring of individuals to assess actual exposures, and data analytics capabilities for linking and evaluating source-exposure and exposure disease relationships'.[102] The realisation of the expected positive effects of the use of BDA in environmental law will take some time.[103]

1.2.2 Challenges Surrounding the Use of BDA in the Environmental Sphere

Despite governments acknowledging the impact of BDA, mainly in providing visibility to environmental injustices, little consideration has been paid to ethical issues. With the constant development of personal and environmental data that is available to everyone, incentives to encourage citizens to provide data became a source of profit, and also created the basis for new groups and political agendas. BDA also provided an opportunity for the use of citizen science to provide support for communities suffering from environmental injustice.[104] Citizens within local communities or in general collecting environmental data, which is then sent to competent authorities, fill information gaps while offering 'early warning of environmental issues and problems, and data and information on problems not adequately covered by monitoring networks'.[105]

BDA also affected the concepts of accountability and expertise in administrative law due to the 'explosion of new facts and the proliferation of new modes of fact-making', further reducing the role of experts, judgements, reason and deliberation. In fact, this trend was occurring before the advent of BDA and in all legal fields associated with the risk assessment methods in the 1970s and the computational methods in the 1980s and 1990s affecting the individual expert judgements and the notion of expertise.[106] The replacement of the technocratic process by expert systems and algorithms raised concerns regarding transparency and accountability. In that sense, who exactly would be held accountable when BDA and algorithms no longer can be evaluated

102 *Id.*, at 551.

103 *Id.*, at 553.

104 *Id.*, at 562–564.

105 National Advisory Council for Environmental Policy and Technology, *Information to Action: Strengthening EPA Citizen Science Partnerships for Environmental Protection* (EPA 220-R-18-001, April 2018) 7.

106 Boyd, *supra* note 91, at 565.

by regulators and scientists and how would the courts look at these cases? A paradox was created as, on one hand, BDA is supposed to solve environmental injustice by reducing uncertainties.[107] For instance, data mining of social media posts concerning pollution and health gathered proof of environmental injustices and raised public awareness, which has provided much needed support for environmental activism.[108] At the same time, its power is in the hands of algorithms that in theory are supposed to be objective, yet in practice, there are various concerns related to their objectivity given the recorded bias from their use, in particular the bias suffered by marginalised groups.[109]

Moreover, there is a need to be careful as to how BDA is an unchecked use, which may lead to conflicts with legal principles and social values. Such use should only be agreed upon after collective political and ethical debates.[110] For instance, debates constantly arise regarding 'fairness', where the legal system continuously attempts to interpret rules while balancing normative and contextual aspects when making fair laws and judgments. Even then, there are conflicting and evolving concepts of fairness over time. Resolving conflicting interpretations is a messy process, as is resolving conflicting values such as equality and freedom that occur through a legitimate process rather than violence. Allowing BDA to influence this process is recipe for disaster given the many considerations that are not taken into account in the data analysis.[111] It is in this context that Devins et al. argued that big data has the potential to 'lull the legal system into accepting opaque, undemocratic decision-making far removed from the value-laden debates that should animate a free society'.[112]

1.2.3 BDA and International Environmental Law

BDA is at the stage of entering environmental law and affecting its development as innovations based on data are being used to tackle global environmental

---

107 *Id.*, at 566.

108 A. Mah, *'Environmental Justice in the Age of Big Data: Challenging Toxic Blind Spots of Voice, Speed, and Expertise'*, 3:2, Environmental Sociology (2017) 122–133, 123.

109 Boyd, *supra* note 91, at 566; AI Myths, *'AI Can Be Objective/Unbiased'*, at https://www.aimyths.org/ai-can-be-objective-or-unbiased, last accessed 14 June 2021; N. Byrnes, *'Why We Should Expect Algorithms to Be Biased'*, 24 June 2016, at https://www.technologyreview.com/2016/06/24/159118/why-we-should-expect-algorithms-to-be-biased/, last accessed 14 June 2021.

110 Lajaunie, Schafer & Mazzega, *supra* note 97, at 541; M. Carabantes, *'Black-Box Artificial Intelligence: An Epistemological and Critical Analysis'*, 35, AI & Society (2019) 309–317.

111 Devins et al., *supra* note 72, at 387–388; H. Giebler & W. Merkel, *'Freedom and Equality in Democracies: There is No Trade-off!'*, 22 February 2018, at https://socialeurope.eu/freedom-equality-democracies-no-trade-off, last accessed 14 June 2021.

112 *Id.*, at 413.

challenges, including climate change, natural disasters, water, energy and food security.[113] According to Lajaunie, Burkhard and Mazzega, 'the mining of massive data sets makes it possible to undertake concrete actions dedicated to the elaboration, production, implementation, follow-up, and adaptation of the environmental targets defined at various levels of decision making (from the international to the subnational level)'.[114] BDAs may enhance the effectiveness of international environmental law especially as the UN Environment Programme (UNEP) called for the use of numbers in tracking the effectiveness of international environmental agreements as 'there is no coherent set of quantified goals, targets and indicators that unfold and measure progress toward environmental sustainability or sustainable development'.[115] UNEP has also called for the use of evidence-based science to measure progress in reaching environmental goals and developed platforms providing information on the progress made towards reaching environmental goals and SDGs.[116]

BDA questions the legal epistemology when it comes to new forms of regulations. In that sense, science is crucial to environmental law, which is partly built on environmental sciences. In theory, environmental science should provide the basis for the content of environmental law, help identify violations of the rules, and support implementation as science is integrated into law. In practice, such integration is often not well assessed and is limited to experts. Climate change is an exception to this rule to the extent that science is used to determine limits of global warming through the various studies providing the necessary basis for drafting climate change binding and nonbinding instruments. BDA supports the scientific process and allows the understanding of this process transformation into legal knowledge.[117]

In this context, the application of BDA and AI in the building of legal targets and evaluating indicators related to environmental challenges and sustainable development is being analysed. Accurate up-to-date data allow the adoption of policies affecting the environment and tackling the existing challenges.[118] Scientific knowledge is built upon accurate data needed for the adoption of environmental goals and targets, which then would be transformed into legal objectives. This can only occur through the combined efforts of various disciplines, including law, social science and environmental science. Data in this

113 Lajaunie, Schafer & Mazzega, *supra* note 97, at 523–524.

114 *Id.*, at 523.

115 *Id.*, at 524.

116 *Id.*

117 *Id.*, at 525; G. T. Farmer & J. Cook, *Climate Change Science: A Modern Synthesis* (Dordrecht: Springer, 2013).

118 Lajaunie, Schafer & Mazzega, *supra* note 97, at 528.

context is very important for environmental lawyers and researchers given the constant changes in the environment to which legal norms apply and where changes need to be considered in the decision-making process.

In fact, legal researchers should play an important role in helping understand the regulation of BDA when it is used in the environmental context. Here, the use of BDA could benefit from the scientific knowledge and data used by decision-makers in the development of environmental policies and targets. This can only be possible by staying engaged and getting informed about the progress being made in science while adopting an integrative understanding of existing connections.[119] The importance of legal researchers stems from the fact that environmental targets are not only based on science and data, but are also political targets that may be vague or unquantifiable, which means unachievable, while accountability cannot be determined. Still, technological innovations can provide much-needed help by building SMART indicators to figure out political interactions.[120] Examples include input indicators measuring the amount of resources being spent on drafting policies (e.g., money, staff) and output indicators measuring the efficiency of the policies generated.[121] These indicators are used in politics to either highlight the need for change or the soundness of adopted policies, especially as some of these indicators show citizens' perceptions.[122]

BDA has a role to play in understanding the architecture of international environmental law and its evolution, as well as contributing to the development of novel environmental law.[123] BDA and AI can be used to 'anticipate how regulation and scientific knowledge will be integrated and interact in the normative complex system constituted by environmental law'.[124] BDA is crucial to the 'understanding of socio-environmental evolutions, the multi-scale and refined knowledge of the open system constituted by "environmental law" (from global to local levels), or the adaptation of this system to environmental

119 *Id.*, at 530–531.

120 *Id.*, at 531–532.

121 A. Schumann, *Using Outcome Indicators to Improve Policies: Methods, Design Strategies and Implementation* (Paris: OECD Regional Development Working Papers 2016/02) 1.

122 R. Kitchin, T. P. Lauriault & G. McArdle, *'Smart Cities and the Politics of Urban Data'*, in S. Marvin, A. Luque-Ayala & C. McFarlane (eds), *Smart Urbanism: Utopian Vision or False Dawn?* (Abingdon: Routledge, 2016) 26; M. Aladalah, Y. Cheung & V. C. S. Lee, *'Towards a Model for Engaging Citizens via Gov2.0 to Meet Evolving Public Value'*, in Information Resources Management Association (ed.), *Civic Engagement and Politics: Concepts, Methodologies, Tools, and Applications* (Hershey: IGI Global, 2019) 286.

123 Lajaunie, Schafer & Mazzega, *supra* note 97, at 534.

124 *Id.*, at 534–535.

changes'.[125] For instance, the US Environmental Protection Agency developed an application entitled 'How's My Waterway?' that 'pulls information from the database of water quality assessments submitted biennially by each state under the Clean Water Act' providing information such as 'whether the water has been assessed for pollution; the assessment findings, if any; and work performed to preserve or restore water quality'.[126] The current model of regulations and case law are not appropriate for dealing with the rapidly-changing challenges and knowledge that we are currently experiencing.[127]

1.2.4 BDA in Transboundary Water Governance

The sustainable management of freshwater resources requires the use of data and information to meet long-term needs such as planning, the development of policies and infrastructure at the national level and in the transboundary context. Data and information are also collected for short- and medium-term decision-making purposes, mainly monitoring water resources[128] for operation of infrastructure assets, for example.

Transboundary water resource data can be classified as 'big data' when it meets the criteria of variety, volume, and velocity. There is variety because data is collected on a 'diverse set of parameters, across different temporal and spatial scales; data types that provide integrated information can be diverse, from point-samples to satellite imagery; and data can come from disciplines ranging from hydrological to social sciences, as well as institutions/entities'.[129] The data is voluminous because it can be 'collected from hundreds or thousands of locations, with long and high resolution time-series; the advent of easily accessible open-source satellite imagery can lead to large volumes of data collated; and the potential for citizen science to contribute data will ideally lead to large volumes of additional data'.[130] Finally, the data has velocity because 'telemetry allows for remote collection of data being transmitted from sensors in the field in near real-time'.[131] Several articles have highlighted how BDA is being used for water management and protection, contributing to the development of policies for the governance of transboundary freshwaters and avoiding conflicts.[132] For instance, Leb highlighted the role of satellites in enhancing transparency

125 *Id.*, at 537.
126 Breggin & Amsalem, *supra* note 17, at 9.
127 Lajaunie, Schafer & Mazzega, *supra* note 97, at 538.
128 Leb (2020), *supra* note 20, at 10.
129 Gemmell et al., *supra* note 27, at 9.
130 *Id.*
131 *Id.*
132 Ndlhovu et al., *supra* note 47, at 9.

and in the production of new datasets and sources, based on which countries sharing water resources can acquire information.[133]

BDA techniques used in water resources management can be grouped into four main types:

1. Descriptive: Explains what has happened in the past based on data presented in graphics and reports, but not why it happened and what might happen in the future.
2. Diagnostic: Based on descriptive analytics, seeks to understand the reasons why any given event took place in the past.
3. Predictive: Uses past data to model future outcome and predict what could happen.
4. Prescriptive: Uses optimisation to advise on how best to manage a system to obtain a desired result.[134]

Machine learning, statistics and visualisation are among the techniques that can be used 'to consolidate transboundary water data and to apply data science approaches to enhance national and transboundary data sets that support water resources security decision-making'.[135]

Water experts and municipal officers have different views concerning the use of BDA and AI in the water sector. One concern is the potential for job losses because of technological developments, while others have noted how complicated these technologies are and the need for mathematical understanding. In contrast, others are highly interested in these technologies and have requested training. All the stakeholders supported the potential of citizen science in complementing existing data, indicating that citizen science should be used as a proxy in the absence of traditional data, although there is a need to verify it as it may contain biases.[136] Moreover, there are concerns over political interference as community involvement may be seen negatively by authorities afraid of causing public panic, especially if such involvement is done by activists. There are also fears over the potential dependence on AI and ignoring the human aspect and natural intelligence. Overall, there is a consensus that human expertise in the water sector would not be replaced by AI and BDA.[137]

133 Leb (2020), *supra* note 20, at 5–20.

134 Ndlhovu et al., *supra* note 47, at 10.

135 *Id.*, at 10–11.

136 *Id.*, at 1–18.

137 Y. Nuapia et al., *Imagining Solutions for Extracting Further Value from Existing Datasets on Surface and Groundwater Resources in Southern Africa: Deliverable 3 – Citizen Science and Advanced Data Analytics* (Water Research Commission, Project No. K5/2881, October 2019) 26–27.

A successful application of BDA in transboundary water governance, according to the South African Water Research Commission (WRC) reports, requires consideration of the following factors:

- Data need to be consistent in terms of spatial and temporal resolution.
- Missing data are likely to occur and appropriate methodologies need to be applied for data patching.
- Realistic limits and constraints need to be set in order to make optimal use of existing data and information (e.g., omit monitoring points that have too little data; set realistic periods of groundwater level response to rainfall events).[138]

So far, there is limited use of disruptive technologies such as BDA in the transboundary water context, which is why numerous questions around its usefulness remain unanswered.[139] For instance, what if each or some of the parties sharing a water resource refuse to acknowledge the results emerging from the use of BDA because it negatively affects water sharing? How can the bias within BDA be addressed, especially by providing all the available data to be processed? What if states do not possess the technological capabilities to implement BDA to improve transboundary water management?[140]

1.3 *Legal Frameworks That May Play a Role*

Keeping in mind the objective of addressing the use of BDA in the transboundary water context through the lens of IWL, this section will point to relevant provisions in other specific global regulatory frameworks. These regulatory frameworks are international space law and international climate change law. The relevance of these frameworks in the context of BDA for environmental management will be highlighted. The role of IWL in the context of data and information exchange will be examined in subsequent sections.

1.3.1 International Space Law

Some developed countries have open data policies that make the information used by policy-makers completely available to the public or limit its restriction. International and regional organisations, such as the World Meteorological Organization (WMO), provide information tools that are based on data generated and provided by their member states. Such information originates mainly

138 Z. Gaffoor et al., *Big Data Analytics and Modelling: Localising Transboundary Data Sets in Southern Africa: A Case Study Approach Deliverable 5: A Comparative Tool for Inventory Datasets* (Report to the Water Research Commission, February 2020) 25.

139 Lcb (2020), *supra* note 20, at 7.

140 Ibrahim, *supra* note 9, at 1139–1153.

from satellite surveillance, which is constantly increasing due to technological advancements and private satellite providers operations.[141] The legal basis for satellite data collection and observation is space law treaties, in particular the Outer Space Treaty,[142] that have been established by the UN since the 1960s, as well as other legal instruments,[143] such as UN Resolution 41/65 on 'Principles Relating to Remote Sensing of the Earth from Outer Space'.[144]

In fact, it is the increasing use of satellites for earth observation that led the UN to clarify the principles in existing space treaties in Resolution 41/65.[145] The Resolution stated that remote sensing should benefit all the countries with a particular focus on the needs of developing countries. The interests and rights of the sensed state must be protected with the sensed state having a right of access to the data collected from its territory on a 'non-discriminatory cost basis and on reasonable cost terms' with consideration of the particular needs and interests of developing countries.[146]

The Resolution also calls for international cooperation and the establishment of data collection, processing and storage facilities, the provision of technical assistance and ensuring the availability of any information, especially to countries that may be affected by the data. It also calls for the promotion of environmental protection and disaster risk reduction through remote sensing. In that sense, this Resolution provides broader freedoms for the sensing states while considering the interests of the sensed states. These freedoms have been criticised by those concerned with the rights of the sensed states as 'data collection does not require prior consent, notification of or consultation with the observed state, there are no geographic limits for data collection and there are no limits for spatial resolution'.[147]

Indeed, states and private entities owning satellites may now have information related to a basin while not being located on that basin. The sensing state must provide data to the sensed state under the space law provision of the 'right to gain access to this information based on non-discriminatory cost basis

141 Leb (2020), *supra* note 20, at 27.

142 Treaty on Principles Governing the Activities of States in the Exploration and Use of Outer Space, including the Moon and Other Celestial Bodies, New York, 27 January 1967, in force 10 October 1967, at https://www.unoosa.org/oosa/en/ourwork/spacelaw/treaties/introouterspacetreaty.html, last accessed 14 June 2021.

143 Leb (2020), *supra* note 20, at 27–30.

144 United Nations General Assembly (UNGA), Resolution 41/65 Principles relating to remote sensing of the earth from outer space, adopted 3 December 1986.

145 *Id.*

146 *Id.*; Leb (2020), *supra* note 20, at 30–31.

147 Leb (2020), *supra* note 20, at 31.

and on reasonable cost terms'.[148] These rights and obligations may change due diligence standards for states sharing fresh water. Earth observation systems are an additional data source that is only available to the sensing state. Where the data are not made public, the sensed state has the right to obtain it. Where it is made public, it should be used on the basis of the principle of equitable and reasonable utilisation and as part of the due diligence obligation to prevent significant harm.[149]

Satellites, through the data collected, can monitor a transboundary basin in the absence of data and information exchange, which is particularly useful for Transboundary Aquifers (TBAs). This has been the case in places like the Middle East, where satellites have measured groundwater depletion. According to Leb, riparian states will continue to benefit and need to exchange data and information on transboundary watercourses. However, data exchange requirements change with availability of satellite data, which can substitute for some datasets that previously had to be exchanged between riparian countries. The data provided by satellites can be used to motivate countries to cooperate, especially when it shows the negative consequences of non-cooperation, such as in the context of TBAs.[150]

Already BDA is seen as an opportunity to better understand space data as various space agencies are using it to rapidly process their data and more efficiently make decisions.[151] This has led to the emergence of a new term, 'space big data', which describes 'large amounts of data generated through or distributed by means of space technology'. These data include earth observation and remote sensing images, as well as information gathered or transmitted by satellite connectivity.[152] This has led to various studies and conferences addressing BDA from space[153] as big data from space has resulted in new legal challenges and the 'need for further developments of standards and interoperable interfaces between the growing number of platforms hosting multi-petabyte

148 *Id.*, at 6869; Resolution 41/65, *supra* note 144, at Principle XII.

149 *Id.*, at 69.

150 *Id.*, at 70.

151 A. Kirkovska, *'Big Data and Its Impact in the Space Sector, One Bit at a Time: Why is Big Data Important for Space Exploration?'*, 14 September 2018, at https://medium.com/spacedecentral/big-data-and-its-impact-in-the-space-sector-one-bit-at-a-time-1e2d378ad4cc, last accessed 14 June 2021.

152 D. Stefoudi, *'Space Big Data: Big Data Troubles in the Final Frontier'*, 16 June 2017, at https://leidenlawblog.nl/articles/space-big-data-big-data-troubles-in-the-final-frontier, last accessed 14 June 2021.

153 European Space Agency, *'Conference on Big Data from Space – BiDS'17'*, 28–30 November 2017, at https://earth.esa.int/web/guest/events/all-events/-/article/conference-on-big-data-from-space-bids-17, last accessed 14 June 2021.

scale data co-located with processing capabilities'.[154] The legal challenges include data privacy and protection, cybersecurity, and intellectual property rights.[155] There are also questions related to state sovereignty as states need to protect the assets within their territories from the eyes of the world.[156] Hence, there is a need for using both international public and private law, in addition to legal mechanisms that are in between, to address these new legal challenges.[157]

Investments in space big data are emerging given the existing opportunities, mainly from the private sector such as SpaceX, but more importantly by companies tackling environmental issues, such as farming and agriculture.[158] Government agencies are also investing in this field. For instance, NASA is looking to create a 'community-driven and supported GIS-based big data analytics platform' as is the Joint Research Centre of the European Commission.[159] As such, the use of BDA to process space data has great potential for improving environmental governance and management.

1.3.2 International Climate Change Law

International climate change law has addressed the topic of data in the framework of transboundary water management,[160] as water resources and climate change are directly interconnected.[161] Climate change is expected to affect

154 P. Soille, S. Loekken & S. Albani, *'Preface'*, in P. Soille, S. Loekken & S. Albani (eds), *Proceedings of the 2019 Conference on Big Data from Space (BiDS'19): Turning Data into Insights* (Munich: Joint Research Centre, 19–21 February 2019) ii.

155 Stefoudi, *supra* note 152.

156 I. Emanuilov, *'From Space Big Data to Big Space Brother: Do States Have a Right to Privacy? (Part I)'*, 23 July 2019, https://www.law.kuleuven.be/citip/blog/from-space-big-data-to-big-space-brother-do-states-have-a-right-to-privacy-part-i/, last accessed 14 June 2021.

157 P. R. Borges de Carvalho, *'Transnational Space Law in the 21st Century: What Laws Govern Data in Outer Space?'*, 3 October 2020, https://tclf.in/2020/10/03/transnational-space-law-in-the-21st-century-what-laws-govern-data-in-outer-space/, last accessed 14 June 2021.

158 A. Wooden, *'Space Data: The Final Analytics Frontier'*, https://www.intel.co.uk/content/www/uk/en/it-management/cloud-analytic-hub/big-data-from-satellites.html, last accessed 14 June 2021.

159 T. Huang, *'A Web of Data Analytics Services'*, in P. Soille, S. Loekken & S. Albani (eds), *Proceedings of the 2019 Conference on Big Data from Space (BiDS'19): Turning Data into Insights* (Munich: Joint Research Centre, 19–21 February 2019) 37; J. Tan & B. Osborne, *'Analysis of Big Data from Space'*, XLII:2/W7, The International Archives of the Photogrammetry, Remote Sensing and Spatial Information Sciences (2017) 1367–1371.

160 Leb (2020), *supra* note 20, at 31.

161 A. Baba et al. (eds), *Climate Change and its Effects on Water Resources: Issues of National and Global Security* (Dordrecht: Springer, 2011); UNESCO, *Water and Climate Dialogue: Adapting to Climate Change: Why We Need Broader and 'Out-of-the-Box' Approaches* (UNESCO World Water Assessment Programme, 2011).

water quality, quantity and timing of availability. This will require specific actions and solutions including 'supplementing natural supplies; using more climate-resilient technologies and processes to provide water of sufficient quality for drinking and ecosystem protection; upgrading water treatment systems; and creating further storage capacity to be able to cope with greater microbial, turbidity and chemical load'.[162]

Climate change law has addressed this topic. Article 4(1)(g) of the United Nations Framework Convention on Climate Change (UNFCCC) states that all parties shall

> [p]romote and cooperate in scientific, technological, technical, socio-economic and other research, systematic observation and development of data archives related to the climate system and intended to further the understanding and to reduce or eliminate the remaining uncertainties regarding the causes, effects, magnitude and timing of climate change and the economic and social consequences of various response strategies.[163]

Article 5 states that in carrying out their commitments under Article 4 (1)(g) parties shall:

(a) Support and further develop, as appropriate, international and intergovernmental programmes and networks or organizations aimed at defining, conducting, assessing and financing research, data collection and systematic observation, taking into account the need to minimize duplication of effort;
(b) Support international and intergovernmental efforts to strengthen systematic observation and national scientific and technical research capacities and capabilities, particularly in developing countries, and to promote access to, and the exchange of, data and analyses thereof obtained from areas beyond national jurisdiction; and
(c) Take into account the particular concerns and needs of developing countries and cooperate in improving their endogenous capacities and capabilities to participate in the efforts referred to in subparagraphs (a) and (b) above.

---

162 A. Rieu-Clarke et al., *Transboundary Water Governance and Climate Change Adaptation: International Law, Policy Guidelines and Best Practice Application* (Paris: United Nations Educational, Scientific and Cultural Organization, 2015) 36.

163 United Nations Framework Convention on Climate Change, New York, 9 May 1992, 1771 UNTS 107.

These commitments have been included also in the Paris Agreement, which bases the effective response to climate change on scientific knowledge. The reiteration of similar obligations can be found in Article 7 of the Agreement which 'calls on states to strengthen scientific knowledge, including through systematic observation and early warning systems that support decision-making' and 'calls on UN specialized organizations and agencies to support the states in these efforts'.[164] Still, it is worth mentioning that water is not mentioned in the Paris Agreement.[165]

International climate change law has led to the emergence of a network of different actors such as intergovernmental organisations that state that data is also important for effective transboundary water cooperation, not only climate change.[166] Still, this does not mean there are no obstacles to data sharing despite the provisions mentioned above.[167] Provisions within other global regulatory frameworks, such as intellectual property rights, limit the exchange of climate data collected through earth observation,[168] and may be relevant for water data and management.

Studies concerning the impact of BDA directly or indirectly on climate change are emerging in the context of issues like climate change adaptation and mitigation,[169] climate resilience, and in other sectors that are connected to climate change, such as agriculture, cleaner production, sustainable cities and communities, water, and biodiversity.[170] Moreover, using BDA for climate change research has intensified in recent years given the opportunities to tackle all aspects of climate change.[171] In 2014, the UN Big Data Climate Challenge was established to 'bring forward data-driven evidence of the economic dimensions

164 Leb (2020), *supra* note 20, at 32.

165 C. Leb, *'General Obligation to Cooperate and Regular Exchange of Data and Information (Articles 8 and 9)'*, in L. B. de Chazournes et al. (eds), *The UN Convention on the Law of the Non-navigational Uses of International Watercourses: A Commentary* (Oxford: Oxford University Press, 2018) 139.

166 Leb (2020), *supra* note 20, at 32.

167 M. W. Carroll, *'Intellectual Property and Related Rights in Climate Data'*, in J. D. Sarnoff (ed.), *Research Handbook on Intellectual Property and Climate Change* (Cheltenham: Edward Elgar Publishing, 2016) 384–398.

168 F. Lyall, *'Climate Change and Space Law'*, in R. G. Rayfuse & S. V. Scott (eds), *International Law in the Era of Climate Change* (Cheltenham: Edward Elgar Publishing, 2012) 184.

169 J. D. Ford et al., *'Opinion: Big Data has Big Potential for Applications to Climate Change Adaptation'*, 113:39, PNAS (2016) 10729–10732.

170 V. Sebestyén, T. Czvetkó & J. Abonyi, *'The Applicability of Big Data in Climate Change Research: The Importance of System of Systems Thinking'*, 9, Frontiers in Environmental Science (2021) 1–26.

171 H. D. Guo, L. Zhang & L. W. Zhu, *'Earth Observation Big Data for Climate Change Research'*, 6:2, Advances in Climate Change Research (2015) 108–117.

of climate change'.[172] In this sense, BDA presents an opportunity to bring to climate science novel data, methods, and evaluation tools.[173]

Still, there are challenges facing its implementation in practice that should not be underestimated. For instance, when it comes to climate data, there are questions over 'sampling bias, autocorrelation, and causal inferences in predictive model'.[174] It is in this context that the UN has been conducting research, organising conferences and issuing calls for innovation challenges related to the impact of BDA on climate change.[175] It has been argued for instance that 'a Big Data architecture can provide all the necessary mechanisms to achieve a transparent flexible and continuous mitigation global market reducing costs and increasing cash flows, transparency and stabilizing in the markets'.[176] Given these developments, one may wonder how future climate change agreements and instruments will address these questions given that BDA is expected to be used for new climate action tools, products and markets.[177] Already, a consortium of agencies supporting implementation of knowledge elements have developed tools for processing big data and big data related to climate change,[178] which is also useful for transboundary water management.

172 United Nations Global Pulse, *'Big Data Climate Challenge, Climate Summit'*, 2014, at https://www.unglobalpulse.org/challenges-hackathons/big-data-climate-challenge-2014/, last accessed 14 June 2021.

173 J. H. Faghmous & V. Kumar, *'A Big Data Guide to Understanding Climate Change: The Case for Theory-Guided Data Science'*, 2:3, Big Data (2014) 155–163.

174 M. I. Espinoza & M. Aronczyk, *'Big Data for Climate Action or Climate Action for Big Data?'*, 8:1, Big Data & Society (2021) 1–15, 4.

175 United Nations, Climate Change, *'Climate Change Data Using Satellites, AI and Big Data: A Multi-Stakeholder Perspective'*, 1 December 2020, at https://unfccc.int/about-us/partnerships/climate-change-data-using-satellites-ai-and-big-data-a-multi-stakeholder-perspective, last accessed 14 June 2021 ; United Nations, Climate Change, *'Data for Climate Invites Researchers to Catalyze Data-Driven Climate Solutions'*, 14 March 2017, at https://unfccc.int/news/data-climate-invites-researchers-catalyze-data-driven-climate-solutions, last accessed 14 June 2021.

176 United Nations Framework Convention on Climate Change, *'Internship Assignment, Sustainable Development Mechanisms (SDM) Programme Regulatory Implementation Unit'*, at https://unfccc.int/secretariat/employment/UserManagement/FileStorage/PN82J3XY5SBKE6HVGOUAWQIR7LT109, last accessed 14 June 2021.

177 United Nations Framework Convention on Climate Change, *'Internship Assignment, Sustainable Development Mechanisms (SDM) Programme Blockchain – Regulatory Development Unit (RDU)'*, https://unfccc.int/secretariat/employment/UserManagement/FileStorage/PR3ADBS05MF2N47CYQZXWJIUK86E1L, last accessed 14 June 2021.

178 See in general, H. Hassani, X. Huang & E. Silva, *'Big Data and Climate Change'*, 3:1, Big Data and Cognitive Computing (2019) 1–12; R. Biesbroek, S. Badloe & I. N. Athanasiadis, *'Machine Learning for Research on Climate Change Adaptation Policy Integration: An Exploratory UK Case Study'*, 20:85, Regional Environmental Change (2020) 1–13.

1.3.3 In Summary

The use of earth observation and data sharing through specific legal regimes that address climate change and outer space provides a huge of volume of information associated with transboundary water resources that directly facilitates the implementation of IWL. These legal regimes make 'basin-level data of hydrological, meteorological, geographic, hydrographic, ecological and other factors of natural character directly available to basin states'.[179] Hence, these legal regimes support the realisation of the principle of equitable and reasonable utilisation and could reduce the importance of the provisions related to data and information exchange among the states sharing fresh water given the availability of the abovementioned information.[180] The rules of these regimes applicable to climate change data or data collected via satellites affect directly or indirectly water resources as the new information generated through BDA can be used for transboundary water resources management.

1.4 *Open Water Data Law as a Framework*

1.4.1 Background

Generally, governments collect data, such as geospatial, for planning, decision-making and service provision purposes. Such data is not made available to the public with limited exceptions. With the emergence of the internet, many public data became available to citizens and the private sector.[181] The origin of open data is the Freedom of Information movement in the 1960s in the US. It is also part of the concept of government making all documents and services available online. The difference is that open data allows a variety of uses while e-government just provides citizens access to a broad range of information and services.[182]

The concept of open data is new, even though it already has been applied in the space field. For instance, satellite earth observation data are in many cases open and free. The term has many definitions depending on the authority defining it, be it the Open Data Institute, the European Union (EU) Open

179 Leb (2020), *supra* note 20, at 68.

180 *Id.*

181 R. E. Sieber & P. A. Johnson, *'Civic Open Data at a Crossroads: Dominant Models and Current Challenges'*, 32:3, Government Information Quarterly (2015) 308–315, 309–310.

182 *Id.*, at 308–312. E-government is 'the use of ICTs [information and communications technologies] to more effectively and efficiently deliver government services to citizens and businesses. It is the application of ICT in government operations, achieving public ends by digital means'. See United Nations, Department of Economic and Social Affairs, *'E-Government'*, https://publicadministration.un.org/egovkb/en-us/about/unegovdd-framework, last accessed 14 June 2021.

Data Portal, or the Open Knowledge Foundation.[183] Open data, according to the Open Knowledge Foundation, should be (1) freely available to the public, (2) re-purposable, (3) re-publishable, and (4) without control mechanisms like use licenses.[184] A key aspect of the definition is the reusability of data. There are three main reasons for the provision of open data sources by governments: '(1) increase democratic control and political participation; (2) foster services and product innovation, recognise the value of data for the development of new products and services in the knowledge economy; and (3) strengthen law enforcement'.[185]

Several types of open data exist. The first is when a government acts as a platform providing online data portals supplying data that others use. The second is when a government acts as an activist by offering the possibility for technical experts such as entrepreneurs, the private sector and civil society organisations to exploit the data and create a benefit. The third type is when citizens provide data to governments by reporting, for instance on problems and crises resulting in policies taking advantage of citizen knowledge of their environment to respond to a problem. Sometimes citizen data are more accurate than government data. Still, their data may be more difficult to use with regards to a transboundary basin given that there is greater room for error and divergence in methodologies versus the controlled methods used by governments. The fourth type of data is participatory open data. Citizens and government engage in a transaction where the objective is not only the provision of data, but ensuring that citizens have a say in the decision-making process. Existing problems are solved and citizens are further encouraged to provide data.[186]

Studies have identified barriers to the implementation of effective open data policies. These barriers include '(1) closed government culture; (2) privacy legislation; (3) limited quality of data; (4) limited user-friendliness/information overload, and (5) lack of standardisation of open data policy'.[187] Moreover, open data has been criticised. First, there are risks emerging as the various actors participating, be they citizens, civil society, private sector and so on, have different motives and interests that affects the entire open data process.

183 R. Harris & I. Baumann, *'Open Data Policies and Satellite Earth Observation'*, 32, Space Policy (2015) 44–53, 45.

184 Sieber & Johnson, *supra* note 184, at 4; Open Knowledge Foundation, *'What is Open?'*, at https://okfn.org/opendata/, last accessed 20 January 2020.

185 B. Pedregal et al., *'Information and Knowledge for Water Governance in the Networked Society'*, 8:2, Water Alternatives (2015) 1–19, 4.

186 *Id.*, at 8–11; M. Kosmala et al., *'Assessing Data Quality in Citizen Science'*, 14:10, Frontiers in Ecology and the Environment (2016) 551–560.

187 Pedregal et al., *supra* note 185, at 5.

Second, and depending on the type of open data chosen, the role of the government may shift over time as a result of increasing efficiency of the private sector, which might also mean that the government cannot keep up with the regulations needed. Thirdly, governments may adopt standard open data provisions and consider that mission accomplished even though such processes require constant updating. Further, it important to make sure that the government does not simply abandon the entire process for some reason.[188]

As discussed above, there are several statements and legal instruments specific to earth observation adopted at the international, regional and national levels.[189] There are also broad policy statements and legal instruments relevant to earth observation.[190] These documents and organisations include exceptions to open data in relation to international law as well as to other fields.[191] They do not each necessarily include all the exceptions listed here.[192]

1.4.2 Open Data in the Water Sector

Water management is characterised by uncertainty and complexity due to different economic and political interests and changing weather patterns and hydrologic variability, with culture and identity also playing an important role. As such, it is necessary to involve all the actors in the decision-making process,

188 *Id.*, at 12–16.

189 Harris & Baumann, *supra* note 183, at 46–49. These international instruments include the Global Earth Observation System of Systems (GEOSS) data sharing principles; the International Disaster Charter and UN remote sensing principles. European measures include the Copernicus data policy; the European Space Agency (ESA) Data Policy; the European Organisation for the Exploitation of Meteorological Satellites (EUMETSAT) Data Policy; the Sentinel data policy and SPOT Data. In the US, measures include the Landsat data policy, the National Environmental Satellite, Data, and Information Service (NESDIS) of the National Oceanic and Atmospheric Administration (NOAA) and the US earth observation strategy.

190 *Id.* International instruments include the G8 Open Data Charter; International Oceanographic Commission data policy; Organisation for Economic Co-Operation and Development guidelines for research data and WMO Resolution 40. European measures include the Aarhus Convention; European environmental information directive; European Infrastructure for Spatial Information in Europe (INSPIRE) directive; and the European public sector information directive. In the US, measures include the US global change research program data policy and the US open data policy.

191 *Id.*, at 52. These fields are 'international relations and foreign policy; national security; defence; national legislation; intellectual property rights; personal data protection; commercial and industrial confidentiality; statistical confidentiality; legal confidentiality; the course of justice; contractual issues; financial viability; proprietary interests; indigenous rights; conservation of sensitive ecological, natural, archaeological, or cultural resources; availability of resources and organizational policies'.

192 *Id.*

making access to information essential for the implementation of a participatory approach. Information must be 'relevant to the specific management questions, easily accessible and understandable for all types of stakeholders, adapted to the decision-making context and time frame, and traceable'.[193] Indeed, access to water data and ensuring the open exchange of water information is essential for addressing water problems.[194] It is in this context that calls for open data in the water sector have been made.

Water data and information are very sensitive, controversial and extremely difficult to manage due to the physical importance of water and the political nature of water decisions. This reality affects or will affect the implementation of an open data policy, in particular in the transboundary water context. Yet, several scholars believe that open data regimes will foster transboundary water governance 'by helping lower nationalistic fervour on water, promoting political contestation in agenda-framing and providing alternative imaginations or narratives'.[195] They see the involvement of information and communication technologies in water governance as a means for eliminating asymmetry of information between nations and for avoiding the hiding of information, which will lead to the development of water management goals that are realistic and acceptable to everyone.[196]

A new water data system is needed to address all the issues related to water governance, be it water supply, quality, or use, while also meeting existing water demands for urban, agricultural, ecological and industrial purposes.[197] A successful water data system requires not only that the data to be open and transparent, but also that it is relevant for the decision-makers who are supposed to use it. The entire process of establishing a water data system should cater to the needs of stakeholders and decision-makers. The system needs to be interoperable and include the different types of data emanating from different sectors to enhance the ability of the decision-maker through the integration of data and data sources. The system needs to address existing data gaps, whether because of the absence of data or the unsuitability of existing data. Moreover, clear and strict rules and standards must be adopted to integrate data from

---

193 Pedregal et al., *supra* note 185, at 2.

194 D. Blodgett et al., *'An Analysis of Water Data Systems to Inform the Open Water Data Initiative'*, 52:4, Journal of the American Water Resources Association (2016) 845–858, 845.

195 Pedregal et al., *supra* note 185, at 6.

196 *Id.*

197 A. Cantor et al., *Data for Water Decision Making: Informing the Implementation of California's Open and Transparent Water Data Act through Research and Engagement* (Center for Law, Energy & the Environment, UC Berkeley School of Law, Berkeley, CA, Jan. 2018) 7.

different sources according to best practices while maintaining the autonomy of the systems from where the data is collected. Given that decision-makers have various data and information needs, the system must be flexible enough to consider these needs through various formats and resolutions. The system must allow the generation of new information from the integration and processing of the collected data, thus providing an added value to decision-makers. A constant conversation between data users, developers, and end users must take place to satisfy the evolving needs of decision-makers. Finally, a successful water data system requires good governance, stable funding and robust cyberinfrastructure.[198]

Examples of open data initiatives include the one 'established by the federal government to enhance water information sharing across the US using standardized web services for geospatial and temporal data'.[199] Other examples include the online portal in the food and water fields launched by the Food and Agriculture Organization of the UN for 'enhancing decision-makers capacity to estimate agricultural potentials and variability under different climate and resources scenarios'.[200] Another example is the Eye on Earth network 'used to create an online site and group of services for scientists, researchers and policymakers in order to share and analyse environmental and geospatial data'.[201] Moreover, the UN has created the Global Pulse, which is a big data programme aiming at 'harnessing today's new world of digital data and real-time analytics in order to foster international development, protect the world's most vulnerable populations, and strengthen resilience to global shocks'.[202]

1.4.3 Open Data and the Law

Uhlir and Schröder argue that 'there are many compelling reasons for developing more comprehensive access regimes at the institutional, national, and international levels, with open access as the default rule. This is the case whether the data are produced within government or by entities funded by

---

198 *Id.*, at 7–9.

199 D. R. Maidment, *'Open Water Data in Space and Time'*, 52:4, Journal of the American Water Resources Association (2016) 816–824, 816.

200 G. Misuraca, F. Mureddu & D. Osimo, *'Policy-Making 2.0: Unleashing the Power of Big Data for Public Governance'*, in M. Gascó-Hernández (ed.), *Open Government: Opportunities and Challenges for Public Governance* (Dordrecht: Springer, 2014) 177.

201 *Id.*

202 *Id.*, at 178.

government sources'.[203] They provide a list of the benefits to having open access data:

- reinforces open scientific inquiry,
- encourages diversity of analysis and opinion,
- promotes new research and new types of research,
- enables the application of automated knowledge discovery tools online,
- allows the verification of previous results,
- makes possible the testing of new or alternative hypotheses and methods of analysis,
- supports studies on data collection methods and measurement,
- facilitates the education of new researchers,
- enables the exploration of topics not envisioned by the initial investigators,
- permits the creation of new data sets, information, and knowledge when data from multiple sources are combined,
- helps transfer factual information to and promote capacity building in developing countries,
- promotes interdisciplinary, inter-sectoral, inter-institutional, and international research, and
- generally helps to maximize the research potential of new digital technologies and networks, thereby providing greater returns from the public investment in research.[204]

There are several considerations for having open access, mainly legal ones, as the public has the right to access data, which is consistent with Article 19 of the Universal Declaration of Human Rights. Indeed, the freedom of opinion and expression mentioned in this provision includes among its key elements the right to access information from various public bodies.[205] 'National law on information rights should include public access to data and information produced by the government, and related freedom of expression by the public'.[206] In addition, the data produced is considered to have public good characteristics. Other considerations are socio-economic (e.g., online dissemination of public data and information online), ethical (e.g., the public has already paid

203 P. F. Uhlir & P. Schröder, *'Open Data for Global Science'*, 6, Data Science Journal (2007) 36–53, 203.

204 *Id.*

205 Global Campaign for Free Expression, *'Statement on the Right to Communicate by Article 19'*, February 2003, at https://www.article19.org/data/files/pdfs/publications/right-to-communicate.pdf, last accessed 14 June 2021.

206 Uhlir & Schröder, *supra* note 203, at 204.

through their taxes for the production of information), and good governance (e.g., transparency cannot be ensured without citizens access to public data and information).[207]

The main international instrument addressing public access to information is the Convention on Access to Information, Public Participation in Decision-making and Access to Justice in Environmental Matters. This convention guarantees 'the rights of access to information, public participation in decision-making, and access to justice in environmental matters'.[208] The Regional Agreement on Access to Information, Public Participation and Justice in Environmental Matters in Latin America and the Caribbean guarantees the 'full and effective implementation in Latin America and the Caribbean of the rights of access to environmental information, public participation in the environmental decision-making process and access to justice in environmental matters, and the creation and strengthening of capacities and cooperation'.[209]

Open data access policies also have been implemented at the national level, including China through its 2002 Scientific Data Sharing Program. In 2004, Canada initiated the National Consultation on Access to Scientific Research Data, while an Interagency Working Group on Digital Data in the White House Office of Science and Technology Policy was put in place in the US in 2005.[210]

A Global Information Commons for Science Initiative is being launched with the objective of accelerating 'the development and scaling up of open scientific data and information resources on a global basis, with particular focus on "common use" licensing approaches'.[211] Specifically, it aims to:

---

207 *Id.* According to Article 19: 'Everyone has the right to freedom of opinion and expression; this right includes freedom to hold opinions without interference and to seek, receive and impart information and ideas through any media and regardless of frontiers'. Universal Declaration of Human Rights, 10 December 1948 (General Assembly resolution 217 A(III)), at https://www.un.org/en/about-us/universal-declaration-of-human-rights, last accessed 20 January 2020.

208 Convention on Access to Information, Public Participation in Decision-making and Access to Justice in Environmental Matters, Aarhus, 25 June 1998, Article 1, at https://unece.org/DAM/env/pp/documents/cep43e.pdf, last accessed 14 June 2021.

209 Regional Agreement on Access to Information, Public Participation and Justice in Environmental Matters in Latin America and the Caribbean,t Escazú, Costa Rica, 4 March 2018, at https://treaties.un.org/doc/Treaties/2018/03/20180312%2003-04%20PM/CTC-XXVII-18.pdf, last accessed 14 June 2021.

210 Uhlir & Schröder, *supra* note 203, at 49.

211 *Id.*, at 52–53.

(1) Improve understanding and increase awareness of the societal and economic benefits of easy access to and use of scientific data and information, especially focusing on those resulting from governmental or publicly funded research activities;
(2) Promote the broad adoption of successful institutional and legal models for providing open availability on a sustainable basis and facilitating reuse of data and information;
(3) Help coordinate the efforts of the many stakeholders in the world's diverse research community who are engaged in devising and implementing effective approaches to attaining these objectives, with particular attention to the circumstances of the developing as well as developed countries;
(4) Develop an online "open knowledge environment" to promote all of the objectives of the Initiative, including providing an online collaboratory for work with different research communities to define, test, analyze, and create new knowledge about the information commons paradigm.[212]

1.4.4 Open Data and Water Law

There are very few examples of open data regulations in the water sector. While some provisions may be found in general regulations, there are two specific regulations adopted at the national level in the US. The first is open water data legislation enacted in California in 2016, and the second was enacted in New Mexico in 2019.

1.4.4.1 *The California Open and Transparent Water Data Act*

California enacted the Open and Transparent Water Data Act in 2016 to create, operate, and maintain an integrated water data platform at the state level. The Act aims to integrate multiple water and ecological data sources, including completed water transfers and exchanges. It also aims to create data sharing, documentation, quality control, and public access protocols. It includes protocols for open-source platforms and decision support tools concerning water data. Reports on the protocols are submitted to the legislature. Finally, the Act requires state funded recipients to adhere to the Act's protocols.[213]

The drafters stated several reasons for why this act was needed.[214] The California drought exposed the need for open water and ecological data to support effective water management and informed user decision-making on

212 *Id.*, at 53.
213 Open and Transparent Water Data Act, *supra* note 41, at 1.
214 *Id.*, Chapter 1 (12401).

water availability and allocation. At the same time, California recognised the unique opportunity whereby political will, multisector awareness, technological capability, and open source platform availability intersect to integrate and increase open water data access. California's state agencies had also been piloting an open data portal that fostered interagency collaboration and data sharing to improve transparency and accountability. An important factor is also California's state agencies policy of promoting open and interoperable water data to foster entrepreneurship, innovation, and scientific discovery. California recognised that water data gathered using public funds requires making the data publicly available. Finally, California used available open source tools to create an inexpensive centralised online-integrated water and ecological data platform.

The Act also created room for government agencies like the water department to create partnerships with existing civil society and non-profit organisations and even create a separate non-profit organisation.[215] California's integrated water data platform required the integration of multiple autonomous databases in different government jurisdictions and academia. These datasets included the following:

(1) The department's information on state water project reservoir operations, groundwater use, groundwater levels, urban water use, and land use.

(2) The state board's data on water rights, water diversions, and water quality through the California Environmental Data Exchange Network (CEDEN).

(3) The California Department of Fish and Wildlife's information on fish abundance and distribution.

(4) The United States Geological Survey's streamflow conditions information through the National Water Information System.

(5) The United States Bureau of Reclamation's federal Central Valley Project operations information.

(6) The United States Fish and Wildlife Service's, United States Forest Service's, and National Oceanic and Atmospheric Administration fisheries' fish abundance information.

Another required task is to provide water data transfers and exchange data with specific requirements, and to provide documentation of data quality and format using metadata. The Act also required adherence to data protocols of state agencies. Finally, the Act required the various stakeholders the ability to receive special and time series data from different sources.[216] The Act also

215 *Id.*, Chapter 2, Article 2 (12410)(b)(c).

216 *Id.*, Chapter 2, Article 3 (12415).

included provisions for the creation of a water data administration fund, to be funded through appropriation or voluntary public and private donations,[217] that makes money available to collect, manage, and improve water and ecological data.[218]

1.4.4.2 *The New Mexico Water Data Act*

The state of New Mexico adopted the Water Data Act in 2019. The Act requires several state agencies to 'standardize data on water levels, quality and use' due the need to manage the scarce water resources of the state.[219] The Act aims to give 'state agencies funding and technical support to standardize water data collection and create tools that help water managers get quick and easy access to information on water resources' by making water data open, accessible, and usable.[220] It represents a first step towards the integration of water data across the state.[221]

Its objective is to 'integrate existing and new water and ecological data and information from multiple databases managed by federal, state, tribal and local entities using consistent and standardized formats',[222] among others. The rationale behind the Act is to improve water and related resource planning and management by requiring relevant state agencies to coordinate and integrate data across multiple governmental and nongovernmental sources.[223]

To reach the objectives of the new regulation, New Mexico formed a water data council which shall be 'jointly convened, coordinated, administered and staffed by the bureau of geology and mineral resources of the New Mexico institute of mining and technology and the interstate stream commission'.[224] The council has many duties, including the identification and collection of water data and tools; the development and establishment of standards and best practices for water data collection, sharing, transparency, documentation, and quality control; the establishment of open water data best practices that

---

217 *Id.*, Chapter 3 (12420.(b)).

218 *Id.*, Chapter 3 (12420.(a)).

219 T. Davis, *'NM Puts Focus on Better Water Data'*, 25 January 2020, at https://www.abqjournal.com/1413327/nm-puts-focus-on-better-water-data.html, last accessed 20 January 2020.

220 M. Myatt, *'Currents: Get to Know 6 Programs Driving Open Water Data'*, 9 July 2019, at https://waterfdn.org/get-to-know-6-programs-driving-open-water-data/, last accessed 20 January 2020.

221 L. Paskus, *'Bill Would Shine a Light on State's Water Situation'*, 1 March 2019, at https://nmpoliticalreport.com/2019/03/01/bill-would-shine-a-light-on-states-water-situation/, last accessed 20 January 2020.

222 House Bill 651, *supra* note 42, at 2.

223 *Id.*, Section 3, pp. 2–3.

224 *Id.*, Section 4(A), p. 3.

make data discoverable, interoperable, and integrated; the development of an integrated water data platform; and the identification and prioritisation of water data and information gaps.[225]

The Act also required adherence to water data standards and best practices developed by the council whenever water research uses state funding. The Act allows the council to collaborate with third parties to integrate and manage water data. Finally, the Act required the council to submit a plan to the legislature that includes an assessment, goals, targets, actions, budgetary needs, and progress and performance metrics.[226]

The Act even established a 'water data account' to 'receive appropriations from the legislature and gifts, grants or donations for the bureau of geology and mineral resources to carry out the purposes of the Water Data Act'.[227] In this context, the council is tasked with the development of 'guidelines to manage and prioritize the use of funds from the water data account to carry out the purposes of the Water Data Act, including contracting with entities to make water data and information open, interoperable and integrated'.[228]

1.4.4.3 *Comparative Analysis of the California and New Mexico Acts*

Upon examination of both Acts, it becomes obvious that the focus is on the establishment of new water data structures that have several different tasks that must be realised, albeit the structures have different names. In the case of the Open and Transparent Water Data Act, the legislator created the integrated water data platform that is tasked with the realisation of all the provisions of the regulation.[229] In the case of the Water Data Act, the legislator created a water data council that is required to implement the provisions of this Act and also developed an integrated water data and information platform.[230] It seems that the Water Data Act is creating two structures, which is unnecessary, as the Open and Transparent Water Data Act shows that one structure, in this case the integrated water data platform, can fulfil the tasks that must be realised by the water data council under the Water Data Act.

Both Acts emphasized the integration of water data. The Open and Transparent Water Data Act focused on integrating 'existing water and ecological data information from multiple databases and provide data on completed

225 *Id.*, at Section 5(A), pp. 4–5.
226 *Id.*, at Section 5(B, C, D), pp. 5–6.
227 *Id.*, at Section 6(A), p. 6.
228 *Id.*, Section 6(b), p. 6.
229 Open and Transparent Water Data Act, *supra* note 41.
230 House Bill 651, *supra* note 42.

water transfers and exchanges'.[231] It mainly deals with the integration of 'existing water and ecological data information from multiple autonomous databases managed by federal, state, and local agencies and academia using consistent and standardized formats'.[232] Similar reasoning occurred in the context of the Water Data Act, which required the 'state to develop a modern, integrated approach to collecting, sharing and utilizing data and information for water management'.[233] The objective is to 'integrate existing and new water and ecological data and information from multiple databases managed by federal, state, tribal and local entities using consistent and standardized formats'.[234]

Both acts also addressed the regulation of water data exchange. The Open and Transparent Water Data Act called for the development of 'protocols for data sharing, documentation, quality control, public access, and promotion of open-source platforms and decision support tools related to water data and to submit to the Legislature a report on those protocols'.[235] In contrast, the Water Data Act called for the development of 'common water data standards and best practices for data collection, sharing, transparency, documentation and quality control' and the establishment of 'best practices to make water data open, discoverable, interoperable and integrated'.[236]

Notably, California seemed to have been a step ahead of New Mexico since California's state agencies have long been working on an integrated open data platform created from open source technology. California's agencies, therefore, had already achieved some form of integration in water data sharing and collaboration.

Finally, both acts addressed financial matters to ensure the existence of sufficient funds to carry out the tasks identified in the regulations. The Open and Transparent Water Data Act created a water data administration fund that shall be 'available, upon appropriation, to the department, the state board, or the Department of Fish and Wildlife for the collection, management, and improvement of water and ecological data for the purposes of this part'.[237] Similarly, as discussed above, the Water Data Act established a 'water data account'.[238] Both Acts also created guidelines to that end. The Open and Transparent Water

231 Open and Transparent Water Data Act, *supra* note 41, at 1.
232 *Id.*, Chapter 2, Article 3 (12415).
233 House Bill 651, *supra* note 42, Section 3, pp. 2–3.
234 *Id.*, Section 2(1), p. 2.
235 Open and Transparent Water Data Act, *supra* note 41, at 1.
236 House Bill 651, *supra* note 42, Section 5(A)2, pp. 4–5.
237 Open and Transparent Water Data Act, *supra* note 41, Chapter 3 (12420. (a)).
238 House Bill 651, *supra* note 42, Section 6(A), p. 6.

Data Act requested that the Department of Finance 'develop a standardized agreement to allow for the voluntary donation to the fund by any person, educational institution, government entity, corporation or other business entity, or organization'.[239] Meanwhile the Water Data Act called on the water data council to 'develop guidelines to manage and prioritize the use of funds from the water data account to carry out the purposes of the Water Data Act, including contracting with entities to make water data and information open, interoperable and integrated'.[240]

1.4.5 In Summary

There have been attempts to establish open data regulations in the water sector. While several open data regulations exist globally, there is a lack of open water data regulations. The Open and Transparent Water Data Act of California and Water Data Act of New Mexico are the most complete regulations that have been adopted. In the authors opinion, such open water data regulations can be replicated in the transboundary water context while considering the specificities surrounding the governance of shared water resources from a legal perspective. This position will be explored using the case study analysis below. It is worth mentioning here that several basins do have data sharing protocols that are similar to the California and New Mexico acts and provide guidance on uniform data standards and development of water data platforms such as the joint 2001 Procedures for Data and Information Exchange and Sharing established by the Mekong River Commission.[241]

2 Case Study

2.1 *Project Description*

This case study provides an overview of the shared water resources in the SADC region and discusses in detail the state of TBAs there. Specifically, it examines BDA that is being used to improve transboundary water management.

---

239 Open and Transparent Water Data Act, *supra* note 41, Chapter 3 (12420. (b)).

240 House Bill 651, *supra* note 42, Section 6(b), p. 6.

241 Leb (2018), *supra* note 165, at 139; Mekong River Commission for Sustainable Development, '*Procedures for Data and Information Exchange and Sharing*', 2001, at https://www.mrcmekong.org/assets/Publications/policies/Procedures-Data-Info-Exchange-n-Sharing.pdf, last accessed 14 June 2021.

2.1.1 Shared Fresh Water in Southern Africa

Africa has a huge number of shared fresh water sources resulting from the colonial era as rivers were used to determine the border between states.[242] Natural resources on the continent, including in the SADC region, are characterised by overexploitation and unsustainable use patterns. The poor usually pays the highest price for this reality, especially when it comes to water access.[243]

SADC countries include Angola, Botswana, Comoros, Democratic Republic of Congo, Lesotho, Madagascar, Malawi, Mauritius, Mozambique, Namibia, Seychelles, South Africa, Eswatini (formerly Swaziland), Tanzania, Zambia and Zimbabwe.[244] Established in 1980, SADC was established with the objective of improving the quality of life in the region, ensuring socio-economic development and pushing towards regional integration.[245] The SADC Secretariat is comprised of four directorates: Food, Agriculture and Natural Resources; Trade, Industry, Finance and Investment; Infrastructure and Services; and Social and Human Development.[246] The Directorate for Infrastructure and Services includes the SADC Water Division, which coordinates and manages the SADC Water Programme.[247] The Division creates a platform for addressing water issues and challenges between the member states. Its responsibilities and functions play an important role at the level of River Basin Organisations (RBOs). Nonetheless, there are challenges when it comes to the realisation of its responsibilities, functions, and roles, such as the absence of direct or clear link with national water ministries.[248]

Water is unevenly distributed in both space and time in the region, while rainfall, and extreme events such as floods and droughts are common. Some of the countries are experiencing high water stress, others medium or low water stress.[249] In terms of climate, hydrological conditions, and governance

---

242 A. R. Turton, M. J. Patrick and F. Julien, *'Transboundary Water Resources in Southern Africa: Conflict or Cooperation?'*, 49:3, Development (2006) 22–31, 22.

243 D. Malzbender & A. Earle, *Water Resources of the SADC: Demands, Dependencies and Governance Responses* (African Centre for Water Research, 2007) 2.

244 T. Manungufala & J. Dini, *'Transboundary Cooperation'*, in L. Filho et al. (eds), *Clean Water and Sanitation* (Dordrecht: Springer, 2022).

245 Limpopo River Awareness Kit, *'Governance: Southern African Development Community, SADC Water Sector'*, http://www.limpopo.riverawarenesskit.org/LIMPOPORAK_COM/EN/GOVERNANCE/SADC/SADC_WATER_SECTOR.HTM, last accessed 20 January 2020.

246 *Id.*

247 *Id.*

248 Limpopo River Awareness Kit, *'Governance: Southern African Development Community, SADC Water Division'*, http://www.limpopo.riverawarenesskit.org/LIMPOPORAK_COM/EN/GOVERNANCE/SADC/SADC_WATER_DIVISION.HTM, last accessed 20 January 2020.

249 Manungufala & Dini, *supra* note 244, at 3–4.

arrangements, there are similarities and differences between the countries of the SADC region given its large territory. Economic growth combined with population growth is expected to result in water stress by 2025, with the most developed economies of the region, including South Africa and Botswana, being the most water stressed.

Given the uneven distribution in rainfall patterns between the countries, water storage and transfer infrastructure has been built in places like South Africa and Zimbabwe. Both countries are ranked among the top dam builders of the world.[250] The region also has a high number of transboundary rivers.[251] Fifteen rivers are shared between the twelve mainland countries, covering almost 80% of the surface area and providing more than 70% of fresh water to the region.[252] The dependency on transboundary rivers varies between countries. Groundwater is relied upon by approximately 70% of the rural population, and numerous important aquifers are transboundary.

The transboundary nature of many rivers and aquifers further complicates the task of managing these resources as cooperation between nations is needed to ensure their good governance. Any action or measure taken by a state has implications for the sharing of water with other states, especially downstream countries.[253] The governance and management of shared water resources in Southern Africa is very complicated given the existing hydrological linkages across borders; the limited water resources in the most developed economies, namely, South Africa and Botswana; the location of the most important cities that are not close to the rivers; the differences between countries in terms of human, financial and technological resources and social challenges such as population increase, urbanisation, climate change threats, refugees and diseases.[254]

As a result of these factors, the SADC region faces numerous challenges related to data collection, organisation and management. These include:

1. Lack of staff numbers and skills capacity and equipment;
2. Lack of clear objectives and procedures for groundwater monitoring;
3. Inconsistencies in collection of data. The spatial and temporal distribution of data is low or uneven (many data gaps);
4. Insufficient quality assurance and quality control of data;

---

250 Malzbender & Earle, *supra* note 243, at 3–4.

251 *Id.*, at 4.

252 Manungufala & Dini, *supra* note 244, at 4–5.

253 *Id.*

254 I. M. Jacobs & S. Nienaber, *'Waters Without Borders: Transboundary Water Governance and the Role of the "Transdisciplinary Individual" in Southern Africa'*, 37:5, Water SA (2011) 665–678, 666.

5. Few functional digital databases. Data are stored in different places in different formats which further compromises the usability of the data;
6. Limited data backup strategies, sometimes non-existent and data are at risk of being lost;
7. Complicated access to the data, sometimes even within the government, departments and data sharing is very limited both at national and regional levels; and
8. Limited capacity to interpret groundwater data and production of information for effective decision-making.[255]

More specifically, there are various issues facing Botswana and South Africa that affect data sharing between the countries. In Botswana, data collected and stored are not of high quality because of the organisational, technical and logistical problems with groundwater monitoring result in data gaps. The low data quality is mainly due to the absence of formal procedures for data quality assurance and quality control. Moreover, the data collected are not easily accessible by regional offices,[256] while 'groundwater data are not widely used for analyses, interpretation and dissemination'.[257] The situation in South Africa is better because of the establishment of a nationwide system for coding boreholes. Nonetheless, there are problems with groundwater monitoring, for instance, regional offices do not have sufficient financial capacity to perform this task, and groundwater abstraction is not monitored.[258]

These challenges with data collection, management and organisation paved the road for the use of BDA. The overall aim is to address existing data gaps to tackle the problems facing transboundary water management in the region.

2.1.2 The State of Transboundary Aquifers

The number of TBAs in Southern Africa exceeds the number of shared river basins.[259] Despite various studies, there is no precise number as it seems that new aquifers are identified regularly. Currently it is estimated that there are 30 TBAs.[260]

---

255 SADC-GMI, IGRAC & IGS, *SADC Framework for Groundwater Data Collection and Management* (SADC-GMI Report, Bloemfontein, South Africa, 2019) 2.

256 A. Sterckx, *State of Groundwater Data Collection and Data Management in SADC Member States* (Capacity Building for Groundwater Data Collection and Management in SADC Member States (SADC-GWdataCoM project), Final Report, 31 January 2019) 11–12.

257 *Id.*, at 12.

258 *Id.*, at 22.

259 SADC-GMI, IGRAC & IGS, *supra* note 255, at viii.

260 Interview with Jonathan Lautze, Research Group Leader: Integrated Management of Basins and Aquifers, 10 June 2021, at https://www.iwmi.cgiar.org/about/staff-list/jonathan-lautze/, last accessed 14 June 2021; M. Gomo & D. Vermeulen, *'A Transboundary*

The SADC region's TBAs are heavily used to satisfy diverse needs such as drinking water and irrigation. Ensuring the good governance of these aquifers requires the cooperation of all stakeholders, namely, the national groundwater department of each country.[261] The heavy use of groundwater in the region means that ensuring water security through cooperation among the SADC countries is a must. Among the challenges facing the sustainable management of TBAs are the absence of strong institutions, the weak functioning of RBOs, the absence of scientific data-sharing between states,[262] and the overexploitation of shared groundwater resources.[263]

Bad governance of TBAs is a reality that must be dealt with. In particular, countries have failed to regulate this resource effectively. This has led to the need for innovation to tackle the problem.[264] The management of shared aquifers is complicated given that it is a hidden resource crossing countries. More research is needed to understand its nature. In particular, TBAs are being used for various purposes, either as a complementary water source or as the only water source, especially in drylands.[265] The different water uses hold the potential for polluting the aquifer, making it difficult to prove the responsible party in the transboundary context. Therefore, more information is needed on these aquifers. Climate change further worsens the situation as it affects precipitation and evaporation and therefore aquifer recharge.[266]

The water resources in the SADC region will continue to be used for the various purposes in addition to meeting new emerging needs such as contributing to biodiversity and building regional peace and security, as well as reducing the

Aquifer of Potential Concern in Southern Africa', 19:6, Water Policy (2017) 1160–1171; Nijsten et al., *supra* note 36.

261 A. Sterckx, C. R. Vargas & A. Gemmell, *Big Data Analytics and Transboundary Water Collaboration: Theme 1: Consolidation of Data and Application of Big Data Tools to Enhance National and Transboundary Data Sets in Southern Africa that Support Decision-Making for Security of Water Resources – Deliverable 4: Groundwater Data Sharing Protocol* (UMVOTO Africa (Pty) Ltd, K5 Number: 2880, 18 December 2019) 6.

262 Gaffoor et al., *supra* notes 38 & 52; Pietersen, Kanyerere & Wanangwa, *supra* note 32, at 1.

263 K. Knüppe, *'The Challenges Facing Sustainable and Adaptive Groundwater Management in South Africa'*, 37:1, Water SA (2011) 67–79.

264 Z. Gaffoor et al., *Big Data Analytics and Modelling: Localising Transboundary Data Sets in Southern Africa: A Case Study Approach: Deliverable 3: Policy Brief on Modeling and Data Analytical Tools for Downscaling in a Transboundary Water Management Context* (University of the Western Cape & CSIR, November 2019) 1.

265 A. Aureli et al., *'Education and Training for Transboundary Groundwater Management as an Instrument of Dialogue and Communication'*, in C. J. G. Darnault, (ed), *Overexploitation and Contamination of Shared Groundwater Resources* (Dordrecht: Springer, 2006) 25–31, 26–28.

266 Malzbender and Earle, *supra* note 243, at 7.

risk to regional peace and security due to looming water conflicts. The majority of water is being used for agriculture.[267] Rapid industrial and urban development in SADC countries will impact the share of water used for agriculture as a greater proportion of water will be used for energy generation with the further development of hydropower throughout the region.[268] Indeed, freshwater resources, be it surface water or groundwater, are being used in Southern Africa in the mining, washing, beneficiation and transportation of coal, plant construction and power generation (cooling coal plants).[269]

The SADC Protocol definition of watercourse links groundwater to surface waters. TBAs that are not connected to surface waters have not been considered in Southern Africa in the context of transboundary water management. Yet, their importance has led to including them in the process.[270]

2.1.3 The Importance of Transboundary Groundwater Data Sharing in Southern Africa

Data on groundwater is needed for the 'assessment and regular monitoring of the state of the resources (quantity and quality), its interaction with other components of the water cycle (e.g. surface water, rainfall and evaporation), its relationship with socio-economic activities and environmental issues, as well as the legal and institutional setting in which it is governed'.[271] The data required for the management of groundwater resources are not collected from the groundwater departments of each state but from entities such as meteorological and agricultural offices. Therefore, there is a need for an active and constant exchange of data and information across different sectors and with the water departments to ensure the development of sound policies for water management.[272] Cooperation in groundwater data and information sharing between organisations collecting groundwater-related data at the national and local levels is critical. At the transboundary level, data collection and format needs to be harmonised. At the regional level where data might benefit other states having similar problems, as well as the general public and civil

267 *Id.*, at 7–8; L. A. Swatuk, *'Water Conflict and Cooperation in Southern Africa'*, 2:3, WIRES Water (2015) 215–230.

268 Malzbender and Earle, *supra* note 243, at 10.

269 T. Mabhaudhi et al., *'Southern Africa's Water – Energy Nexus: Towards Regional Integration and Development'*, 8:6, Water (2016) 1–21, 1–2.

270 P. S. V. H. Heyns, M. J. Patrick & A. R. Turton, *'Transboundary Water Resource Management in Southern Africa: Meeting the Challenge of Joint Planning and Management in the Orange River Basin'*, 24:3 International Journal of Water Resources Development (2008) 371–383, 372; Revised SADC Protocol, *supra* note 44, Article 1.

271 SADC-GMI, IGRAC & IGS, *supra* note 255, at 10.

272 *Id.*, at 12.

society, access to data is important.[273] There is a need to create incentives and encourage stakeholders (government officials, officials from other public or semi-public organisations, consultants, borehole owners) to participate in the acquisition of essential data from borehole drilling, siting and testing. Strategies to promote groundwater data collection include 'simplifying recording and submitting of data, training stakeholders, providing stakeholders access to the data, addressing issues related to sensitive data, [and] raising awareness on the benefits of the data'.[274]

The collection of groundwater data is expensive and in some instances is impossible to repeat, especially with regards to collecting historical groundwater data. Therefore, the quality of the data collected must be checked and protected against potential changes from users.[275] There are measures that states can take to reduce potential errors in data collection and strengthen the quality and consistency of the data gathered. These measures are used during all phases of data collection and can have different objectives. Among the measures that can be taken are training and capacity development of staff involved in coordination, supervision and/or interpretation, field technicians and external parties (drillers, consultants, lab services); providing guidelines for data collection by different states and the development of data collection forms/field-forms to be used by technicians; using mobile applications for data recording in the field; constantly calibrating, testing and using the equipment; using automated data collection techniques; and defining target/acceptable data quality and corrective measures.[276]

Data sharing can be improved through having open data, which means that data can be available to anyone. However, this is not the case in the SADC region as data is either explicitly restricted (need to request data or pay for access to it) or implicitly restricted (absence of online platforms). Restricted data is less efficient as it takes time since the parties need to request the data. Hence, investing in emerging technologies is important to promoting a culture of open data. The sharing of data must also include the metadata (data about the data). Metadata becomes more relevant in the transboundary and international contexts given that states have different methods of data collection and storage; metadata can help ensure harmonisation.

273 *Id.*, at 57–58.
274 *Id.*, at 19–20.
275 *Id.*, at 49.
276 *Id.*, at 39–42.

In the SADC region, it has been suggested that a working group can be created to facilitate data sharing.[277] Some of the options available for funding groundwater data collection and management are through

1. The national budget, however, such funding must be secured in each budget cycle even though such activities are long-term.
2. Groundwater tax funding measures related to the management of groundwater where the tax is set by the entity responsible for groundwater management, however, this option requires proper law enforcement.
3. Cost recovery fees, for instance, for 'registration and licensing of the drilling of boreholes and/or for groundwater abstraction' or for 'providing data from the groundwater databases'.
4. Licensing conditions forcing, for instance, the holders of a drilling permit or groundwater abstract permit to collect data for the water departments.
5. External funding through international donor organizations, which requires continued funding, especially at the end of the project as experience shows that data collection stops once the funding ends.[278]

Good transboundary groundwater management requires that all stakeholders actively participate in the process. Awareness of the challenges and issues surrounding such management is a critical. Therefore, groundwater departments must provide data to all stakeholders, especially when they request specific data.[279] There is a need to understand the role and responsibilities of each groundwater department and facility at the national level, ensure the harmonisation of their roles, reduce gaps in data collection, figure out whether in practice they are fulfilling their roles and how their role can be strengthened to ensure better data collection and management. Moreover, departments must have the legal means to enforce collection of data from all the stakeholders. Overall, groundwater management and collection activities must be clearly defined.[280]

2.2 *Legal Framework Applicable to the Region*

This section provides a detailed description of the main legal mechanisms governing transboundary water resources in the SADC region, in particular the Revised SADC Protocol.

277 *Id.*, at 58–59.
278 *Id.*, at 75–76.
279 *Id.*, at 56.
280 *Id.*, at 77–78.

2.2.1 The SADC Protocol

The Southern African Development Coordination Conference was established in 1980 between several African countries looking to facilitate economic development and integration. The Conference did not have a legal status, which led to the adoption of the SADC Treaty in 1992 which established SADC as an official international organisation having a legal personality.[281] The countries of the region adopted several other agreements, including the 1987 Agreement on the Action Plan for the Environmentally Sound Management of the Common Zambezi River System between Botswana, Mozambique, Tanzania, Zambia and Zimbabwe,[282] the 1992 Treaty on the Development and Utilization of the Water Resources of the Komati River between Swaziland and South Africa,[283] and the 1994 agreement on the establishment of a Permanent Okavango River Basin Commission between Angola, Botswana and Namibia.[284] These agreements have shortcomings, notably some of them do not include all the riparian states and none of them are comprehensive.[285]

The aim of the SADC treaty is the promotion of policies and frameworks for securing economic integration. The treaty sets out general principles to guide the members behaviour, including the objectives of utilisation of natural resources in a sustainable manner and the need for effectively protecting the environment.[286] The main mechanisms for cooperation are protocols, which must be established in each necessary area in accordance with Article 22.

---

281 S. M. A. Salman, *'Shared Watercourses in the Southern African Development Community: Challenges and Opportunities'*, 6:1, Water Policy (2004) 25–38, 25–26.

282 Agreement on the Action Plan for the Environmentally Sound Management of the Common Zambezi River System, Harare, 28 May 1987, http://www.fao.org/3/w7414b/w7414boj.htm, last accessed 14 June 2021.

283 Treaty on the Development and Utilisation of the Water Resources of the Komati River Basin Between the Government of the Kingdom of Swaziland and the Government of the Republic of South Africa, 13 March 1992, at http://www.fao.org/3/w7414b/w7414b14.htm, last accessed 14 June 2021.

284 Agreement between the Governments of the Republic of Angola, the Republic of Botswana, and the Republic of Namibia on the Establishment of a Permanent Okavango River Basin Water Commission (OKACOM), Windhoek, 16 September 1994, http://www.fao.org/3/w7414b/w7414bom.htm, last accessed 14 June 2021.

285 Salman (2004), *supra* note 281, at 30; Protocol on Shared Watercourse Systems in the Southern African Development Community (SADC) Region, Johannesburg, 28 August 1995, http://www.fao.org/3/w7414b/w7414bon.htm, last accessed 14 June 2021.

286 S. M. A. Salman, *'Legal Regime for Use and Protection of International Watercourses in the Southern African Region: Evolution and Context'*, 41:4, Natural Resources Journal (2001) 981–1022, 990–991. Other instruments were also adopted including the SADC Regional Indicative Strategic Development Plan (RISDP), a '15-year regional integration development plan, setting the priorities, policies and strategies for achieving the long-term goals of SADC'. Limpopo River Awareness Kit, *'Governance: Southern African Development*

Because members share numerous freshwater sources, attention has been directed to regulating the use and protection of these water resources. The Protocol on Shared Watercourse Systems was concluded in 1995 (SADC Protocol).[287] It entered into force in 1998. Thc Protocol recognised several international instruments and documents, including the 1966 Helsinki Rules and the work of the ILC on the non-navigational uses of international watercourses, together with concepts such as sustainable development and equitable utilisation.[288]

The provisions of the Protocol establish rules that must be followed by the parties. Articles are mainly devoted to the creation of procedures and the establishment of rules for institutions and their operations.[289] The Protocol has several shortcomings. For instance, it did not include a provision related to the obligation not to cause significant harm and several procedural elements are missing.[290]

The conclusion of the Convention on the Law of the Non-Navigational Uses of International Watercourses (UNWC) in 1997 highlighted the limitations of the SADC Protocol.[291] As a result, the latter was amended and updated to reflect provisions in the UNWC. The revision process started in 1998 and ended with the signature of the Revised Protocol on Shared Watercourses in 2000 (SADC Revised Protocol).[292] Similar to the 1995 Protocol, the Revised Protocol recognised developments in IWL, but it did not acknowledge the existence of the 1995 Protocol in the preamble.[293] This led to inconsistencies as Article 16(1) recognises the existence of the 1995 Protocol.[294] The main objectives of the Revised Protocol according to Article 2 are 'to foster closer cooperation for judicious, sustainable and coordinated management, protection and utilization of shared watercourses, and advance the SADC's agenda of regional integration and poverty alleviation'.[295] The remaining Articles mention several

Community, Instruments of the Sector', http://www.limpopo.riverawarenesskit.org/LIMPOPORAK_COM/EN/GOVERNANCE/SADC/INSTRUMENTS_OF_THE_SECTOR.HTM, last accessed 20 January 2020.

287 Salman (2001), *supra* note 286, at 996.

288 *Id.*, at 998.

289 *Id.*, at 1000–1001.

290 *Id.*, at 1001.

291 Convention on the Law of the Non-navigational Uses of International Watercourses, New York, 21 May 1997, https://legal.un.org/ilc/texts/instruments/english/conventions/8_3_1997.pdf, last accessed 14 June 2021 [UNWC].

292 Revised SADC Protocol, *supra* note 44.

293 Salman (2001), *supra* note 286, at 1004.

294 *Id.*, at 1004–1005.

295 Revised SADC Protocol, *supra* note 44, at Article 2.

matters that are similar to the 1995 Protocol, but several new principles have been added.[296]

The Revised Protocol includes the principles of equitable and reasonable utilisation and the obligation not to cause significant harm in a similar manner to the UNWC.[297] It also includes provisions on planned measures, environmental protection, and management of shared watercourses.[298] The Revised Protocol states that the rights and obligations arising from agreements adopted before the Protocol are not affected by this mechanism, where the members to both agreements can consider harmonising these treaties. The Protocol does not allow future agreements to amend its provisions but rather only apply them.[299] The application of the Protocol without amending it provides stability and predictability, especially since it is a regional instrument. Future agreements may cover all or a part of the watercourse or apply to a particular project or program. While the rights of the riparian states that are not parties to an agreement are not affected, these states can also negotiate to becoming a member to the agreement.[300] It is worth mentioning that the Protocol applies to navigational uses in accordance with Article 1(1)[301] and freedom of navigation was extended to all riparian states. Article 5 of the Protocol established several committees, including the Committee of the Water Ministers, the Committee of Water Senior Officials, the Water Sector Coordinating Unit, and the Water Resources Technical Committee and Sub-Committees.[302] These committees have a hierarchal order. States under the Protocol are

296 Salman (2001), *supra* note 286, at 1005.

297 *Id.*, at 1007–1010. Concerning the principle of equitable and reasonable utilization, see Articles 2(b); 3 (7) a, b & (8)(a)(b); 4 (1)(g)(i); and 4 (3)(b)(ii) of the SADC Revised Protocol. Concerning the obligation not to cause significant harm, see Articles 2(d); 3 (10)a, b, c; 4 (2)(b)(i), (c); and 4(b) of the SADC Revised Protocol, *supra* note 44.

298 Salman (2001), *supra* note 286, at 1011–1013. On planned measures, see Articles 3 (8)(vii) & 9 and 4(1) of the SADC Revised Protocol, *supra* note 44. On environmental protection, see Articles 2(c); 3 (2), (4), (6), (8)(ii); 4 (1)(b), 2(b)(i), (d); and 4(b) of the SADC Revised Protocol. On water management, see Articles 2(a), (c), & (e); 3(3); 4(3)(a); and. 5 (2)(c) of the SADC Revised Protocol.

299 Salman (2001), *supra* note 286, at 1013–1014. On the rights and obligations arising from agreements, see Articles 6 (1)(5); and 16 of the SADC Revised Protocol, *supra* note 44.

300 Salman (2001), *supra* note 286, at 1014–1015. On the shared watercourse agreements, see Article 6 of the SADC Revised Protocol, *supra* note 44.

301 Salman (2001), *supra* note 286, at 1017; See also Article 1(1) of the SADC Revised Protocol, *supra* note 44.

302 Salman (2001), *supra* note 286, at 1018; See also Article 5 of the SADC Revised Protocol, *supra* note 44.

obliged to establish the necessary commissions, water authorities, etc.[303] The Protocol states that disputes that are not settled between the parties should be addressed by the Tribunal established under the 1992 Treaty.[304]

2.2.2 Other Important Documents

The main regional documents addressing water management are the SADC Regional Water Policy (RWP) and the Regional Water Strategy (RWS). Both documents recognise Integrated Water Resources Management (IWRM).[305] Among their many aims, the RWP and RWS have the objectives of providing 'a framework for sustainable, integrated and coordinated development, utilisation, protection and control of national and transboundary water resources in the region'.[306] These documents recognize the importance of regional cooperation in an integrated manner and the involvement of all the sectors related to water management.[307] They also promote regional integration and poverty alleviation within the SADC region.[308] These documents were adopted to support the implementation of the Revised SADC Protocol.[309] Some states in the SADC region have already revised their domestic laws and regulations to incorporate their provisions while other states are in the process of doing so. Such amendments should result in the harmonisation of water laws between the SADC states, leading to a coherent regional framework for the management of water resources.[310]

---

303 Salman (2001), *supra* note 286, at 1018; See also Article 5 of the SADC Revised Protocol, *supra* note 44.

304 Salman (2001), *supra* note 286, at 1019–1020; See also Article 7 of the SADC Revised Protocol, *supra* note 44.

305 Malzbender and Earle, *supra* note 243, at 14. There are specific tools also established mainly the SADC Water Sector ICP Collaboration Portal; Southern African Development Community, *'Regional Water Policy'*, August 2005, at https://www.sadc.int/files/1913/5292/8376/Regional_Water_Policy.pdf, last accessed 14 June 2021; Southern African Development Community, *'Regional Water Strategy' Final Draft*, June 2006, at https://www.sadc.int/files/2513/5293/3539/Regional_Water_Strategy.pdf, last accessed 14 June 2021.

306 Manungufala & Dini, *supra* note 244, at 7–8.

307 Malzbender and Earle, *supra* note 243, at 14.

308 Limpopo River Awareness Kit, *'Governance: Southern African Development Community, SADC Water Policy and Strategy'*, http://www.limpopo.riverawarenesskit.org/LIMPOPORAK_COM/EN/GOVERNANCE/SADC/SADC_WATER_POLICY_AND_STRATEGY.HTM, last accessed 20 January 2020.

309 Limpopo River Awareness Kit, *'Governance: Southern African Development Community, SADC Protocol'*, http://www.limpopo.riverawarenesskit.org/LIMPOPORAK_COM/EN/GOVERNANCE/SADC/SADC_WATER_PROTOCOL.HTM, last accessed 20 January 2020.

310 Malzbender and Earle, *supra* note 243, at 14–15.

SADC adopted the SADC Regional Strategic Action Plan (RSAP) in 2010.[311] The RSAP comprises four guidelines for strengthening RBOs and assisting in the decision-making process in areas such as stakeholder participation, environmental management, funding, and financing.[312] The RSAP has the objective of implementing the RWP and the RWS.[313] States also adopted the SADC Vision for Water, Life and Environment in 2000.[314] Finally, as noted above, numerous RBOs have been established in the SADC region.[315]

The SADC region has policies, strategies and technical guidelines on groundwater data collection. However, these policies and technical guidelines are not connected, because of the lack of an organisational framework on how the technical guidelines can be used for policy-making. States adopted the SADC Framework for Groundwater Data Collection and Data Management.[316] The general objective of the Framework is 'to provide organisational and planning structures for collection and management of groundwater data in strategic,

311 Limpopo River Awareness Kit, *supra* note 286; Southern African Development Community Secretariat, *Regional Strategic Action Plan on Integrated Water Resources Development and Management Phase IV* (2016).

312 Limpopo River Awareness Kit, *'Governance: Southern African Development Community, SADC Guidelines'*, http://www.limpopo.riverawarenesskit.org/LIMPOPORAK_COM/EN/GOVERNANCE/SADC/GUIDELINES_FOR_STRENGTHENING_RB.HTM, last accessed 20 January 2020.

313 Limpopo River Awareness Kit, *'Governance: Southern African Development Community, SADC Action Plan'*, http://www.limpopo.riverawarenesskit.org/LIMPOPORAK_COM/EN/GOVERNANCE/SADC/SADC_ACTION_PLAN.HTM, last accessed 20 January 2020.

314 Limpopo River Awareness Kit, *'Governance Instruments'*, *supra* note 286; Southern African Development Community, *Southern African Vision for Water Life and Environment in the 21st Century* (2009).

315 Limpopo River Awareness Kit, *'Governance: Southern African Development Community, River Basin Organisations'*, http://www.limpopo.riverawarenesskit.org/LIMPOPORAK_COM/EN/GOVERNANCE/SADC/RIVER_BASIN_ORGANISATIONS.HTM, last accessed 20 January 2020. These are the Tripartite Permanent Technical Committee (TPTC) between South Africa, Mozambique and Swaziland; International Commission for the Congo-Oubangui-Sangha Basin (CICOS) between Cameroon, Central African Republic, Democratic Republic of Congo and the Republic of Congo; Pangani Basin Water Board (PBWB) between Kenya and Tanzania; Permanent Okavango River Basin Water Commission (OKACOM) between Angola, Botswana and Namibia; Orange-Senqu River Commission (ORASECOM) between Botswana, Lesotho, Namibia and South Africa; Lake Tanganyika Authority (LTA) between Burundi, the Democratic Republic of Congo, Tanzania, and Zambia; Zambezi Watercourse Commission (ZAMCOM) between Angola, Namibia, Zimbabwe, Botswana, Malawi, Tanzania and Mozambique; and Ruvuma Joint Water Commission between Mozambique and the United Republic of Tanzania.

316 Groundwater Management Institute, *SADC Framework for Groundwater Data Collection and Management* (April 2019).

innovative and cost-effective ways'.[317] The Framework aims to assist SADC member states to develop procedures tailored to their financial and human capacities that address challenges in groundwater data collection and management. Additionally, the Framework aims to harmonise data collection, management, and exchange practices across member states and enhance transboundary and regional cooperation.[318]

The Framework is intended to benefit all member states regardless of their capacity in data collection and management, and addresses aspects related to 'borehole siting, groundwater monitoring, field data collection and databases and data sharing'.[319] It is expected that the Framework will contribute to the implementation of regional protocols and strategies. For example, it is expected that the Framework will contribute to the implementation of the provision of the SADC Revised Protocol on the sharing of hydrogeological data and information as well as the realisation of the targets in the SADC Regional Water Policy.[320] The Framework is aimed at officials that have coordinating roles, such as managers and directors of a department.[321] The key pillars of the Framework are the SADC Revised Protocol, the RWP, the RWS, the RSAP as well as other institutions, in particular the 'African Ministers' Council on Water (AMCOW) (Groundwater Committee); SADC Groundwater Management Institute; Water Resources Technical Committee; Water Resources Technical Committee hydro-geology sub-committee; SADC Water Division and River Basin Organisations'.[322]

2.2.3 Shortcomings of the SADC Protocol

The SADC Revised Protocol defined watercourses as 'systems of surface and ground waters consisting by virtue of their physical relationship a unitary whole normally flowing into a common terminus such as the sea, lake or aquifer'.[323] This definition acknowledges the hydrological connections between surface water and groundwater and conjunctive water use. Yet, it creates limitations on sharing TBAs and aquifer systems. The focus on systems of transboundary surface water and groundwater means that the Protocol only applies to those aquifers that are connected to surface water, excluding

317 SADC-GMI, IGRAC & IGS, *supra* note 255, at viii.
318 *Id.*, at viii.
319 *Id.*, at 3.
320 *Id.*, at 4.
321 *Id.*, at 6.
322 SADC-GMI, *Framework for Institutionalising Groundwater Management in the SADC Region* (SADC GMI Report, Bloemfontein, South Africa, 2019) 21.
323 *Id.*

solitary, non-recharging and fossil TBAs. The focus of the Protocol is on surface water, which raises the question of whether an aquifer must be connected to an international river or lake to be considered transboundary, or whether a domestic source of surface water connected to a TBA can be covered under the provisions of the Protocol.[324] Even though international water principles apply to transboundary groundwater, the latter has unique characteristics that must be considered in any policy or instrument seeking to regulate groundwater. First, since aquifers flow at a slower pace, they become more vulnerable to surface pollution and contamination with longer recovery time. Second, the underground location of aquifers makes them difficult to access, leading to extremely difficult reclamation that is costly and takes years to accomplish. Third, aquifers that are non-recharging will require specific protection. Finally, groundwater regulation must consider the cost and difficulty of groundwater monitoring.[325]

There is a need for 'specific management regimes and regulatory interventions tailored to the context of groundwater that represent major gaps in current international, regional and basin-specific legislation governing shared watercourses'.[326] The SADC Revised Protocol is a framework agreement that seeks to provide guidance to the member states in their quest to establish basin specific water agreements. Yet, very few water agreements in the region include groundwater within their scope.[327]

2.2.4 In Summary

Cooperation among the countries of the SADC region is much better when compared to cooperation over the sharing of freshwater resources globally. The SADC Revised Protocol enables cooperation that goes beyond the water sector, connecting it to other related sectors such as energy and agriculture.[328] Challenges remain, however, including the clear interpretation of the principles of the Protocol, the implementation of its provisions through domestic laws across the SADC countries, the shortage of human and financial resources which affects the implementation of the Protocol, addressing the groundwater gap in governance, and improving the management of this resource.[329]

---

324 *Id.*

325 *Id.*

326 *Id.*

327 *Id.*

328 Manungufala & Dini, *supra* note 244, at 8.

329 *Id.*, at 9–10.

2.3 *The Ramotswa Aquifer as a Case Study*

This section provides a case study of the Limpopo River Basin and the Ramotswa Aquifer. It examines the legal and institutional developments in the basin as well as the means to harmonise the national laws of the basin states. The analysis of the application of BDA to the Ramotswa aquifer is followed by a discussion of the ways to improve the legal and institutional governance of TBAs in the SADC region in general and of the Ramotswa aquifer in particular.

2.3.1 The Limpopo River Basin

The Limpopo River basin is one of the main river basins in Africa, along other river basins such as the Congo (Zaire), Nile, Lake Chad, Niger, Zambezi, Orange, Senegal and Volta.[330] Approximately 18 million people located in four different states (Botswana, Mozambique, South Africa and Zimbabwe) rely on the Limpopo River basin as it constitutes 'an important agricultural area, has extraordinary mineral resources and is exceptionally rich from a biodiversity point of view'.[331] The river originates from the highlands separating three of the four countries (Botswana, Mozambique, and South Africa) and passes through the four countries into the Indian Ocean. 'By area, 45 percent of the basin is in South Africa, 19 percent in Botswana, 21 percent in Mozambique, and 15 percent in Zimbabwe'.[332] Botswana is the upstream state of the basin, South Africa and Zimbabwe 'are in the middle reaches of the basin with the border between them being formed by the main stem of the Limpopo River'.[333] Mozambique is a downstream state where 'the Limpopo meanders across a huge flood plain'. So far, there are no dams on the main parts of the river constituting the international border, but there are possibilities of future dams on

330 K. Frenken (ed.), *Irrigation in Africa in Figures: AQUASTAT Survey* (Rome: Food and Agriculture Organization of the United Nations, FAO Water Reports 29, 2005) 21.

331 B. Petrie et al., *Risk, Vulnerability & Resilience in the Limpopo River Basin: Climate Change, Water and Biodiversity – A Synthesis* (For the USAID Southern Africa "Resilience in the Limpopo River Basin" (RESILIM) Program, One World Sustainable Investments, Cape Town, South Africa, 2014) viii.

332 T. Zhu & C. Ringler, *'Climate Change Impacts on Water Availability and Use in the Limpopo River Basin'*, 4:1, Water (2012) 63–84, 64.

333 A. Turton, *'The Southern African Hydropolitical Complex'*, in O. Varis, C. Tortajada & A. K. Biswas et al. (eds), *Management of Transboundary Rivers and Lakes* (Dordrecht: Springer, 2008) 47–48.

specific tributaries of the basin.[334] Moreover, major dam projects have been established on the tributaries of the river basin.[335]

With the exception of Mozambique, the border states are the most economically developed in the region. Their urban centres are major users of water resources of the basin, with water used for various purposes, including supplying industries and power stations. Water is also used in the rural areas of these countries for domestic purposes, irrigation, and livestock watering.[336] The most important urban and industrial sectors of South Africa are located in the basin. Economic growth is increasing in some basin countries due to a boom in extractive industries. Further, the population is witnessing significant growth, resulting in further urbanisation. All these developments face an increasingly scarce water resource in the basin. This water scarcity 'poses the biggest threat to the livelihoods, economies and ecosystems of the river basin system'.[337]

The basin is important for each country sharing it for different strategic reasons.[338] The basin has approached a critical point as there is no more water that can be allocated for additional uses or increasing demands from existing water users. Hence, difficult choices must be made concerning the future governance of the basin. Future policies, strategies and laws must have as an objective the promotion of resilience and the strengthening of the 'basin's ability to recover quickly from disturbances and shocks'.[339] Irrigated agriculture and mining, which require a lot of water, have been the main activities. This has resulted in water scarcity, leaving no room for other water uses, while water demands continue to grow. The interaction between the three biophysical sub-systems (water, climate and biodiversity) is creating further pressure as a change in one of these sub-systems will heavily affect the other sub-systems. Human actions, whether in the form of activities or governance measures, also add to the complexity.[340] Improving water management in the basin

---

334 *Id.*, at 48.

335 A. E. Mohamed, *'Comparing Africa's Shared River Basins – The Limpopo, Orange, Juba and Shabelle Basins'*, 2:7 Universal Journal of Geoscience (2014) 200–211, 202.

336 A. Earle et al., *Indigenous and Institutional Profile: Limpopo River Basin* (International Water Management Institute, IWMI Working Paper 112, 2006) 1.

337 Petrie et al., *supra* note 331, at viii; 'The basin is mostly semi-arid, with a highly variable climate, and is periodically exposed to severe droughts and floods. It has widely divergent land-use patterns, ecosystems and social, economic and governance systems. Its water resources are already over-subscribed; rainfed agriculture relies heavily on the basin for food production and livelihoods are largely based on climate-sensitive natural resources'.

338 Turton, *supra* note 333, at 48.

339 Petrie et al., *supra* note 331, at viii.

340 *Id.*

is also needed given the high dependence on rain-fed agriculture, resulting in food insecurity and higher poverty levels. Improved water management of the basin would contribute to 'raising the standards of human welfare and socio-economic development'.[341] It would also support the nations ability to respond to extreme events, such as floods, disasters and climate change triggered events that occur in the basin.[342] Still, the basin states lack robust institutions to manage the shared water resource.[343] Enhancing water management and infrastructure changes may improve the situation of the river basin for these four countries.[344]

2.3.2 The Aquifer

Groundwater is a very important source of fresh water for Botswana and South Africa since they are semi-arid countries. This is especially true for rural communities that rely on this water resource. The Ramotswa TBA provides freshwater resources to rural communities, local municipalities, and cities.[345] The aquifer area contains the most densely populated area of Botswana, as well as rural areas in South Africa.[346] The groundwater levels in the aquifer vary between the northern and southern portions; the groundwater table in the northern portion is shallower.[347]

341 C. C. Mabiza, *Integrated Water Resources Management, Institutions and Livelihoods under Stress: Bottom-Up Perspectives from Zimbabwe* (Dissertation submitted in fulfilment of the requirements of the Board for Doctorates of Deft University of Technology and of the Academic Board of the UNESCO-IHE Institute for Water Education for the degree of Doctor; CRC Press, 2013) at 1.

342 S. T. Mubako & N. Mintz-Habib, *'Climate Change Adaptation and Water in Semi-Arid Regions: A Case Study of the Limpopo Basin, Southern Africa'*, in D. Stucker & E. Lopez-Gunn (eds), *Adaptation to Climate Change through Water Resources Management: Capacity, Equity and Sustainability* (Abingdon: Routledge, 2015) 208.

343 N. Mirumachi, *Transboundary Water Politics in the Developing World* (Abingdon: Routledge, 2015).

344 T. Zhu & C. Ringler, *Climate Change Implications for Water Resources in the Limpopo River Basin* (IFPRI Discussion Paper 0096, April 2010).

345 Ndlhovu et al., *supra* note 47, at iii. Ramotswa's name originates from the town of Ramotswa, in the South-East District of Botswana, southwest of the capital Gaborone, see Gemmell et al., *supra* note 27, at 12. Ramotswa is located in 'North West Province in South Africa and in the South East District in Botswana' in the Upper Limpopo River Basin, in the Marico and Ngotwane river subcatchment areas. See M. Magombeyi et al., *Agricultural Water Management Solutions for Smallholder Farmers in the Ramotswa Transboundary Aquifer Area* (Integrated Water Management Institute, December 2018) 2–13.

346 J. Lautze et al., *Joint Strategic Action Plan for the Ramotswa Transboundary Aquifer Area – Roadmap* (SAP Roadmap Report, December 2016) 8.

347 *Id.*, at 12–13.

The neighbouring areas to the aquifer in Botswana are urban, with high economic and population growth, in contrast to South Africa, where these areas have low economic growth and low population density. Yet, there is a great interest in the aquifer from the South African side because of the rising water demands in numerous cities, including Mafikeng, Zeerust and Lichtenburg. The Ramotswa Wellfield represents the main location from which groundwater is being abstracted in Botswana, despite being decommissioned in the 1990s because of pollution. It reopened in 2014 due to water shortages. Along with this wellfield, there are three others: Lobatse Wellfield, Pitsanyane Wellfield and Woodland Wellfield. In South Africa, there are more than 700 boreholes in the Ramotswa study area and thousands of boreholes in wider Ramotshere Moiloa local municipality, with water being used mostly for agricultural (both crops and livestock) and domestic purposes.[348]

The Ramotswa aquifer faces several challenges when it comes to its management. These challenges are a result of existing data gaps affecting the adoption of sound policies on the basis of reliable information. They also resulted from existing risks from groundwater contamination that previously occurred in some parts of the aquifer. Further, there is insufficient water in the aquifer to meet the demands in both countries. Botswana suffers from physical water scarcity, and both countries, though mainly South Africa, suffers from economic water scarcity due to 'low levels of infrastructure and service delivery [that] constrains the use of water to meet requirements'.[349] Moreover, there are challenges facing the implementation of and compliance with the policies adopted affecting water management because of a 'lack of capacity due to limited staff and financial resources, as well as constraints related to the technical skills or expertise of staff'.[350] Finally, access to water and sanitation for the vulnerable people near the aquifer is inadequate 'due to a lack of financial resources to ensure sufficient and continuous service during drought conditions or infrastructure/service delivery failure'.[351]

2.3.3 Legal and Institutional Developments in the Limpopo River Basin

Several regional initiatives, agreements and institutions paved the way for cooperation between the countries of the basin. These include the Tripartite Permanent Technical Committee established in 1983 between Mozambique,

348 Gemmell et al., *supra* note 27, at 13.

349 J. Lautze et al., *Joint Strategic Action Plan for the Ramotswa Transboundary Aquifer Area* (Integrated Water Management Institute, May 2019) 5.

350 *Id.*

351 *Id.*

South Africa, and Swaziland.[352] It had the objective of 'making recommendations on the management of the water shortages being experienced in the Limpopo, Incomati and Maputo Rivers at that time'.[353] Botswana, Mozambique, South Africa and Zimbabwe formed the Limpopo Basin Permanent Technical Committee (LBPTC) in 1986. The same countries also signed the Agreement on the Limpopo Basin Permanent Technical Committee in 1986,[354] which provided the legal framework for the LBPTC.[355] In 1987, Botswana and South Africa established the Joint Permanent Technical Committee (JPTC) concerning the Limpopo, Molopo and Nossob Rivers,[356] resulting initially in an agreement over water transfers from South Africa's Molatedi dam in 1988. Both countries also established the Tswasa agreement in 1998 which was revised and updated in 2014.[357] This revision also covered the agreement over water transfers from South Africa's Molatedi dam, which was needed due to the variations in political governance structures near the border.[358] The same nations formed the Joint Permanent Commission for Co-operation in 1997 to 'deal with a variety of issues, including the transfer of water from the Molatedi Dam on the Marico River'.[359]

The JPTC established a bilateral forum between South Africa and Botswana, which was updated with the signing of a memorandum of understanding. The JPTC 'acts as a formalized and functional forum for cooperation across the border regarding matters of transboundary water management between the two countries'.[360] Already, the JPTC has had an impact. For instance, in 2015, it established 'a subcommittee on the joint management of water quality

352 Agreement between the Government of the Republic of South Africa, the Government of the Kingdom of Swaziland and the Government of the People's Republic of Mozambique Relative to the Establishment of a Tripartite Permanent Technical Committee, Pretoria, 17 February 1983, at http://www.fao.org/3/w7414b/w7414b0h.htm, last accessed 14 June 2021.

353 Limpopo River Awareness Kit, *'Governance: Water Governance in the Limpopo Basin, History of LIMCOM'*, http://www.limpopo.riverawarenesskit.org/LIMPOPORAK_COM/EN/GOVERNANCE/WATER_GOVERNANCE_IN_THE_LIMPOPO/LIMCOM.HTM, last accessed 20 January 2020.

354 Agreement Relative to the Establishment of the Limpopo Basin Permanent Technical Committee, 1986, at https://iea.uoregon.edu/treaty-text/4452, last accessed 14 June 2021.

355 *Id.* The LBPTC provides advice to the parties on matters related to transboundary water issues in the Limpopo.

356 *Id.*

357 Lautze et al. (2019), *supra* note 349, at 21.

358 J. Lautze et al., *Draft Joint Strategic Action Plan for the Ramotswa Transboundary Aquifer Area* (IWMI; DWA - Botswana; DWS – South Africa, March 2018) 21.

359 *Id.*

360 *Id.*

and aquatic weeds in the Upper Limpopo River Basin, which has proposed practical measures to reduce proliferation of water hyacinth'.[361]

Botswana, Mozambique, South Africa, and Zimbabwe signed the 2003 Agreement on the Establishment of the Limpopo Watercourse Commission (LIMCOM) to address the entire Limpopo Basin, where the Ramotswa aquifer is located. The 2003 Agreement was based on the 1986 Agreement on the Establishment of the Limpopo Basin Permanent Technical Committee.[362] The Commission has the main task of advising 'the Contracting Parties and provide recommendations on the uses of the Limpopo, its tributaries and its waters for purpose and measures of protection, preservation and management of the Limpopo'.[363] The Agreement created a council as the principal organ of the Commission while numerous provisions of the treaty addressed the functions and structure of the council.[364] The implementation of the 2003 Agreement is slow. Still, a secretariat and three technical task teams (legal, technical and floods) have been created. A Limpopo River Basin IWRM Plan 2016–2020 has been adopted furthering 'LIMCOM's operations, and creating a monitoring and evaluation framework for implementation'.[365] Each of the agreements mentioned above include specific IWL principles. For instance, the 2003 LIMCOM Agreement includes the following principles: 'sustainable development; intergenerational equity; prevention principle; transboundary impact assessment principle; equitable and reasonable utilisation; harmonisation of policies and exchange of information'.[366]

Cooperation over the Ramotswa aquifer has been attempted in the context of the JPTC and LIMCOM. A decision was made in a 2016 JPTC meeting that progress concerning the aquifer shall be regularly reported. After presenting the project to LIMCOM in 2017, there was a proposal that the 'RAMOTSWA project could serve as a pilot in the context of a to-be-developed groundwater task team for the Limpopo basin'.[367] In fact, the JPTC in 2016 started engaging more actively in the Ramotswa aquifer through project activities with

361 *Id.*

362 *Id.*

363 Agreement on the Establishment of the Limpopo Watercourse Commission (2003), Article 3, at https://iea.uoregon.edu/treaty-text/4453, last accessed 14 June 2021.

364 *Id.*; Limpopo River Awareness Kit, *'Governance: Water Governance in the Limpopo Basin, LIMCOM Objectives and Structure'*, http://www.limpopo.riverawarenesskit.org/LIMPOPORAK_COM/EN/GOVERNANCE/WATER_GOVERNANCE_IN_THE_LIMPOPO/OBJECTIVES_AND_STRUCTURE.HTM, last accessed 20 January 2020.

365 Lautze et al. (2019), *supra* note 349, at 20.

366 *Id.*, at 22.

367 *Id.*, at 22–23.

the development of a strategic action plan for the aquifer,[368] while supporting the institutionalisation of its cooperative management. It was recognised that the JPTC already has an operational institutional platform.[369] Concerning the JPTC and LIMCOM, the JPTC was first to identify the need to resolve issues concerning the Moletedi dam; LIMCOM came later with a much wider mandate. In practice, many of the experts and policy-makers in the JPTC also participate in LIMCOM structures.[370]

2.3.4 Harmonizing National Laws of the Limpopo Basin Countries

Each of the four countries of the Limpopo basin has its own national, domestic, and local water rules. For instance, among the many water regulations and policies, Botswana has the Water Act of 1968, which regulates water management; the Water Utilities Corporation Act of 1970 as amended in 1978;[371] and the Water Utilities Corporation (Vesting of Assets) Order of 2008.[372] Water laws and policies of South Africa include the National Water Act of 1998, the Water Services Act of 1997, and the Water Use Licence Application and Appeals Regulations of 2017.[373]

It is important to harmonise the national water legislations of the riparian countries given the 'highly uneven development of policy, legislative and strategy between Member States' and the 'inadequate institutional capacity and governance arrangements, particularly for implementation of policy, legislation and strategies'.[374] This situation is worsened by the uneven human and financial resources at the national level because of the absence of political awareness and support.[375] For instance, in its National Water Act, South Africa addressed international water management, establishing 'guidelines for bi-national or multi-national bodies to be established to implement international

368 SADC-GMI, *supra* note 322, at 28.

369 *Id.*, at 28.

370 Interview with Jonathan Lautze, *supra* note 260.

371 Limpopo River Awareness Kit, *'Governance; Water Governance in the Limpopo Basin, National Policies & Laws'*, http://www.limpopo.riverawarenesskit.org/LIMPOPORAK_COM/EN/GOVERNANCE/WATER_GOVERNANCE_IN_THE_LIMPOPO/NATIONAL_POLICIES_AND_LAWS/BOTSWANA.HTM, last accessed 20 January 2020.

372 Food and Agricultural Organization of the United Nations, *'FAOLEX Database, Botswana – Country Profiles'*, http://www.fao.org/faolex/country-profiles/general-profile/en/?iso3=BWA, last accessed 20 January 2020.

373 Food and Agricultural Organization of the United Nations, *'FAOLEX Database, South Africa – Country Profiles'*, http://www.fao.org/faolex/country-profiles/general-profile/en/?iso3=ZAF, last accessed 20 January 2020.

374 SADC Regional Water Strategy, *supra* note 305, at 24.

375 *Id.*

agreements related to the management and development of transboundary water resources'.[376] Similarly, Mozambique considered transboundary water resources in Article 14 of its 1991 National Water Law focusing, for example, on integrated water resource management in shared river basins which takes into account 'the interests of all riparian states, proper allocation and joint utilisation of shared water, and joint planning and implementation of studies and infrastructural projects'.[377] In contrast, Botswana lacks a formal policy framework addressing transboundary water resources, despite the establishment of water agencies tackling shared water resources.[378] Zimbabwe still needs to consider shared water resources in its national water laws despite its participation in water commissions and focus on addressing regional water resources.[379]

2.3.5 The Application of BDA to the Ramotswa Aquifer

The Ramotswa aquifer case study will be used to examine the impact of BDA from a legal perspective. Testing big data in this context will be based on a previous Ramotswa project conducted from 2015 to 2019 to 'support a long-term joint vision and cooperation on the shared groundwater resources of the Limpopo River Basin and to build a community of practice around TBA

---

376 Limpopo River Awareness Kit, *'Governance, Water Governance in the Limpopo Basin, National Policies & Laws, South Africa'*, at http://www.limpopo.riverawarenesskit.org/LIMPOPORAK_COM/EN/GOVERNANCE/WATER_GOVERNANCE_IN_THE_LIMPOPO/NATIONAL_POLICIES_AND_LAWS/SOUTH_AFRICA.HTM, last accessed 14 June 2021; National Water Act, South Africa, 1998, http://www.limpopo.riverawarenesskit.org/LIMPOPORAK_COM/_SYSTEM/DMSSTORAGE/3461EN/RSA_NATIONALWATERACT_1998.PDF, last accessed 14 June 2021.

377 Limpopo River Awareness Kit, *'Governance, Water Governance in the Limpopo Basin, National Policies & Laws, Mozambique'*, at http://www.limpopo.riverawarenesskit.org/LIMPOPORAK_COM/EN/GOVERNANCE/WATER_GOVERNANCE_IN_THE_LIMPOPO/NATIONAL_POLICIES_AND_LAWS/MOZAMBIQUE.HTM, last accessed 14 June 2021; Republic of Mozambique, Act No. 16/91 Regulating Water Resources Belonging to the Public Domain, at https://www.ecolex.org/details/legislation/act-no-1691-regulating-water-resources-belonging-to-the-public-domain-lex-faoc003125/, last accessed 14 June 2021.

378 Limpopo River Awareness Kit, *'Governance, Water Governance in the Limpopo Basin, National Policies & Laws, Botswana'*, at http://www.limpopo.riverawarenesskit.org/LIMPOPORAK_COM/EN/GOVERNANCE/WATER_GOVERNANCE_IN_THE_LIMPOPO/NATIONAL_POLICIES_AND_LAWS/BOTSWANA.HTM, last accessed 14 June 2021.

379 Limpopo River Awareness Kit, *'Governance, Water Governance in the Limpopo Basin, National Policies & Laws, Zimbabwe'*, at http://www.limpopo.riverawarenesskit.org/LIMPOPORAK_COM/EN/GOVERNANCE/WATER_GOVERNANCE_IN_THE_LIMPOPO/NATIONAL_POLICIES_AND_LAWS/ZIMBABWE.HTM, last accessed 14 June 2021.

management in the SADC region'.[380] The main outcomes of the Ramotswa project were

1. Developing 'a solid base of knowledge on the Ramotswa Transboundary Aquifer in terms of hydrogeology and socio-economics'.
2. Defining 'five priority areas, including the developing of tools for a joint and harmonized management and monitoring of the groundwater resources considering present and future climate and demographic changes'.
3. Developing 'a joint information management system: the Ramotswa Information Management System (RIMS) hosted by IGRAC as an on-line portal providing access to maps, data, and information related to groundwater in the Ramotswa project'.[381]

The Ramotswa project focused on BDA and went through several steps. The first step was preliminary data collection, primarily data and data sets from the ministries discussed above, in addition to other authorities that were identified in Botswana and South Africa respectively. Several other databases were also identified, including the International Groundwater Resources Assessment Centre (IGRAC) database.[382] Various data analytical tools were used, with 'the volume, variety, velocity, veracity and value of the sourced data' guiding the choice of tools and approaches. Alternative data sources were expected to play a significant role given that groundwater data concerning the aquifer was expected to be scarce. First, there was a need for data quality control, integration and reformatting, given that the collected data was 'incomplete, contain[s] duplicates, or contain[s] errors and require[s] integration and reformatting'.[383] Therefore, data was 'integrated and reformatted into a consolidated database'. This included tasks such as 'record matching, identifying inaccuracy of data, overall quality of existing data, deduplication, and column segmentation'.[384] Then data was analysed, which required the collection of additional data that was not related directly to the particularities of groundwater. The aim was to 'increase data variety and volume and to be able to sufficiently test identified data tools'.[385]

The project identified three major challenges: automating data quality control, filling in sparse datasets, and deriving additional value from available and/

380 Gemmell et al., *supra* note 27, at 5.
381 *Id.*
382 *Id.*, at 17–18.
383 *Id.*, at 18.
384 *Id.*, at 18–19.
385 *Id.*, at 19.

or 'alternative' data.[386] This is why machine learning is more appropriate than standard statistical analysis as machine learning tools 'continuously learn from new data, becoming more effective over time, as well as [having] the potential for identifying patterns and/or clusters in the data'.[387] The project made use of three pre-existing Geographic Information System (GIS) platforms to visualise data products for decision-making and water resources management. These GIS platforms were RIMS, the Global Groundwater Monitoring Network, and the Global Freshwater Quality Database GEMStat. Each of these platforms has its own characteristics and key functions and tasks within the project. The project aimed at

> a unification of different policies / legalities through a common scientific approach – allowing for holistic management of the aquifer; coordination of future research and monitoring of the aquifer and increased awareness of the importance of groundwater in the region. The information gathered and tools provided facilitated informed and transparent decision making in a sphere where policies and agendas were often conflicting across national borders.[388]

BDA requires a huge amount of energy for data storage, communication and processing purposes. This means countries must have a large energy budget while simultaneously investing in energy efficiency.[389] Yet, South Africa and Botswana currently are facing energy challenges related to production, reliance on conventional energy resources, difficulties in transitioning to clean energy sources, and poor management practices and planning.[390] This reality will affect the use of BDA in the Ramostwa aquifer in the long term, as

---

386 *Id.* 'Machine learning, which is a large field of study but is only one of a number of subfields within AI, are AI programmes that can self-learn from a given set of data'. See J. Truby, R. D. Brown & A. Dahdal, *'Banking on AI: Mandating a Proactive Approach to AI Regulation in the Financial Sector'*, 14:2, Law and Financial Markets Review (2020) 110–120, at 111.

387 Gemmell et al., *supra* note 27, at 19.

388 *Id.*, at 24.

389 B. Parhami, *'Energy Implications of Big Data'*, in S. Sakr & A. Y. Zomaya (eds), *Encyclopaedia of Big Data Technologies* (Dordrecht: Springer, 2019).

390 K. Kotze, *'South Africa's Energy Conundrum'*, 8 April 2019, at https://globalriskinsights.com/2019/04/south-africas-energy-conundrum/, last accessed 14 June 2021; World Bank, *'Botswana: Issues and Options in the Energy Sector'*, 2010, at http://documents.worldbank.org/curated/en/396731468742179889/Botswana-Issues-and-options-in-the-energy-sector, last accessed 14 June 2021.

well as in other shared water resources between South Africa and Botswana. Similar challenges and many others exist in the rest of the African countries that will also affect the implementation of BDA in the context of shared water resources.[391]

2.3.6 Improving the Legal and Institutional Governance of TBAs in the SADC Region

Numerous suggestions have been made to improve the management of TBAs in the SADC region. These include strengthening shared watercourses agreements and institutions, developing targeted groundwater management and development strategies, and undertaking pathfinder projects to manage and develop groundwater resources.[392]

Very few water agreements mention groundwater specifically or treat it as part of the water resource. This is very important to promote conjunctive water use as well as addressing the characteristics of transboundary groundwater. As such, the development of specific water agreements must be done when it is appropriate, and strengthening existing water agreements may be more effective.[393]

The establishment of new water institutions faces several challenges and complex administrative processes. Therefore, strengthening existing shared watercourse institutions could facilitate the division of roles and responsibilities. State support is crucial to develop institutional capacities, especially as essential staff must have technical, financial or institutional skills. Indeed, the governance of TBAs requires technical expertise. Access to information and ensuring data and information exchange is essential so that institutions can provide advice and facilitate decision-making. In fact, institutions need to act as a broker for data and information management, and create a platform through which countries can agree on a specific understanding for sharing the water resource. States must be willing to provide such data and information while engaging in conversation with other institutions, the private sector and civil society organisations.

River basin organisations have already developed IWRM strategies and plans that include groundwater. These strategies and plans must be further strengthened and enhanced. Doing so requires engaging with all the stakeholders. There is also a need to undertake initial joint projects to implement

391 M. Hafner, S. Tagliapietra & L. de Strasser, *Energy in Africa: Challenges and Opportunities* (Dordrecht: Springer, 2018).

392 SADC-GMI, *supra* note 322, at 28.

393 *Id.*, at 29.

strategies and plans related to groundwater.[394] One has to keep in mind though the existence of political, technical and economic challenges. There is a need to address the significant internal and systemic issues such as 'strengthening existing institutions and focal points to drive awareness and capacity building programmes (staff and skills) and support the sourcing of sustainable funding for these institutions to undertake studies that support improved groundwater management'.[395] There is a need also to engage key experts and networks of expertise.[396]

2.3.7 Improving the Legal and Institutional Governance of the Ramotswa Aquifer

Both Botswana and South Africa have stated the need to develop a joint agreement for the management of the Ramotswa aquifer and made several recommendations to this end. The most relevant ones in the transboundary context are those related to institutional harmonisation and agreements focused on transboundary issues.[397] These recommendations were summarised in a Draft Joint Strategic Action Plan for the Ramotswa Transboundary Aquifer Area along with other recommendations addressing its implementation and capacity and tailored training.[398] Recommendations related to institutional harmonisation include internal harmonization within national government departments, harmonising plans (and planned activities) across countries, and adopting a joint management structure through the establishment of local operational joint management committees comprising local based institutions. Recommendations related to agreements on focused transboundary issues include an 'agreement establishing Joint Management Structure – operational committee' where various protocols will be established and 'creation of a Memorandum of Understanding for groundwater monitoring, specific to the Ramotswa Aquifer and RIMS' with associated protocols.[399]

394 *Id.*, at 30.
395 *Id.*, at 33.
396 *Id.*, at 34.
397 Lautze et al. (2018), *supra* note 358, at 15.
398 *Id.*
399 *Id.*, at 15–17.

3 Data and Information Exchange in IWL

3.1 *Data and Information Exchange in the Transboundary Water Context*

Information and data exchange are considered in the general framework of cooperation obligation. This monograph adopts the definition provided by Gerlak, Lautze and Giordano for the term 'data', namely, '"hard" numbers relating to water resources, such as rates of river flow and levels of water quality'.[400] They defined 'information' as 'general qualitative information, such as communication that a flood is impending or other conclusions reached from the analysis of hard data'.[401]

3.1.1 History of Water Information and Data Exchange

Information and data exchange provisions are part of the procedural mechanisms for treaty implementation. Until the 1920s, information exchange provisions within water agreements were rare.[402] Data and information exchange mechanisms were in less than 20% pre-World War II instruments, but there was a sharp increase in their inclusion from the 1930s to the 1940s and a continuous increase from the 1970s onward.[403] Between the 1980 and 2000, 61% of treaties signed had a data and information exchange obligation.[404] Currently, at least 40% of water agreements have specific provisions related to data and information exchange. This percentage is constantly rising.[405] About 37% of water agreements signed between 1900 and 2007 resulted in the creation of a platform or water institution for data and information exchange.[406]

---

400 A. K. Gerlak, J. Lautze & M. Giordarno, *'Greater Exchange, Greater Ambiguity: Water Resources Data and Information Exchange in Transboundary Water Treaties'*, in R. Q. Grafton et al. (eds), *Global Water: Issues and Insights* (Canberra: Australian National University, 2014) 58.

401 *Id.*, at 58–59.

402 M. Giordano et al., *'A Review of the Evolution and State of Transboundary Freshwater Treaties'*, 14, International Environmental Agreements: Politics, Law and Economics (2014) 245–264, 251–258.

403 A. K. Gerlak, J. Lautze & M. Giordano, *'Water Resources Data and Information Exchange in Transboundary Water Treaties'*, 11 International Environmental Agreements: Politics, Law and Economics (2011) 179–199, 188.

404 K. Conca, F. Wu & C. Mei., *'Global Regime Formation or Complex Institution Building? The Principled Content of International River Agreements'*, 50:2, International Studies Quarterly (2006) 263–285.

405 Giordano et al., *supra* note 402, at 258–259.

406 H. N. Thu & U. Wehn, *'Data Sharing in International Transboundary Contexts: The Vietnamese Perspective on Data Sharing in the Lower Mekong Basin'*, 536, Journal of Hydrology (2016) 351–364, 353.

There are many differences as to how the information is shared. Some treaties require regular exchange, while others require it upon request, as needed, or for specific events. Half the treaties are not clear about when a provision related to data and information exchange occur.[407] Moreover, more than half of the water agreements call for information exchange through 'technical cooperation such as joint research, investigation and assessments that suppose some aspects of data and information exchange'.[408] Many other agreements call for indirect methods for data sharing such as 'prior notification provisions or formalized communication procedures'.[409] Hence, there are many methods and issues involved when it comes to data and information sharing in transboundary water laws that require careful reading and interpretation as to how data sharing is being included. Where data sharing is not directly mentioned, treaties may still have related mechanisms.[410]

The importance of information exchange has increased over time with the international community understanding its significance with each instrument adopted. Instruments and documents adopted since the 1960s include Article XXIX of the 1966 Helsinki Rules on the Uses of the Waters of International Rivers[411] and the 1982 Montreal Rules.[412] Even the inclusion of a provision within the UNWC related to regular information exchange occurred gradually during the decades before the adoption of the Convention.[413] The obligation to exchange data and information between states sharing transboundary fresh water sources can be found in international declarations such as the Rio Declaration 1992,[414] the Dublin Statement of the International Conference on Water

407 Giordano et al., *supra* note 402, at 258–259.

408 *Id.*, at 259.

409 *Id.*

410 *Id.*

411 Helsinki Rules on the Uses of the Waters of International Rivers Helsinki, August 1966, Article XXIX, at https://www.internationalwaterlaw.org/documents/intldocs/ILA/ILA-HelsinkiRules1966-as_amended.pdf, last accessed 14 June 2021.

412 International Law Association, Rules on the Water Pollution in an International Drainage Basin, Montreal, 1982, Article 5, at https://www.internationalwaterlaw.org/documents/intldocs/ILA/ILA-Rules_on_the_Water_Pollution_in_an_International_Drainage_Basin-Montreal1982.pdf, last accessed 14 June 2021.

413 C. Leb, *Cooperation in the Law of Transboundary Water Resources* (Cambridge: Cambridge University Press, 2013) 115–116.

414 United Nations General Assembly, *Report of the United Nations Conference on Environment and Development* (*Rio de Janeiro, 3–14 June 1992*), Annex 1: Rio Declaration on Environment and Development, Principles 10 & 19, at https://www.un.org/en/development/desa/population/migration/generalassembly/docs/globalcompact/A_CONF.151_26_Vol.I_Declaration.pdf, last accessed 14 June 2021 [Rio Declaration].

Accurate and up-to-date data are needed for the development of policies and programmes. Indeed, the good governance of a basin is extremely difficult when reliable data are absent. For instance, 'high-flow data are needed for the design of major structures such as bridges and dams and for flood plain management, while low flow and yield data are required for water supply investigation and design, environmental studies, and low-flow forecasting'.[427] Effective and reliable data and information is needed to ensure the management of water resources globally and represents one of the key principles of the global regulatory framework addressing water governance in the transboundary context. The gathering of water data and information jointly can prevent disputes and conflict. Understanding complex problems through data and information is perceived as a means to enhancing the governance of common resources.[428]

Sharing data and information helps dealing with uncertainties and provides a further step toward cooperation among nations as 'a solid information base is necessary to delineate areas of agreement and disagreement and to structure and inform debate'.[429] In contrast, the absence of reliable data and information affects negotiations among the parties. Once a treaty is established, the exchange of information can form the basis for coordinated management and can help in the implementation of the convention. Moreover, such exchange would create much needed trust among the parties for the long-term implementation and compliance with the treaty, while at the same time develop a sense of reciprocity between states and promote further understanding and communication between them. In addition, data and information can help solve potential disputes between nations.[430]

There are different sources for data and information. The first source is the national agencies of the states sharing freshwater resources. In this case, there are usually certain rules or procedures to follow to obtain access to these data for national use and special arrangements are needed for others requesting these data. The second source is the shared data and information collected by mutual agreement and participation of the states and available to them all.[431] Finally, there are data available to everyone, such as satellite images and derived data products obtainable from the worldwide web.[432]

427 J. Chenoweth, *'Effective Multi-Jurisdictional River Basin Management'*, 24:4, Water International (1999) 368–376, 368.

428 Gerlak, Lautze & Giordarno (2014), *supra* note 400, at 57.

429 Gerlak, Lautze & Giordano (2011), *supra* note 403, at 183.

430 *Id.*, at 183–184.

431 Paisley & Henshaw, *supra* note 416, at 203.

432 *Id.*, at 209.

3.1.3 Factors and Obstacles Affecting Data and Information Exchange

One has to keep in mind that data collection in itself is not very useful as enormous amounts of data have been collected globally but remain unused, creating a data graveyard. Additionally, the data and information collected in many places is not helping or influencing the decision-making process. The lack of tangible benefits as a result is affecting trust between the parties.[433] Several factors affect the way this data is being used after being shared between the parties. These factors affect the governance of shared fresh water even in the context of data and information exchange.[434] In fact, data and information sharing is most likely going to occur when the parties perceive that there are more benefits than costs in doing so. Naff summarised the complicated relation between data and water in the following manner:

> flowing water carries within itself its own information, and because watercourses tend to be very dynamic systems, water data are consequently almost always in one degree or another estimates, extrapolations, and, sometimes, even speculation. Consequently, consistently reliable and accessible water data for international and transboundary riven are frustratingly rare.[435]

Since water matters are complicated, water data will always reflect this complexity. The quantity and quality of data are both very important. Historical data is also important even though it is usually inconsistent or inaccurate due to problems related to measurement, collection, processing, and natural or human changes.[436]

Numerous factors affect the exchange of data and information. They can be divided into either primary or secondary factors. Primary factors are those related to river or groundwater basins and cannot be changed by any force and as such must be always accepted. Secondary factors are matters that individual countries or the basin as a whole have minimal capacity to modify. The factors determine whether effective data and information exchange can occur. Some primary or secondary factors are considered interrelated in certain basins,

433 Chenoweth & Feitelson, *supra* note 421, at 499.

434 S. Gallaher & T. Heikkila, *'Challenges and Opportunities for Collecting and Sharing Data on Water Governance Institutions'*, 153:1, Journal of Contemporary Water Research & Education (2014) 66–78.

435 T. Naff, *'Information, Water, and Conflict: Exploring the Linkages in the Middle East'*, 22:1 Water International (1997) 16–28, 16.

436 *Id.*

but usually they are independent from each other.[437] Primary factors include 'compatible needs; absence of legacies of mistrust; political stability; common language and culture; sufficient levels of economic development; [and] increasing water resources stress'.[438] Secondary factors include 'perception by basin countries that cooperation is of mutual benefit; external pressure and funding for cooperative initiatives; comparable levels of institutional capacity; popular and political concern about water resources management; [and] existence of a functional formal or informal cooperative arrangement'.[439] Usually, not all these factors will be present in a shared basin, thus, 'tradeoffs between the different factors are critical in determining whether or not effective exchange processes are likely to be established'.[440]

States have different abilities when it comes to data and information gathering. A combination of human resources, financial capabilities and technological innovation provides certain nations with precise information on the state of the transboundary fresh water source, including hydrometeorological, socio-economic and environmental conditions. In contrast, other nations do not have such capacities.[441] Data is fragmented across numerous national agencies and institutions often require official permission to release data, meaning that access to data is usually restricted. Such restrictions are often due to considering water a matter of national security, especially in the transboundary context. Data affects a country's bargaining and negotiating position. The lack of data prohibits a state from assessing the real impact of a planned measure on the shared freshwater source and thus controlling whether the other state is complying with the obligation to not cause significant harm and the principle of equitable and reasonable utilisation.[442]

There are limitations to accessing water and climate data 'due to the increasing cost of data collection, licence conditions, data politicisation, and national regulations'.[443] Others argue that 'a range of contextual differences, including cultural, political, intentional, organisational, relational, knowledge, resource, physical and technical, strongly influence transnational information sharing'.[444] There are also limitations because data sharing may be perceived as weakening the negotiation position of a particular state or even blaming the

---

437 Chenoweth & Feitelson, *supra* note 421, at 500.
438 *Id.*, at 500–501.
439 *Id.*, at 501–502.
440 *Id.*, at 502.
441 Leb (2020), *supra* note 20, at 24–25.
442 *Id.*, at 25–26.
443 Thu & Wehn, *supra* note 406, at 353.
444 *Id.*

parties for any potential damage caused to the shared water resource.[445] States may decide not to share data fearing that the costs may outweigh the benefits of cooperation as negotiations may hinder their bargaining power. Data may be used as a weapon through which they can blame the other party for negative consequences. In fact, states may adopt vague mechanisms for data and information exchange to have further flexibility for purposes such as domestic politics. Also, the cost of collecting and exchanging the data is high, especially given contrasting economic, social, and political interests.[446]

3.2 *Data and Information Exchange within International Water Conventions and Instruments*

In IWL, there are three specific obligations related to information exchange: (1) the regular exchange of data and information, (2) notice of natural and human triggered emergencies, and (3) notice of planned measures.[447] Notification is not necessarily an 'exchange' obligation; the former concerns unilateral provision of information, while the latter implies mutual exchange of information and data. This section will examine each of these specific obligations. Data and information exchange or notification is extremely important for BDA given the various sources from which big data is created. Figure 1 shows the diverse sources of groundwater data and information.

Many of the sources set out in Figure 1 are collected at the national and local level by each state. For instance, data related to monitoring, drilling and pumping are collected by the national water departments. Moreover, states may have reports, maps and documents that are not shared with other parties and computer-based simulation results, all of which need to be shared.[448] These are a few examples of data and information that once collected is referred to as big data. This data need to be shared between countries. Notification of emergencies and planned measures through data should also occur so that any BDA among the parties or by one or more party considers this information. This is

---

445 *Id.*

446 Gerlak, Lautze & Giordano (2011), *supra* note 403, at 184. Water as a resource has already be used as a weapon for political reasons to show the dominance of one party over water access, for tactical reasons to show the ability to use water for military gain and for psychological reasons to highlight the control of a party over the local population. See J. Schillinger et al., *'Water in War: Understanding the Impacts of Armed Conflict on Water Resources and their Management'*, 7:6, WIREs Water (2020) 1–19, 10–11.

447 Leb (2013), *supra* note 413, at 114.

448 *Id.*

Source	Description	Characteristics
Field activities	Data generated from field activities such as monitoring, drilling and pumping activities	Structured data format Limited coverage (spatially and temporally) Local
Historical	Legacy reports, maps and documents	Unstructured Local or regional Text or images
Remote sensing	Satellite, airborne or ground-based earth observation	Unstructured and structured Multidimensional Voluminous Regional
Computer simulation	Data generated through computer-based models	Unstructured and structured Multidimensional Voluminous Regional
Social media and the web	Data available on webpages and social media post	Unstructured Textual, images, videos or audio Multidimensional Heterogeneous Voluminous Local
Internet of Things	Data available from connected devices	Unstructured and structured Heterogeneous Multidimensional Local

FIGURE 1 Sources of data in the groundwater domain from a big data context
GAFFOOR ET AL., SUPRA NOTE 38.

extremely important given that any data processing depends on the type and amount of data fed to the algorithm.

This has been noticed in various instances in the private sphere when the data fed to the algorithm did not reflect current situation and reality.[449] For example, some algorithms recognised that doctors are predominantly male although currently there is a high percentage of female doctors in the workforce globally, especially in the Organisation for Economic Co-operation and Development countries where it almost reaches 50%. Yet, the data fed to the algorithm did not only reflect the current situation, but also included historical data, when doctors were predominantly male. As such, this predominance resulted in a bias in the algorithm processing the information.[450]

Clearly, data and information in the transboundary water context remains extremely important. Accurate processing of data and information to produce a new result with an added value requires having all the possible data for processing. Otherwise, there is a risk of having biased results. Hence, the provisions within IWL and transboundary water agreements related to data and information exchange, as well as notification of emergencies and planned measures through data, are essential when it comes to the use of BDA.

3.2.1 Regular Exchange of Data and Information

Regular exchange of data and information is essential for effective cooperation. When only partial information is exchanged, it is not possible to assess whether a water use can be carried out.[451] Information exchange is also key to the implementation of other principles of IWL, such as equitable and reasonable use, no significant harm and cooperation.[452] The regular exchange

---

449 N. T. Lee, P. Resnick & G. Barton, *'Algorithmic Bias Detection and Mitigation: Best Practices and Policies to Reduce Consumer Harms'*, 22 May 2019, at https://www.brookings.edu/research/algorithmic-bias-detection-and-mitigation-best-practices-and-policies-to-reduce-consumer-harms/, last accessed 14 June 2021; J. Manyika, J. Silberg & B. Presten, *'What Do We Do About the Biases in AI?'*, 25 October 2019, at https://hbr.org/2019/10/what-do-we-do-about-the-biases-in-ai, last accessed 14 June 2021.

450 A. Brown, *'Biased Algorithms Learn From Biased Data: 3 Kinds Biases Found In AI Datasets'*, Forbes, 7 February 2020, at https://www.forbes.com/sites/cognitiveworld/2020/02/07/biased-algorithms/?sh=55bfdfe976fc, last accessed 14 June 2021; OECD, *'Women Make Up Most of the Health Sector Workers But They Are Under-Represented in High-Skilled Jobs'*, at https://www.oecd.org/gender/data/women-make-up-most-of-the-health-sector-workers-but-they-are-under-represented-in-high-skilled-jobs.htm, last accessed 14 June 2021.

451 Leb (2013), *supra* note 413, at 115.

452 See in general, S. M. A. Salman, *'Equitable and Reasonable Utilization and the Obligation Against Causing Significant Harm – Are they Reconcilable?'*, 115, American Journal of International Law (2021) 183–188; S. Schmeier, *'International Water Law Principles in*

of data and information as a customary obligation is still debated, as such exchange is not a universal practice. Such an obligation only occurs in treaties or other arrangements.[453] The information that must be provided must meet specific quality standards so that a state has more information about a shared basin. The end goal is the 'standardisation of information and data collection systems'.[454] Yet, this obligation is limited, as states often claim national defence and security considerations to avoid sharing data and information.[455]

Article 9 of the UNWC deals with the exchange of data and information. States are required to regularly exchange available data and information related to a given watercourse. States are especially asked to exchange those of 'hydrological, meteorological, hydrogeological and ecological nature and related to the water quality as well as related forecasts'.[456] If a state cannot immediately comply with another state's request to supply available data and information, the former needs to make best efforts to this end. The supplying state may also ask the requesting state for payment of the 'reasonable costs of collecting and, where appropriate, processing such data or information' to ensure compliance with its demand.[457] States are required to make their best efforts to collect and process data and information to facilitate the use of this newly acquired data and information by other watercourse states.[458]

The idea of exchanging readily available data, as mentioned by Article 9 of the UNWC, was cause for great debate during the negotiation of the convention. Ultimately, it 'was inserted in the Convention to reflect that the obligation should not become too onerous for individual States to carry out and that it should correspond to the respective capacities of States to produce data'.[459] Article 9 of the UNWC does not indicate the timing and frequency of data and information exchange; the term regular means an 'ongoing and systematic process'.[460] Similarly, very few treaties have included provisions specifying timing and frequency. In contrast, the treaties 'point towards a general duty to establish a continuous process of State cooperation over shared water resources'.[461] Finally, states are under an obligation of due diligence to provide

Negotiations and Water Diplomacy', 115, American Journal of International Law (2021) 173–177.

453 Leb (2013), *supra* note 413, at 118.

454 *Id.*, at 119.

455 *Id.*, at 118–120; UNWC, *supra* note 291, Article 31.

456 UNWC, *supra* note 291, Article 9(1).

457 *Id.*, Article 9(2).

458 *Id.*, Article 9(3).

459 Leb (2013), *supra* note 413, at 120.

460 *Id.*, at 122.

461 *Id.*

the data requested by another state even when it is not readily available. In case of hostilities, or when other obstacles prevent the direct exchange of data in accordance with Article 30 of the UNWC, states must still exchange such data through mutually acceptable indirect procedures.[462]

In contrast to the UNWC, the 1992 Convention on the Protection and Use of Transboundary Watercourses and International Lakes (UNECE Water Convention) did not mention the term regular in its provisions. Article 6 states that '[t]he Parties shall provide for the widest exchange of information, as early as possible, on issues covered by the provisions of this Convention'.[463] States also have a right to protect 'information related to industrial and commercial secrecy, including intellectual property, or national security' regardless of the provisions of this convention in accordance with national and international regulations.[464] Perhaps the closest provision related to regular exchange of data and information is Article 9, requiring the establishment of joint bodies based on agreements or arrangements between basin states. Among their tasks, these joint bodies are required to '(a) collect, compile and evaluate data in order to identify pollution sources likely to cause transboundary impact; (c) draw up inventories and exchange information on the pollution sources mentioned in paragraph 2 (a) of this article; (i) promote cooperation and exchange of information on the best available technology'.[465] Article 13 explicitly states the reasonable available data that must be exchanged which include, *inter alia*, '(a) environmental conditions of transboundary waters; (b) experience gained in the application and operation of best available technology and results of research and development; [and] (c) emission and monitoring data'.[466] States are even required to exchange information on their national regulations.[467] The novelty of this convention is stating that 'information on the conditions of transboundary waters, measures taken or planned to be taken to prevent, control and reduce transboundary impact, and the effectiveness of those measures' must be made available to the public where a specific procedure has been added to that end.[468] There are other articles that are

462 *Id.*, at 123–124; UNWC, *supra* note 291, Article 30.

463 Convention on the Protection and Use of Transboundary Watercourses and International Lakes, (Helsinki, 17 March 1992), Article 6, at https://unece.org/fileadmin/DAM/env/water/pdf/watercon.pdf, last accessed 14 June 2021 [UNECE Water Convention].

464 *Id.*, Article 8.

465 *Id.*, Article 9(2)(a), (c), (i).

466 *Id.*, Article 13 (a)–(c).

467 *Id.*, Article 13(2).

468 *Id.*, Article 16.

related to the exchange of data and information but would not be considered regular exchange.[469]

Finally, Article 8 of the ILC Draft Articles on the Law of Transboundary Aquifers covered data and information exchange in detail. States are required to exchange data and information on a regular basis 'on the condition of their transboundary aquifers or aquifer systems, in particular of a geological, hydrogeological, hydrological, meteorological and ecological nature and related to the hydrochemistry of the aquifers or aquifer systems, as well as related forecasts'.[470] In case of absence or inadequate knowledge with regards to the aquifers or the aquifer systems, states are required to employ their best efforts to gain this knowledge based on existing practices and standards. Such actions can be done unilaterally or jointly and when needed through or with international organisations.[471] Where an aquifer state requests data and information about an aquifer or aquifer systems that are not immediately available, the requested state must use its best efforts to comply. This state may ask for payment of the 'reasonable costs of collecting and, where appropriate, processing such data or information' as a condition for compliance.[472] Where appropriate, aquifer states are requested to use their best efforts in the collection of data and information 'in a manner that facilitates their utilization by the other aquifer States to which such data and information are communicated'.[473]

Two provisions related to data and information exchange within the UNWC and the Draft Articles are almost identical. The Draft Articles use the term 'and related to the hydrochemistry' in the first paragraph in contrast to the UNWC, which uses 'and related to the water quality'.[474] The Draft Articles also adds new categories related to geological and hydrogeological data and a new paragraph that examines data collection in detail.[475] Like the UNWC, the exchange of data and information obligation according to the Draft Articles is constrained when it comes to data and information that is considered vital to national defence and security as states are not obliged to share such information. Nonetheless, states need to cooperate to share as much information as possible in good faith

469 *Id.*, Article 17(2)(b).

470 Draft Articles on the Law of Transboundary Aquifers (2008), Article 8(1), at https://legal.un.org/ilc/texts/instruments/english/draft_articles/8_5_2008.pdf, 14 June 2021.

471 *Id.*, Article 8(2).

472 *Id.*, Article 8(3).

473 *Id.*, Article 8(4).

474 Leb (2013), *supra* note 413, at 117.

475 *Id.*, at 117.

and depending on the circumstances.[476] Like the UNWC, the Draft Articles do not specify the frequency of data exchange.[477]

As discussed above, data and information exchange is needed to ensure that data processing through BDA leads to unbiased outcomes. Whether the decision to process the data occurs between the countries at the basin level or by one or more parties, data processing resulting in a new outcome that is biased can complicate transboundary water management. On one hand, states may not be willing to accept the outcome as it may lead to new favourable conditions for one party over others. On the other hand, changing water management practices because of data processing that is biased may lead to poor water management, new challenges and problems.[478] In both cases, the party processing the data will claim that it used science, existing data and BDA to exonerate itself from responsibility. It is in this context that the regular exchange of data and information is of utmost importance in preventing situations that will further complicate transboundary water management instead of improving it.

3.2.2 Notice of Natural and Human Triggered Emergencies

IWL pushes states to work together in case of emergency situations.[479] This was the main reason for the ILC to include provisions related to emergency situations in international water conventions.[480] Emergencies occur because of natural causes, such as floods and ice conditions, or human activity conducted near a transboundary basin. To address such emergencies, water agreements usually refer to two broad categories of events: (1) emergencies due to natural causes or human conduct, and (2) measures planned by individual water system states.[481]

The obligation to notify about an emergency is a general obligation under international environmental law, and is not related to IWL.[482] Principle 18 of the Rio Declaration provides that 'States shall immediately notify other States of any natural disasters or other emergencies that are likely to produce sudden

476 *Id.*, at 119; Draft Articles, *supra* note 471, Article 19.

477 Leb (2013), *supra* note 413, at 122.

478 Ibrahim, *supra* note 9.

479 D. Ziganshina, *'Procedural System of Transboundary Water Cooperation in the Aral Sea Basin'*, in A. Kibaroglu et al. (eds), *Water Law and Cooperation in the Euphrates-Tigris Region: A Comparative and Interdisciplinary Approach* (Leiden: Brill/Nijhoff, 2013) 281.

480 C. B. Bourne, *International Water Law: Selected Writings of Professor Charles B. Bourne* (London: Kluwer Law International, 1997) 85.

481 Leb (2013), *supra* note 413, at 125.

482 *Id.*, at 126.

harmful effects on the environment of those States'.[483] This duty also applies before the occurrence of an emergency as states have an obligation to prevent the occurrence of emergencies. The risks related to natural emergencies can be mitigated by regular exchange of data and information. For example, national and joint monitoring and information exchange systems can help address emergencies related to the spread of diseases.[484] When it comes to pollution incidents, notification obligations emerge in case of '(1) emergencies in the case of accidents, and (2) planned measures that will or could pollute waters'.[485]

Article 28 (1) of the UNWC defined emergency as a 'situation that causes, or poses an imminent threat of causing, serious harm to watercourse States or other States and that results suddenly from natural causes, such as floods, the breaking up of ice, landslides or earthquakes, or from human conduct, such as industrial accidents'.[486] In an emergency, the state must immediately notify the potentially affected states, as well as international organisations, of the emergency originating from its territory using all available expeditious means.[487] The state from where the emergency originates must cooperate with the potentially affected states and, when needed, appropriate international organisations to 'immediately take all practicable measures necessitated by the circumstances to prevent, mitigate and eliminate harmful effects of the emergency'.[488] Finally, contingency plans shall be developed jointly by the watercourse states. Such cooperation can extend to affected states and competent international organisations when appropriate.[489]

The UNECE Water Convention addressed emergencies under Article 14:

> The Riparian Parties shall without delay inform each other about any critical situation that may have transboundary impact. The Riparian Parties shall set up, where appropriate, and operate coordinated or joint communication, warning and alarm systems with the aim of obtaining and transmitting information. These systems shall operate on the basis of compatible data transmission and treatment procedures and facilities to be agreed upon by the Riparian Parties. The Riparian Parties shall inform

483 Rio Declaration, *supra* note 414, Principle 18.
484 Leb (2013), *supra* note 413, at 127.
485 *Id.*, at 128.
486 UNWC, *supra* note 291, at Article 28(1). This article is located within Part V which deals with harmful conditions and emergency situations.
487 *Id.*, Article 28(2).
488 *Id.*, Article 28(3).
489 *Id.*, Article 28(4).

> each other about competent authorities or points of contact designated for this purpose.[490]

The UNECE Water Convention is more explicit when it comes to promptly executing notification than the UNWC, even though in practice their provisions are more or less similar.[491] This provision constitutes the basis for Article 15, which provides that states should provide mutual assistance upon request in case of a critical situation.[492]

The Draft Articles cover the notification of emergencies under Article 17. It defines emergency as a 'situation, resulting suddenly from natural causes or from human conduct, that affects a transboundary aquifer or aquifer system and poses an imminent threat of causing serious harm to aquifer States or other States'.[493] The state where the emergency occurs is asked to notify other states and international organisations without delay using the fastest means possible. It is also required to 'take all practicable measures necessitated by the circumstances to prevent, mitigate and eliminate any harmful effect of the emergency' while cooperating with potentially affected states and international organisations as needed.[494] Article 17 added a novel element to emergency measures as aquifer states must take into account vital human needs when an emergency may threaten such needs and adopt measures that are strictly necessary to that end while considering the principle of equitable and reasonable utilisation and the obligation not to cause significant harm.[495] States are also required to provide 'scientific, technical, logistical and other cooperation to other States experiencing an emergency'.[496] Such cooperation can include 'coordination of international emergency actions and communications, making available emergency response personnel, emergency response equipment and supplies, scientific and technical expertise and humanitarian assistance'.[497] One of the main reasons for including a provision on emergency situations within the Draft Articles was the events that occurred during the drafting process, such as the tsunami along the coast of the Indian Ocean in

490 UNECE Water Convention, *supra* note 464, Article 14.

491 R. Moynihan & B. O. Magsig, *'Prevention and Mitigation of Harmful Conditions and Emergency Situations (Articles 27 and 28)'*, in L. B. de Chazournes et al. (eds), *The UN Convention on the Law of the Non-navigational Uses of International Watercourses: A Commentary* (Oxford: Oxford University Press, 2018) 296.

492 UNECE Water Convention, *supra* note 464, Article 15.

493 Draft Articles, *supra* note 471, Article 17(1).

494 *Id.*, Article 17.2(a)–(b).

495 *Id.*, Article 17.3.

496 *Id.*, Article 17.4.

497 *Id.*, Article 17.4.

2004 where there were fears of destruction or flood of seawater to the aquifers. Hence, there was a need to clarify the potential impact of tsunamis and earthquakes on aquifers, for example, through saltwater intrusion.[498]

Communities and nations surrounding the areas where a natural or a human made disaster has occurred are vulnerable to floods and chemical spills, for example, especially in the transboundary water context. Such events have environmental as well as economic effects in the surrounding basin. Currently, the storage and processing of disaster and emergency data is a great challenge facing government organisations managing disasters such as public health authorities. Yet, reaction to a disaster and emergency requires fast processing of disaster and emergency data. BDA can be used to support the quick processing of data for decision-making purposes during and after the occurrence of the event to ensure the adoption of effective disaster response and recovery measures.[499] BDA can be used at various stages in this process. These include the preparedness stage before the occurrence of an event, through early detection and disaster monitoring as well as early warning. It can be used at the mitigation phase to conduct risk assessment and forecasting and prediction. At the response stage, BDA is used for damage assessment, coordination for post-disaster management, and recovery.[500] The obligation of notice of natural and human triggered emergencies in IWL is important as nations must be notified as soon as possible before using BDA to address the disaster or emergency at the various stages set out above. Data processing can also provide information to the state facing the event and other states seeking to protect their territory.

3.2.3 Notice of Planned Measures

The notification of co-riparians of planned measures on shared watercourses is a key principle of IWL.[501] The duty to notify 'stems from good faith, good neighbourliness, and reciprocity', and represents the only method for figuring

---

498 F. Sindico & L. M. Pateiro, *'The Interplay between the UN Watercourses Convention and the Law on Transboundary Aquifers (Article 2)'*, in L. B. de Chazournes et al. (eds), *The UN Convention on the Law of the Non-navigational Uses of International Watercourses: A Commentary* (Oxford: Oxford University Press, 2018) 403.

499 M. Arslan et al., *'A Review on Applications of Big Data for Disaster Management'* (The 13th International Conference on Signal Image Technology & Internet Based Systems, December 2017) 2.

500 Md. N. I. Sarker et al., *'Disaster Resilience through Big Data: Way to Environmental Sustainability'*, 51 International Journal of Disaster Risk Reduction (2020).

501 S. M. A. Salman, *Notification Concerning Planned Measures on Shared Watercourses: Synergies between the Watercourses Convention and the World Bank Policies and Practice* (Leiden: Brill, 2019) 1.

out whether unilateral activities of riparians may affect negatively a watercourse.[502] The importance of notification was highlighted by the International Court of Justice in the *Pulp Mills* case in 2010,[503] where it considered 'notification as a *sine qua non* of cooperation, in addition to being a vital method for protecting the shared watercourse'.[504] It is worth mentioning that the duty to notify rests on both upstream and downstream countries.[505]

In accordance with Article 11 of the UNWC, '[w]atercourse States shall exchange information and consult each other and, if necessary, negotiate on the possible effects of planned measures on the condition of an international watercourse'.[506] The state planning the measures must notify the other watercourse states in a timely manner and provide the available data and information so that the rest of the watercourse states can assess whether the measures will have negative consequences.[507] Notification in accordance with this Article is required in case of potential significant adverse effects, a term that has been subject to several interpretations over the years.[508] The notified state then has a 'period of six months within which to study and evaluate the possible effects of the planned measures and to communicate the findings to it'.[509] This period can be extended for another six months upon the request of the notified state in case of special difficulties in making the evaluation. Still, the UNWC provides watercourse states with the flexibility in this regard, as they can agree on different terms and durations.[510] The notifying state during the six or twelve months period should provide, upon the request of the notified state, additional data and information needed to help making an accurate assessment. The notifying state cannot implement or allow the implementation of the planned measures during this period without the consent of the notified state.[511] Some have commented that this period is too long and may delay measures that do not cause actual harm.[512] The notified state must communicate the results of the assessment within the specified period

---

502 *Id.*, at 2.

503 *Case Concerning Pulp Mills on the River Uruguay* (*Argentina v. Uruguay*), Judgment, ICJ Reports 2010, p. 14.

504 Salman (2019), *supra* note 502, at 3.

505 *Id.*, at 21.

506 UNWC, *supra* note 291, Article 11.

507 *Id.*, Article 12.

508 Salman (2019), *supra* note 502, at 23.

509 UNWC, *supra* note 291, Article 13.

510 *Id.*

511 *Id.*, Article 14. There is an exception to this rule spelled out in Article 19 UNWC, as explained further below.

512 Salman (2019), *supra* note 502, at 24.

and explain in an official document whether it finds the planned measures in violation of the principle of equitable and reasonable utilisation or the obligation not to cause significant harm.[513]

If the notifying state does not receive a response within the specified period, it can proceed with the planned measures taking into account the two principles mentioned above as well as the notification and data and information provided.[514] If the planned measures were found to be problematic by the notified state, consultations and negotiations should follow between the notifying and the notified state to reach an equitable solution. During this period, the planned measures should not be implemented if the notified state so requests.[515] If a state decides to implement planned measures without notification, even after an official request from a concerned state, negotiations and consultations can follow at the request of the state that was supposed to be notified. During this time, the other state can ask the state planning the measure to refrain from implementing the measure for a period of six months unless otherwise agreed.[516] Finally, a state has the right in an utmost emergency for the protection of public health, public safety or other emergency reasons to immediately implement measures, taking into account the principle of equitable and reasonable utilisation and the obligation not to cause significant harm as well as specific Articles related to planned measures within the UNWC. A formal declaration must be submitted to the other states with the necessary data and information, and consultations and negotiations may take place upon the request of the other states.[517] Additionally, Article 30 of the UNWC provides for the use of indirect procedures for fulfilling the duty of cooperation between states, including 'exchange of data and information, notification, communication, consultations and negotiations' when there is no direct contact between states.[518] This Article was not discussed above because it deals with indirect procedures between riparians where notification is only one of the many aspects mentioned.[519]

The UNECE Water Convention has fewer provisions addressing the notification of planned measures when compared to the UNWC. Article 9 regarding the establishment of joint bodies based on agreements or arrangements states that these bodies have among their tasks serving 'as a forum for the exchange

513 UNWC, *supra* note 291, Article 15.
514 *Id.*, Article 16(1).
515 *Id.*, Article 17.
516 *Id.*, Article 18.
517 *Id.*, Article 19.
518 *Id.*, Article 30.
519 Salman (2019), *supra* note 502, at 27.

of information on existing and planned uses of water and related installations that are likely to cause transboundary impact'.[520] This Article 'provides for different types of notification and the role of joint bodies (or RBOs) without defining the process of notification'.[521] Article 13 states that nations must exchange reasonably available data related to, *inter alia*, '(d) [m]easures taken and planned to be taken to prevent, control and reduce transboundary impact'.[522] If the party cannot provide data and information upon the request of a state, the party must comply but can ask 'reasonable charges for collecting and, where appropriate, processing such data or information'. This obligation is applied to all types of data and information exchange, not only the notification of planned measures.[523] Analysis of the provisions of the UNECE Water Convention related to planned measures shows that it addressed this matter lightly.[524]

The Draft Articles addressed the question of planned measures in Article 15. Accordingly, states are required to assess the potential negative consequences of a planned activity on the rest of the aquifer states when there is a reason to believe that such consequences may occur.[525] Before implementing or permitting the implementation of activities that may have negative consequences, the other aquifer states must be notified in a timely manner. The notifying state must provide the technical data and information as well as the environmental impact assessment report so that the notified state can assess the potential impact of the planned activities.[526] When there is disagreement between the notifying and the notified state over the impact of the planned measures, they should enter into consultation and, if needed, negotiation to find an equitable solution. A third party, called an independent fact-finding body, can be used to make an objective assessment of the potential impact of the proposed measures.[527] Also, Article 5 related to factors relevant to equitable and reasonable utilisation addresses planned measures. Accordingly, the equitable and reasonable utilisation of an aquifer or an aquifer system requires consideration of many factors, including 'the availability of alternatives to a

520 UNECE Water Convention, *supra* note 464, Article 9.2(h).

521 N. C. Odili, *Shared Water Resources in West Africa: Relevance and Application of the UN Watercourses and the UNECE Water Convention* (Leiden: Brill, 2018) 56.

522 UNECE Water Convention, *supra* note 464, Article 13.1(d).

523 *Id.*, Article 13.3.

524 Other relevant provisions include Article 3.1.(h). See G. Baranyai, *European Water Law and Hydropolitics: An Inquiry into the Resilience of Transboundary Water Governance in the European Union* (Dordrecht: Springer, 2020) 144.

525 Draft Articles, *supra* note 471, Article 15.1.

526 *Id.*, Article 15.2.

527 *Id.*, Article 15.3.

particular existing and planned utilization of the aquifer or aquifer system'[528] and 'the development, protection and conservation of the aquifer or aquifer system and the costs of measures to be taken to that effect'.[529] The ILC considers the fragility of aquifers in the text of the provisions, including those on planned measures.[530]

BDA can play an important role in the assessment of whether the planned measures have short- or long-term negative consequences on other states sharing the same water basin. Already, states in many places are having disputes over planned measures that are either taking place or will take place in the future. Examples include the Grand Ethiopian Renaissance dam currently being built by Ethiopia, which faces objections from Egypt and sometimes Sudan. Both countries claim that the dam will have negative consequences on their economies and the local population living near the Nile.[531] Another example relates to the measures concerning the release of water by upstream nations to downstream countries in water basins in Central Asia and in the Mekong River basin.[532] In all these cases, BDA can be used to assess the actual impact in both the short and long term of the planned measures on water basins, especially because the other states can demand more data and information from the state undertaking these measures in accordance with IWL. This may resolve many of the current controversies surrounding planned measures and provide a means for the adoption of measures that can be realistically assessed in terms of their impact.

3.3 *Data and Information Exchange within the SADC Revised Water Protocol*

This section provides a brief overview of the different provisions within the SADC Protocol addressing data and information exchange in accordance with the general classification discussed above, including regular exchange,

528 *Id.*, Article 5.1(g).

529 *Id.*, Article 5.1(h).

530 L. B. de Chazournes, *Fresh Water in International Law* (Oxford: Oxford University Press, 2013) 122.

531 S. M. A. Salman, *'The Grand Ethiopian Renaissance Dam: The Road to the Declaration of Principles and the Khartoum Document'*, 41:4, Water International (2016) 512–527.

532 S. Burchi, *'International and Domestic Water Law in Central Asia – Implementing International Law Obligations Regarding Transboundary Waters: The Role of Domestic Water Legislation'*, 4:2, Central Asian Journal of Water Research (2018) 59–68; I. A. Ibrahim, *'Water Governance in the Mekong after the Watercourses Convention 35th Ratification: Multilateral or Bilateral Approach?'*, 36:1, International Journal of Water Resources Development (2020) 200–220.

notification of emergencies caused by nature or human activities and notification of planned measures.

3.3.1 Regular Exchange of Data and Information

The SADC Revised Protocol does not contain a provision addressing the regular exchange of data and information. In fact, the Protocol mentions such exchange in provisions that are scattered throughout the instrument. The first time data and information exchange is mentioned is in Article 2, which states the overall objectives of the Protocol and the measures that it is seeking to take to achieve these objectives. These measures include information exchange.[533] The Protocol then includes the exchange of data and information as one of the general principles stated in Article 3. Accordingly, states must exchange data and information concerning 'hydrological, hydrogeological, water quality, meteorological and environmental condition of shared watercourses'.[534] The only time the exchange of data and information must be regular is in the context of shared water institutions, which must provide 'on a regular basis or as required by the Water Sector Co-ordinating Unit, all the information necessary to assess progress on the implementation of the provisions of this Protocol, including the development of their respective agreements'.[535]

3.3.2 Notification of Natural Emergencies and Those Caused by Human Activity

Emergency situations are covered under Article 4. 5 of the Protocol, according to which a state, in case of an emergency situation originating from its territory, must notify 'potentially affected States, the SADC Water Sector Co-ordinating Unit and competent international organisations'.[536] The state also must immediately provide the needed information to these stakeholders and 'co-operate in the prevention, mitigation, and elimination, of harmful effects of the emergency'.[537] An emergency situation was defined by Article 1 of the Revised Protocol as a 'situation that causes or poses an imminent threat of causing serious harm to Watercourse States and which results suddenly from natural causes, such as torrential rains, floods, landslides or earthquakes or from human conduct'.[538]

533 Revised SADC Protocol, *supra* note 44, Article 2(e).
534 *Id.*, Article 3.6.
535 *Id.*, Article 5.3(c).
536 *Id.*, Article 4.5.
537 *Id.*
538 *Id.*, Article 1.1.

3.3.3 Notification of Planned Measures

The revised Protocol discussed planned measures in detail under Article 4.1. Accordingly, states are required to exchange information, and if needed, negotiate the potential effects of the planned measures on a given watercourse.[539] States are required to notify other nations before the implementation of measures that may have an adverse effect and provide 'technical data and information, including the results of any environmental impact assessment' so that the notified states can make a proper assessment.[540] States have six months to assess the potential effects of the planned measures unless agreed otherwise. The notified state can request an extension of six months in case of difficulties in making the assessment.[541] During this period, the notifying state must cooperate with the notified state by providing, on request, further data and information needed to make the proper assessment, as well as by refraining from the implementation or allowing the implementation of the measures without the consent of the notified state.[542] The notified state must provide its findings within the specified period and attach a document explaining the reasons in case the findings highlight that the planned measures are inconsistent with specific provisions of the Protocol.[543]

The notifying state can proceed with the implementation of the measures in case of no response by the notified state within the period mentioned above.[544] A claim of compensation by the notified state in this context 'may be offset by the costs incurred by the notifying State for action undertaken after the expiration of the time for a reply which would not have been undertaken if the notified State had objected within that period'.[545] If the notified state mentions the existence of problems with the planned measures, the notified and notifying state must enter into consultations and, if needed, negotiations with the objective of reaching an equitable solution.[546] Such consultation must be conducted in good faith, with each state considering the rights and legitimate interests of the other state.[547] During consultation, the notifying state shall refrain from implementing or allowing the implementation of the

539 *Id.*, Article 4.1(a).
540 *Id.*, Article 4.1(b).
541 *Id.*, Article 4.1(c).
542 *Id.*, Article 4.1(d).
543 *Id.*, Article 4.1(e).
544 *Id.*, Article 4.1(f)(i).
545 *Id.*, Article 4.1(f)(ii).
546 *Id.*, Article 4.1(g)(i).
547 *Id.*, Article 4.1(g)(ii).

planned measures for a six-month period, if requested by the notified state unless agreed otherwise.[548] If a state believes that another state is seeking to implement planned measures that may have adverse effects, it may ask that state to follow the procedure of notification stipulated in Article 4.1(b) and explain it reasons through a document.[549] The state planning the measures must provide a documented explanation if it believes that it is not obliged to provide notification in accordance with Article 4.1(b). If this response is unsatisfactory for the concerned state, then both states shall enter into consultations and negotiations in accordance with Article 4.1(g)(i)–(ii).[550] During this time, the state planning the measures shall refrain from implementing them or allowing their implementation if such a request is made by the concerned state for a period of six months unless agreed otherwise.[551] If there is urgency for the implementation of the planned measures, such as protecting public health, public safety or other important interests, the state planning the measures can proceed to implement them while complying with specific provisions within this Article.[552] 'In such case, a formal declaration of the urgency of the measures shall be communicated without delay to the other Watercourse States referred to in paragraph (b) together with the relevant data and information'.[553] The state planning the measures shall enter into consultations and negotiations upon the request of any watercourse state, while also complying with specific provisions of this article.[554]

Article 3 also mentions planned measures as states are required to consider the 'availability of alternatives, of comparable value, to a particular planned or existing use' to ensure that a watercourse is shared in an equitable and reasonable manner.[555] It also referred parties to Article 4 when dealing with planned measures.[556]

548 *Id.*, Article 4.1(g)(iii).
549 *Id.*, Article 4.1(h)(i).
550 *Id.*, Article 4.1(h)(ii).
551 *Id.*, Article 4.1(h)(iii).
552 *Id.*, Article 4.1(i)(i).
553 *Id.*, Article 4.1(i)(ii).
554 *Id.*, Article 4.1(i)(iii).
555 *Id.*, Article 3.8(a)(viii).
556 *Id.*, Article 3.9.

4 Establishing an Open Data Regulation for the Ramotswa Aquifer

4.1 *Current Suggestions for Addressing Water and Information Exchange in the Ramotswa Aquifer*

It has been suggested that a protocol be developed to address transboundary water governance in the Ramotswa aquifer. A protocol would provide 'guidance on the data that need to be exchanged and the metadata necessary to make use of the data that must be shared'.[557] It would also provide 'various technical solutions to organise the exchange of data and suggestions on the frequency of data exchange as well as the policy for sharing data outside of the departments'.[558]

In fact, a protocol on transboundary groundwater data sharing currently is being drafted by South Africa and Botswana for the Ramotswa transboundary aquifer area. It aims at 'improving the flow of data exchange between the national (ground)water departments and ease the harmonisation of data'.[559] The objective is to provide guidance to national groundwater departments in South Africa and Botswana on how to best share groundwater data, as well as providing 'quality assurance and quality control measures to prevent erroneous data to be exchanged'.[560]

Protocols on groundwater data exchange also have been developed by Umvoto and IGRAC.[561] Both entities are focusing on sharing these protocols with all stakeholders to gain feedback and recommendations. The next step is drafting a 'prototype of transboundary groundwater data and information sharing protocols' that can be adopted in the context of the Ramotswa and, potentially, other places in the SADC region.[562] However, it is unclear whether the objective is to adopt one or multiple protocols to address groundwater data

557 Sterckx, Vargas & Gemmell (Deliverable 4), *supra* note 261, at 6–7.

558 *Id.*

559 A. Sterckx, C. R. Vargas & A. Gemmell, *Big Data Analytics and Transboundary Water Collaboration, Theme 1: Consolidation of Data and Application of Big Data Tools to Enhance National and Transboundary Data Sets in Southern Africa that Support Decision-Making for Security of Water Resources – Deliverable 3: Quality Control System Report* (IGRAC & Umvoto, 29 November 2019) 5.

560 *Id.*

561 'Umvoto was established in 1992 as a water resource development and management consultancy and plays a key role in the successful exploration, resource estimation and environmentally sustainable implementation of several turnkey groundwater supply schemes'. See, International Groundwater Resources Assessment Centre, 'UMVOTO', at https://www.un-igrac.org/donor-partner/umvoto, last accessed 20 January 2020.

562 Virtual Workshop, *'Advancing Protocols on Transboundary Groundwater Data Sharing in the Ramotswa Transboundary Aquifer Area (RTBAA)'*; Date: 20–21 January 2021.

and information exchange between the parties to the Ramotswa aquifer. The protocol is a legal agreement developed to guide departments in managing and organising the continuous exchange of groundwater data in the context of TBA.[563] This protocol is in addition to the obligations of South Africa and Botswana stipulated within the SADC Protocol as a framework instrument. The drafters of the protocol hope that other countries will apply the protocol to surface water resources like TBAs or to international lake and river basin organisations.[564] At the same time, the legal status of such protocols is unclear. For instance, Umvoto and IGRAC provide that the 'upload of data in the transboundary database should follow a protocol that specifies what data and metadata must be shared, in which format, and at what frequency'. However, it is not clear if such a protocol will represent an actual legal agreement or a technical document.[565]

Generally, a protocol is adopted as a follow-up to a convention that established general principles. The protocol tackles specific obligations in specific areas. To be able to sign the protocol, a state must first sign the related convention. Parties are not required to comply with a protocol to a convention unless they sign and ratify it.[566] The protocol can take the form of a protocol of signature, addressing additional matters such as interpreting specific clauses of a convention. It can be an optional protocol to an existing convention establishing additional rights and obligations. Such a protocol allows the parties to 'establish among themselves a framework of obligations which reach further than the general treaty and to which not all parties of the general treaty consent, creating a 'two-tier system'.[567] A protocol can also take the form of a supplementary treaty, including additional provisions to an existing convention. Finally, a protocol can be based on an existing framework convention whose objectives are further 'elaborated and incorporated by a Protocol, with specific substantive obligations, according to rules agreed upon in the basic treaty'.[568] Examples of protocols to framework conventions include the Basel Protocol on Liability and Compensation for Damage Resulting from Transboundary

563 Sterckx, Vargas & Gemmell (Deliverable 3), *supra* note 560, at 5.

564 *Id.*

565 *Id.*, at 8.

566 S. Barrett, *Environment and Statecraft: The Strategy of Environmental Treaty-Making* (Oxford: Oxford University Press 2005) 146.

567 United Nations Forum on Forests, *An Overview of International Law: Working Draft* (Ad hoc expert group on Consideration with a View to Recommending the Parameters of a Mandate for Developing a Legal Framework on All Types of Forests, New York, 7–10 September 2004, Background Document No. 3) 5.

568 *Id.*

Movements of Hazardous Wastes and their Disposal, the Cartagena Protocol on Biosafety to the Convention on Biological Diversity, the Kyoto Protocol to the UNFCCC, and the Montreal Protocol on Substances that Deplete the Ozone Layer.[569]

The adoption of water protocols has been examined in the literature, especially since the 1990s with the adoption of international protocols on shared watercourses.[570] Protocols addressing water resources have been adopted at the international level and in the transboundary water context at the basin level. At the international level, the Protocol on Water and Health was adopted by the UNECE in 1995 and entered into force in 2005. The Protocol aims to 'protect human health and well-being by better water management, including the protection of water ecosystems, and by preventing, controlling and reducing water-related diseases'.[571] The Civil Liability and Compensation for Damage Caused by the Transboundary Effects of Industrial Accidents on Transboundary Waters Protocol was adopted in 2003. This protocol 'will give individuals affected by the transboundary impact of industrial accidents on international watercourses (e.g. fishermen or operators of downstream waterworks) a legal claim for adequate and prompt compensation'.[572] The idea of adopting a protocol has also been examined in the context of international non-binding instruments addressing shared water resources. For instance, Dellappenna and Loures suggested the adoption of the Draft Articles on the Law of Transboundary Aquifers of 2008 as a protocol to the UNWC.[573]

569 H. F. Kuehl, *'UPDATE: A Basic Guide to International Environmental Legal Research'*, May/June 2017, at https://www.nyulawglobal.org/globalex/International_Environmental_Legal_Research1.html, last accessed 14 June 2021; Kyoto Protocol to the United Nations Framework Convention on Climate Change, Kyoto, 11 December 1997, 2303 UNTS 162; Basel Protocol on Liability and Compensation for Damage Resulting from Transboundary Movements of Hazardous Wastes and their Disposal Basel, Basel, 10 December 1999, UN Doc. UNEP/CHW.1/WG/1/9/2 ; Cartagena Protocol on Biosafety to the Convention on Biological Diversity, Montreal, 29 January 2000, 2226 UNTS 208 ; Montreal Protocol on Substances that Deplete the Ozone Layer, Montreal, 16 September 1987, 1522 UNTS 29.

570 R. K. Paisley & M. Curlier, *'Creating Basin Mechanisms in Southern Africa'*, in S. C. McCaffrey, C. Leb & R. T. Denoon (eds), *Research Handbook on International Water Law* (Cheltenham: Edward Elgar Publishing, 2019) 344.

571 United Nations Economic Commission for Europe (UNECE), *'Protocol on Water and Health'*, January 2014, at http://www.unece.org/index.php?id=35086#:~:text=The%20UNECE%20%E2%80%93%20WHO%2FEurope%20Protocol,and%20reducing%20water%2Drelated%20diseases, last accessed 20 January 2020.

572 UNECE, *'Protocol on Civil Liability and Compensation for Damage'*, at https://www.unece.org/env/civil-liability/welcome.html, last accessed 20 January 2020.

573 J. W. Dellappenna & F. R. Loures, *'Filling Gaps: A Protocol to Govern Groundwater Resources of Relevance to International Law'*, in F. R. Loures & A. Rieu-Clarke (eds), *The*

Water protocols in transboundary basins have been adopted over the decades. Examples include the 1987 protocol signed between Turkey and Syria 'as an interim agreement for sharing the waters of the Euphrates River'[574] and the SADC Protocol discussed above.[575] Water protocols have also been adopted in the domestic context. For instance, the government of Canada adopted a Protocol for Safe Drinking Water in First Nations Communities[576] and a Protocol for Centralised Drinking Water Systems in First Nations Communities.[577]

The adoption of protocols addressing shared freshwater resources follows a general trend of the international community, which has been adopting conventions and protocols in various fields.

4.2 *Effectiveness of Transboundary Water Agreements and Protocols*

The multiple political, economic and social boundaries present complex challenges in the management of transboundary waters and require strong policies and regulations.[578] In fact, even the transfer of successful water management models from one basin to another is extremely difficult.[579] Biswas clarified the complexities by posing the question of 'how to develop and manage the various transboundary water sources sustainably and efficiently in full agreement and cooperation between the appropriate co-basin countries so that they result in

UN Watercourses Convention in Force: Strengthening International Law for Transboundary Water Management (Abingdon: Routledge, 2013) 263–269.

574 A. Kibaroglu, *'An Analysis of Turkey's Water Diplomacy and its Evolving Position vis-à-vis International Water Law'*, in P. Wouters, H. Chen & J. E. Nickum (eds), *Transboundary Water Cooperation: Principles, Practice and Prospects for China and its Neighbors* (Abingdon: Routledge, 2018).

575 S. M. A. Salman, *'Introductory Note to SADC: Revised Protocol on Shared Watercourses in the Southern African Development Community'*, 40:2, International Legal Materials (2001) 317–319.

576 Government of Canada, *'Protocol for Safe Drinking Water in First Nations Communities'*, at https://www.sac-isc.gc.ca/eng/1100100034913/1533666029471, last accessed 20 January 2020.

577 Government of Canada, *'Protocol for Centralised Drinking Water Systems in First Nations Communities'*, at https://www.sac-isc.gc.ca/eng/1100100034998/1533666593873, last accessed 20 January 2020.

578 J. D. Petersen-Perlman, J. C. Veilleux & A. T. Wolf, *'International Water Conflict and Cooperation: Challenges and Opportunities'*, 42:2 Water International (2017) 105–120, 105; see also A. Tayia, *'Transboundary Water Conflict Resolution Mechanisms: Substitutes or Complements'*, 11:7, Water (2019) 1337.

579 A. K. Biswas, *'Preface'*, in A. K. Biswas (eds), *Managing Transboundary Waters of Latin America* (Abingdon: Routledge, 2013) ix.

a "win-win" situation for all the parties concerned?'[580] The main issues constraining the management of transboundary water resources are usually related to national sovereignty and the absence of water agreements in many places globally,[581] and, in many instances, IWL was non-implementable.[582] Still, water agreements are essential for the management of shared freshwater resources in basins around the globe.[583] External assistance and encouragement play a role in establishing and ensuring the implementation of water agreements.[584] Yet, frequently, water agreements that are adopted are neither enforced nor effective when a crises occurs, leading to disputes between countries.[585] This is because implementation of water agreements is voluntary. Agreements 'must be sustainable and self-enforced if they are to have lasting benefits'.[586]

The adoption of water agreements is not an indication of effective implementation.[587] Water data has been exchanged even in the absence of such agreements, as evidenced by a study conducted on 25 international watercourses establishing and implementing a data-exchange assessment framework.[588] Treaties are important for building institutional capacity, but not sufficient to ensure the effectiveness of water agreements. In a 2005 study, Lautze and Giordano examined 153 water-related agreements in Africa. They found that only 108 are substantive, and a number of these treaties were not implemented or no longer enforced.[589] The main factor that affects the

580 A. K. Biswas, *'Management of Transboundary Waters: An Overview'*, in O. Varis, C. Tortajada, & A. K. Biswas (eds), *Management of Transboundary Rivers and Lakes* (Dordrecht: Springer, 2008) 5.

581 *Id.*, at 8–9.

582 J. A. Allan & N. Miramuchi, *'Why Negotiate? Asymmetric Endowments, Asymmetric Power and the Invisible Nexus of Water, Trade and Power that Brings Apparent Water Security'*, in A. Earle et al. (eds), *Transboundary Water Management: Principles and Practice* (London: Earthscan, 2010) 21.

583 Y. Khudayberganov, *'Security and Water Resources Management Problems and Experience in the Amudarya Basin'*, in C. Madramootoo & V. Dukhovny (eds), *Water and Food Security in Central Asia* (Dordrecht: Springer, 2011) 65–66.

584 World Bank, *'Water Resources Management'* (Policy Paper 1993) 63.

585 F. A. Ward, *'Forging Sustainable Transboundary Water-sharing Agreements: Barriers and Opportunities'*, 15:3, Water Policy (2013) 386–417, 387–388.

586 R. E. Just & S. Netanyahu, *'Preface'*, in R. E. Just & S. Netanyahu (eds), *Conflict and Cooperation on Trans-Boundary Water Resources* (Dordrecht: Springer, 1998) xv.

587 OECD, *Environmental Management in Eastern Europe, Caucasus and Central Asia* (Paris: OECD Publishing, 2005) 79.

588 P. Mukuyu et al., *'The Devil's in the Details: Data Exchange in Transboundary Waters'*, 45:7/8, Water International (2020) 884–900.

589 Petersen-Perlman, Veilleux & Wolf, *supra* note 579; J. Lautze & M. Giordano, *'Transboundary Water Law in Africa: Development, Nature, and Geography'*, 45:4, Natural Resources Journal (2005) 1053–1087.

effectiveness of an agreement is whether states negotiating a water treaty will benefit more from cooperation than from unilateral actions.[590] In addition, parties enter into agreements when the opportunities outweigh the risks of not cooperating.[591] There are many factors that render a water agreement ineffective.

> They may be considered partial in that they related only to certain aspects of transboundary water management, or because important riparian countries are not party to the agreement; or because the legal agreement is widely ignored and there is no effective enforcement mechanism.[592]

Water agreements are especially ineffective when some parties perceive that the agreement is not fair and that they had to sign it due to their weaker status in comparison to other nations. These parties will often try to delay or avoid its implementation.[593] Moreover, there are many variables that play a role in ensuring the effectiveness of water agreements or protocols. These are mostly related to the need to respond to the changes over time in water supply, and demands such as population growth and economic development, as well as changes affecting the water flow, like climate change.[594] The adoption of a water agreement does not mean that cooperation between states will take place in the future as 'these contracts can solidify power imbalances between states and give the illusion of cooperation'.[595] Rather, treaties provide states with the means to organise their inter-state relations and manage disputes. Nations are more likely to manage the shared waters with treaties, especially when negotiations are needed, than without.[596]

Therefore, an effective agreement must include 'measures that allow for adaptation to changes in water supplies, population, climate, technology, infrastructure, and economic activity while also guiding water use patterns'.[597] A flexible water agreement offers 'a more predictable water supply for all riparians, greater incentives to develop needed water infrastructure and more open,

590 Ward, *supra* note 586, at 388.

591 Petersen-Perlman, Veilleux & Wolf, *supra* note 579.

592 OECD, *International Regulatory Co-operation Addressing Global Challenges* (Paris: OECD Publishing, 2013) 52.

593 S. Islam & L. E. Susskind, *Water Diplomacy: A Negotiated Approach to Managing Complex Water Networks* (Abingdon: Routledge, 2013).

594 Ward, *supra* note 586, at 387.

595 S. M. Mitchell & N. A. Zawahri, '*The Effectiveness of Treaty Design in Addressing Water Disputes*', 52:2 Journal of Peace Research (2015) 187200, 187.

596 *Id.*

597 Ward, *supra* note 586, at 386.

transparent and accountable water institutions'.[598] It should also encourage 'increased food production, water security, environmental protection, reduced flood damage, better adaptation to the costs of extreme weather and variable climate, and a reduced need for complex legal, administrative and enforcement activities'.[599] Other factors that play a role in ensuring the effectiveness of a water treaty are water allocation and institutional mechanisms to deal with potential disputes or tensions arising from, for example, water scarcity or competing water interests.[600] States should include mechanisms that facilitate cooperation such as the establishment of RBOs, monitoring, a conflict resolution mechanism, enforcement, and data and information exchange,[601] as treaty design is important to the effectiveness of a water agreement.[602] These mechanisms are not always 'obvious in international water agreements, nor are they clearly defined in environmental agreements'.[603]

4.3 *Addressing Data and Information Sharing between States in the Context of BDA and Other Emerging Disruptive Technologies*

Ibrahim called for the inclusion of new provisions within transboundary water agreements related to BDA and emerging disruptive technologies at the basin level given that the existing traditional data and information provisions, if they exist at all, are not sufficient to address these technologies.[604] Ibrahim also acknowledged that provisions within water agreements usually have a general nature to ensure that states sign, ratify and implement the agreement. Hence, Ibrahim called for balancing the need for the adoption of flexible and general provisions within water agreements and the need to address all the matters surrounding the use of BDA and emerging disruptive technologies. To that end, he called for the adoption of further legal mechanisms, in particular framework water conventions at the basin level. These mechanisms also include follow-up agreements and protocols where states already have adopted framework treaties. The alternative is the adoption of memorandums of understanding where the existing agreement is not a framework convention.

---

598 *Id.*

599 *Id.*

600 S. Dinar & A. Dinar, *International Water Scarcity and Variability: Managing Resource Use Across Political Boundaries* (Oakland: University of California Press, 2017) 102–103.

601 Mitchell & Zawahri, *supra* note 596, at 188.

602 A. Dinar & Y. Tsur, *'Introduction and Conclusion'*, in A. Dinar & Y. Tsur (eds), *Management of Transboundary Water Resources Under Scarcity: A Multidisciplinary Approach* (Singapore: World Scientific Publishing, 2017).

603 P. A. Jones, *'Compliance Mechanisms of International Water Agreements'*, 25:4 Water International (2000) 554–564, 554.

604 Ibrahim, *supra* note 9, at 1147–1148.

Other suggestions include the establishment of collective institutions, such as a joint commission.[605]

Ibrahim acknowledged that existing water agreements are not flexible enough to deal with social, political or economic changes that occur after they have been adopted. Water agreements are not drafted with the thought of considering changes as that potentially would require renegotiation of the entire agreement. This could open a 'Pandora's box' that could worsen the situation, as some parties might not be satisfied with the agreement, look to change existing provisions, gain further benefits, or even eliminate the agreement entirely. Hence, changes such as variation of water flows or new disruptive technologies like BDA will not be considered within existing agreements.[606]

Thus, scholars like Drieschova, Fischhendler and Giordano called for the inclusion of flexible mechanisms within water agreements,[607] such as 'provisions for consultation, a broadening of cooperation, mutual assistance, indirect allocation, or include a reliance on the ambiguous language of international law'.[608] Cooley and Gleick[609] provided examples of potential flexible mechanisms that can be included, namely, '(1) adjustable allocation strategies and water-quality standards; (2) response strategies for extreme events; (3) amendment and review procedures; and (4) joint management institutions'.[610] Meanwhile Jafroudi[611] suggested shortening water agreements. Other scholars who developed new mechanisms include Kilgour and Dinar,[612] who mainly assessed the 'possibility of practical schedules for water allocation that vary according to anticipated flow volumes'.[613] Still, it is important to point out that the mere adoption of flexible mechanisms will not necessarily facilitate the

605 *Id.*

606 *Id.*, at 1148–1149.

607 A. Drieschova, I. Fischhendler & M. Giordano, *'The Role of Uncertainties in the Design of International Water Treaties: An Historical Perspective'*, 105 Climatic Change (2011) 387–408.

608 *Id.*, at 392.

609 H. Cooley & P. H. Gleick, *'Climate-proofing Transboundary Water Agreements'*, 56:4, Hydrological Sciences Journal (2011) 711–718.

610 *Id.*, at 711.

611 M. Jafroudi, *'Enhancing Climate Resilience of Transboundary Water Allocation Agreements: The Impact of Shortening the Agreement's Lifetime on Cooperation Stability'*, 18, International Environmental Agreements: Politics, Law and Economics (2018) 707–722.

612 M. Kilgour & A. Dinar, *'Flexible Water Sharing Within an International River Basin'*, 18, Environmental and Resource Economics (2001) 43–60.

613 *Id.*, at 58.

task of amending an agreement to include new provisions, such as inclusion of emerging technologies like BDA.[614]

It seems that the suggestion of adopting a protocol or protocols to an existing agreement on transboundary groundwater data sharing between South Africa and Botswana is a good start for the regulation of data and information sharing in the context of BDA. First, both countries have signed and ratified the SADC Revised Protocol that established the general and procedural principles applicable to shared water resources in the SADC region.[615] Hence, a new protocol could address the specific aspects related to data and information exchange in the context of emerging technologies such as BDA. Such a protocol would allow detailed consideration of all the elements related to data and information exchange and BDA in the context of the general substantive and procedural principles established within the SADC Revised Protocol. A new instrument could address the sophisticated technicalities of BDA, explain the various terms and roles and consider how to deal with their constant development and progress. Based on this protocol, further instruments and mechanisms could be adopted to address specifically the application of BDA to the Ramotswa aquifer.

A protocol can be considered as a stepping stone document(s) based on which all parties can form initial consensus needed to move forward in ensuring information and data exchange to support BDA. States agreeing to take part in a big data initiative and research, and adopting relevant protocols demonstrates their willingness to engage seriously in the exchange of data and information, particularly if they invest in emerging technologies to ensure the availability of the most valuable and up-to-date information.[616] However, these protocols should only be seen as instruments initiating cooperation between states over information and data sharing given the need to consider the future changes occurring in the basin.[617] There may be further developments in BDA and other emerging technologies that surpass the capacity of legislators to

614 S. Cohen, *Understanding Environmental Policy* (New York: Columbia University Press, 2014).

615 Revised SADC Protocol, *supra* note 44.

616 See all the reports mentioned in monograph related to the application of big data to the Ramotswa aquifer.

617 J. G. Timmerman & S. Langaas, *'Water Information: What Is It Good For? The Use of Information in Transboundary Water Management'*, 5:4, Regional Environmental Change (2005) 177–187; Mukuyu et al., *supra* note 589, at 884–900.

adopt rules to address such developments.[618] Because of these changes, states may change positions over the years concerning the management of a transboundary water resource.[619]

The California Open and Transparent Water Data Act of 2016 and the New Mexico Water Data Act of 2019 can be applied in the transboundary water context to provide further flexibility and clarity. Indeed, despite the focus of these acts on the states of California and New Mexico in the US, some of their provisions can be adapted to address data and information exchange at the basin level while considering BDA and other emerging technologies.

It is important to point out, however, the difference between open data and big data. Open data is described as 'information that is available to the public to use, no matter the intended purpose'. Big data is defined as 'datasets that are on a huge scale; so much so that they cannot usually be handled by the usual software'.[620] Hence, they have different characteristics as 'open data is defined by its use and big data by its size'.[621] This monograph focuses on applying specific provisions from open data regulations in the transboundary water context where BDA is being used. States must consider the need for constant monitoring and updating of water data, information exchange, and the inability of the law to catch up with the constant changes created by climate change, other ecological factors, human conduct, and technological developments.

The idea of developing an integrated open water data platform that employs disruptive technologies like open source BDA platforms between or among riparian states can best address these issues. A transboundary open water data law that employs BDA would be consistent with international data exchange obligations, as discussed above. To address the issue of data and information exchange at the basin level where states are using BDA and other emerging technologies, this monograph proposes the adoption of conventions and protocols that include provisions and features akin to the Open and Transparent Water Data Act and the Water Data Act. These features include the integration of multiple water and ecological data sources, including water data transfers and

---

618 See generally, Ebers & Navas, *supra* note 45; Mak, Tai & Berlee, *supra* note 45; Corrales, Fenwick & Forgo, *supra* note 88.

619 J. Williams, *'Stagnant Rivers: Transboundary Water Security in South and Southeast Asia'*, 10:12, Water (2018) 1819; A. Dinar et al., *Bridges Over Water: Understanding Transboundary Water Conflict, Negotiation and Cooperation* (Singapore: World Scientific Publishing, 2013).

620 Global Database, *'Big Data vs Open Data: What's the Difference?'*, at https://uk.globaldatabase.com/article/big-data-vs-open-data-what-s-the-difference, last accessed 14 June 2021.

621 *Id.*

exchanges; the creation of data sharing, documentation, quality control, and public access protocols; and the creation of open-source platforms and decision support tools to implement open water data.

Specific provisions of these open water data acts can be applied to the transboundary water context while at the same time considering IWL and existing transboundary water agreements at the regional or basin level, as well as the particularities of shared freshwater resources. In Ramotswa aquifer, there is a need to consider the addition of specific provisions of these water data acts considering IWL, the SADC Protocol, especially its provisions on data and information exchange, and the future protocol or protocols on transboundary groundwater data sharing between South Africa and Botswana.

4.4 *Practical Implementation in the Ramotswa Aquifer*

This section will examine the various conventions and instruments that must be considered to regulate the use of BDA in the Ramotswa aquifer. It should be noted that there is lack of clarity over the types of protocols to be adopted. It is most likely that the states sharing the Ramotswa aquifer will adopt a protocol to the SADC Protocol, considering it to be a framework convention. They may also adopt a framework protocol. The former needs to consider the substantive and procedural provisions of the SADC Protocol. The latter would probably also follow these rules, but not necessarily. In both cases, follow-up protocols (a series of several protocols that have binding force; strict legal, technical or hybrid protocols) could be adopted. The following suggestions should be seen in this context, with the authors seeking to provide recommendations while the stakeholders (Botswana, South Africa with the support of agencies and organisations such as Umvoto and IGRAC) are in the process of negotiating potential protocol(s). Hence, the suggestions made should be tailored in accordance with the final outcomes of the negotiations, for example, the adoption of a framework protocol first, and then a series of protocols, or several protocols adopted simultaneously, as well as the nature of the protocol or protocols adopted (strictly legal, technical or hybrid).

4.4.1 Data and Information Exchange Provisions within the SADC Protocol and Relevant Water Provisions

As discussed above, the SADC Protocol is a regional framework instrument applicable in the SADC region to which both Botswana and South Africa are parties. The SADC Protocol includes numerous provisions that could be considered when adopting other binding documents between the states of the region sharing freshwater resources. These include the general principles mentioned in Article 3, such as the principle of unity and coherence of each shared watercourse;[622] the principle of cooperation;[623] the exchange of data and information concerning the 'hydrological, hydro geological, water quality, meteorological and environmental conditions of shared watercourses';[624] and the utilisation of the shared watercourse in an equitable and reasonable manner.[625]

In fact, the relation between the protocol and other conventions adopted by the parties is stipulated in Article 6 on shared watercourse agreements. It states that 'nothing in this Protocol shall affect the rights or obligations of a Watercourse State arising from agreements in force for it on the date on which it became a party to the Protocol'.[626] The parties to such agreements can harmonise them with this protocol[627] and can even 'enter into agreements, which apply the provisions of this Protocol to the characteristics and uses of a particular shared watercourse or part thereof'.[628] Given the importance and relevance of the SADC Protocol, both Botswana and South Africa should implement the provisions of the Protocol that are relevant to data and information exchange.

Moreover, the provisions related to data and information exchange should be replicated within any new protocol. Provisions that should be replicated include Article 2, which states the overall objectives of the Protocol and the measures that it is seeking to take to achieve the mentioned objectives including information exchange;[629] Article 3, which makes the exchange of data and information a general principle;[630] and Article 5.3(c), according to which, exchange of data and information must be regular in the context of shared water institutions.[631] Other provisions that mention data and information exchange include notification in case of natural or human triggered emergencies under Article 4.5,[632] planned measures under Article 4.1, and other measures under the same Article where information and data exchange is required.[633]

These provisions, whether general or specific, relate to data and information exchange under the SADC Protocol. They provide the necessary background

622 SADC Protocol, *supra* note 44, Article 3(1).
623 *Id.*, Article 3(5).
624 *Id.*, Article 3(6).
625 *Id.*, Article 3(8)a.
626 *Id.*, Article 6(1).
627 *Id.*, Article 6(2).
628 *Id.*, Article 6(3).
629 *Id.*, Article 2(e).
630 *Id.*, Article 3.6.
631 *Id.*, Article 5.3(c).
632 *Id.*, Article 4.5.
633 *Id.*, Article 4.1(a); see generally, Article 4.

for the adoption of traditional data and information exchange provisions and disruptive technology driven open water data provisions that employ BDA within any future protocol or protocols on transboundary groundwater data sharing between South Africa and Botswana. Both countries can benefit from existing sophisticated regional water law provisions that consider the particularities and characteristics of the SADC region and that were agreed upon by both countries and the other countries of the region. Such an approach will also provide further legitimacy to the proposed protocol.

4.4.2 The Protocol or Protocols Must Consider Data and Information Exchange Provisions within the Draft Articles on the Law of Transboundary Aquifers

One may wonder why the new protocol(s) needs to consider IWL conventions and instruments that contain provisions addressing data and information exchange since the SADC Revised Protocol was heavily influenced by the UNWC and its provisions.[634] Despite the provisions related to data and information exchange within the UNWC that were the basis for similar provisions within the SADC Revised Protocol, the UNWC was focused on transboundary surface water. The shared aquifers covered within the Protocol were principally the unconfined ones; other types such as confined aquifers were covered in a separate Resolution to the agreement. This resulted in the adoption of provisions that do not take into account the particularities and characteristics of TBAs.[635] Indeed, there are intrinsic differences between groundwater and surface water.

> Groundwater is typically more vulnerable than surface water to pollution and other forms of contamination because it generally flows at much slower rates than surface water. The slow flow can result in contamination and other problems manifesting at equally slower rates, compared with contamination of surface waters, as well as reduction in an aquifer's natural recuperative abilities. Additionally, reclamation of a polluted aquifer, if at all possible, can be extremely difficult and expensive and can render the aquifer unusable for years, decades, or longer. Furthermore, due to its physical location, often at considerable depths,

634 Salman (2004), *supra* note 281; Salman (2001), *supra* note 286; Salman, *supra* note 576.

635 G. Eckstein & Y. Eckstein, *'A Hydrogeological Approach to Transboundary Ground Water Resources and International Law'*, 19:2, American University International Law Review (2003) 201–258; International Law Commission, Resolution on Confined Transboundary Groundwater, adopted by the Commission at its forty-sixth session, in 1994, and submitted to the General Assembly as a part of the Commission's report covering the work of that session on the topic Law of the non-navigational uses of international watercourses.

> groundwater can be substantially more difficult and costly to monitor than surface waters.[636]

As such, specific provisions addressing these characteristics need to be adopted.

Such provisions have only been adopted in the 2008 Draft Articles, well after the adoption of the SADC Revised Protocol. Therefore, the new protocol needs to consider these provisions. In particular, the protocol should incorporate Article 8 of the Draft Articles, which requires states to exchange data and information on a regular basis 'on the condition of their transboundary aquifers or aquifer systems, in particular of a geological, hydrogeological, hydrological, meteorological and ecological nature and related to the hydrochemistry of the aquifers or aquifer systems, as well as related forecasts'.[637] These provisions address the issue of data and information exchange and only focus on TBA because the sole focus of the instrument is on such aquifers.

Such provisions are most appropriate for the planned protocol(s) between South Africa and Botswana given the focus of the said protocol(s) on the regulation of data and information exchange concerning the Ramotswa aquifer. The combination of specific provisions addressing TBAs on the basis of the Draft Articles and provisions addressing the specificities of the SADC on the basis of the SADC Protocol is the most appropriate for the initial elements related to data and information exchange. However, neither the Draft Articles nor the SADC Protocol address BDA and emerging technologies, so these provisions are not sufficient. Adding BDA driven open water data provisions, like those in the Open Water Data Act of California and the Water Data Act of New Mexico, are also necessary.

4.4.3 The Protocol or Protocols Must Include Provisions Replicating the Ones in the Open and Transparent Water Data Act and the Water Data Act

4.4.3.1 *Developing an Integrated Water Data Platform*

Increasingly, water experts are recognising the negative impact of fragmentation of water and ecological data on the adoption of effective and timely water management decisions. This has resulted in calls for building water data

636 G. Eckstein, *The International Law of Transboundary Groundwater Resources* (Abingdon: Routledge, 2017) 81–82.

637 Draft Articles, *supra* note 471, Article 8(1).

platforms by developers.[638] These platforms include 'the U.S. Department of the Interior's Open Water Data Initiative; the Bureau of Reclamation's Reclamation Water Information System; open data actions taken by the states of Texas, Utah and Arizona; the Water Data Exchange; the Internet of Water and numerous others'.[639] The literature addressing the issues surrounding these platforms is growing and highlights the complexities in achieving the objectives of these platforms. Still, further research is needed to understand how and when open data platforms can be used to improve the decision-making process related to water management.[640]

An example of a successful water platform is Colorado's Decision Support Systems (CDSS), an online water data and modelling platform. The CDSS has three main components: '(1) a database, including groundwater data stream-flow data, climate station data, water rights data, and other information, (2) web tools and data management interfaces, and (3) modelling platforms/software. All data, tool and models are publicly available on the CDSS website'.[641] Initially developed in 1990s, currently the CDSS covers ten basins in Colorado. The CDSS is being used for various 'decision-making purposes, including reservoir operation decisions by water commissioners, water availability assessments, decisions about water rights transfers, and long-term water planning by the state and others'.[642] This platform is considered a success.

> The State of Colorado tackled several challenges during tool development and implementation, including (1) development of robust data protocols and standards; (2) concerns over the collection, use and public reporting of data; (3) state agency capacity and staffing issues; (4) model code maintenance; and (5) concerns about intellectual property. Some of these challenges remain ongoing issues.[643]

638 T. Moran et al., *'Evaluating the Use of Data Platforms for Water Management Decisions'*, 8 June 2020, at https://waterinthewest.stanford.edu/publications/evaluating-use-data-platforms-water-management-decisions, last accessed 20 January 2020.

639 T. Moran et al., *'Evaluating the Use of Data Platforms for Water Management Decisions: Key Findings and Recommendations'*, 4 June 2020, at https://purl.stanford.edu/cb612zf3515, last accessed 20 January 2020.

640 T. Moran et al., *Evaluating the Use of Data Platform for Water Management Decisions* (Final Report submitted to the S. D. Bechtel, Jr. Foundation, 9 August 2019, revised 10 January 2020) 4; T. Moran et al., *Evaluating the Use of Data Platform for Water Management Decisions: Supplemental Material* (Water in the West; Stanford Digital Repository, submitted 9 August 2019, revised 10 January 2020).

641 Moran et al. (Final Report), *supra* note 641, at 15.

642 *Id.*, at 16.

643 *Id.*

Analysis of several open water data platforms led to several findings that must be considered when establishing and implementing new platforms. The findings are:

1. The social and political complexities surrounding water data should not be underestimated. In complex water management situations involving many different organisations it can be difficult to discern who the "key" decision-makers are, how (or if) they will use the tool, and what factors may hinder tool adoption.
2. Defining tool objectives and the boundaries of the physical system necessary to meet those objectives can be challenging, particularly when there are many agencies and stakeholders involved in tool development. Clear objectives, planning and metrics are necessary to ensure successful tool development.
3. It is important to ensure short- and long-term agency commitment to tool development prior to initiating tool construction.
4. Securing support for ongoing tool maintenance and hosting can be challenging in retrospect.
5. Agencies may be reluctant to make data publicly available for a variety of reasons, including concerns that increased data transparency may lead to greater scrutiny or the risk of misinterpretation by parties external to the decision making processes; protection of proprietary data; and a lack of capacity to adequately QA/QC [quality assurance/quality control] data in a timely manner.
6. Agencies commonly lack resources (technical, financial and capacity) to make data publicly available.
7. Agencies are often more willing to release primary data than higher-value processed data or model outputs. Legal or regulatory steps may need to be taken to make certain types of data publicly available.[644]

Numerous recommendations have been made to address these findings. For instance, it was recommended that 'the tool development team should work with decision-makers and other potential end users to establish clear objectives for the tool, including the tool's purpose, intended use and users (and their associated priorities), the boundaries of the physical system (tool scale and components), and the data necessary to meet those objectives' to address the second finding.[645] Further, it was recommended that the development team 'work with agencies to (1) understand any potential concerns

644 *Id.*, at 17–18.
645 *Id.*, at 17.

related to increasing data transparency and (2) consider the pros and cons of developing an open and transparent decision support tool'.[646]

The CDSS represents one example of water data platforms. Attempts are being made to establish new platforms for other purposes, including the improvement of water, sanitation and hygiene services,[647] water data gathering,[648] ensuring transparent decision-making,[649] and as a 'benchmarking and monitoring tool to incentivise stakeholders to use data collaboratively to end unnecessary resource waste'.[650]

Like the above-mentioned water data platforms, others were established for the Ramotswa aquifer. Over the last decade, the Potential Role of the Transboundary Ramotswa Aquifer (Ramotswa Project) was conducted under the auspices of the Resilience in the Limpopo Basin Program (RESILIM) project funded by the US Agency for International Development (USAID). The Ramotswa Project had several key components and objectives including RIMS, which 'seeks to compile, house and display mappable data from the Ramotswa Aquifer'.[651] RIMS is an online portal and a 'user friendly tool enabling access to groundwater relevant data and information for stakeholders in both countries and beyond' and provides 'users online access to a map-based platform for storing, organising, sharing and analysing spatial information related to the transboundary Ramotswa aquifer'.[652] Unlike traditional databases, RIMS provides a 'single portal to information originating from many different sources and disciplines and whenever possible it displays data and information in maps'.[653] IGRAC has developed other water data platforms addressing TBAs, including the Stampriet-Kalahari/Karoo aquifer shared between Namibia,

646 *Id.*, at 18.

647 E. Greggio & E. Stewart, *'How Can Online Data Platforms Improve Management of Water, Sanitation and Hygiene Services?'*, 9 February 2019, at https://washmatters.wateraid.org/blog/how-can-online-data-platforms-improve-management-of-water-sanitation-and-hygiene-services, last accessed 20 January 2020.

648 Systematic, *'Water Companies Develop Joint Data Platform'*, 20 April 2020, at https://systematic.com/about/news/2020/water-informatics-platform/, last accessed 20 January 2020.

649 World Resources Institute, *'Data Platforms'*, at https://www.wri.org/resources/data-platforms, last accessed 20 January 2020.

650 UNLEASH, *'The Open Water Data Index'*, at https://unleash.org/solutions/open-water-data-index/, last accessed 20 January 2020.

651 IGRAC, *'RAMOTSWA'*, at https://www.un-igrac.org/special-project/ramotswa, last accessed 20 January 2020.

652 Ramotswa Information Management System (RIMS), *'Ramotswa Information Management System'*, 2, at https://www.un-igrac.org/sites/default/files/resources/files/RIMS%20final%20version.pdf, last accessed 14 June 2021.

653 *Id.*

Botswana and South Africa within the general framework of the Groundwater Resources Governance in Transboundary Aquifers (GGRETA) project. GGRETA developed an information management system where the maps prepared were uploaded online.[654]

The current BDA project in the Ramotswa aquifer builds upon the experience and work conducted in previous projects by IGRAC, including RIMS, to reach its objectives. For instance, the partners in the BDA project, including IGRAC, are seeking to further expand 'RIMS as a shared data repository in which to capture, store and process data and information for the countries sharing the same water resource and make a recommendation on the long-term hosting of this repository'.[655] One wonders whether RIMS can constitute an integrated water data platform to be used for the management of the Ramotswa aquifer or whether there is a need for the development of a new one.

The California and New Mexico acts operate at the national level; in contrast, the Ramotswa aquifer has a transboundary nature. Nonetheless, the provisions of both acts would help address water challenges that are common to the Ramotswa aquifer as well as California and New Mexico, such as filling existing data gaps. Still, California and New Mexico have a specific context, motivations and water challenges that were considered when drafting the acts.[656] Similar challenges exist with the Ramotswa aquifer. Hence, a replication of the provisions of these acts in the context of the Ramotswa must consider this reality.

---

654 IGRAC, *'GGRETA'*, at https://www.un-igrac.org/special-project/ggreta, last accessed 20 January 2020; IGRAC, *'Stampriet Aquifer'*, at https://www.un-igrac.org/case-study/stampriet-aquifer, last accessed 20 January 2020.

655 IGRAC, *supra* note 34.

656 Water Education Foundation, *'California Water Issues Overview'*, at https://www.watereducation.org/aquapedia/california-water-issues-overview, last accessed 14 June 2021; J. Addison, *'An Overview of California's Water Challenges and Solutions'*, 29 October 2018, at https://meetingoftheminds.org/an-overview-of-californias-water-challenges-and-solutions-28860, last accessed 14 June 2021; K. Chamberlain, *'Water Reckoning Looms in New Mexico's Future: "We're not Prepared for What's Ahead of Us"'*, NM Political Report (19 September 2020), https://nmpoliticalreport.com/2020/09/19/water-reckoning-looms-in-new-mexicos-future-were-not-prepared-for-whats-ahead-of-us/, last accessed 14 June 2021; M. McFall-Johnsen, *'New Mexico Faces Extreme Water Scarcity on Par with the United Arab Emirates. Experts Warn More "Day Zeros" are Looming'*, 7 August 2019, https://www.businessinsider.com/new-mexico-faces-extreme-water-stress-2019-8, last accessed 14 June 2021.

4.4.3.2 *Integrating Existing Water and Ecological Data Information from Multiple Databases*

The Open and Transparent Water Data Act of California justifies the regulation by the need to 'integrate existing water and ecological data into an authoritative open-access platform to help water managers operate California's water system more effectively and help water users make informed decisions based on water availability and allocation'.[657] Similarly the Water Data Act of New Mexico justifies the use of a 'modern, integrated approach to collecting, sharing and utilizing data and information for water management' by the need to 'improve water resources planning and management and water security'.[658] The task of data integration in the Open and Transparent Water Data Act is delegated to the Integrated Water Data Platform that has among its tasks the integration of 'existing water and ecological data information from multiple autonomous databases managed by federal, state, and local agencies and academia using consistent and standardized formats'.[659] Data integration in the Water Data Act is delegated to a water data council that has among its tasks establishing 'best practices to make water data open, discoverable, interoperable and integrated'[660] and the development of an integrated water data and information platform.[661]

The focus on integrating water and ecological data is a result of increasing recognition that management issues cannot be addressed by a single discipline.[662] Such a focus has emerged because of strategic policies seeking to address environmental issues such as natural resources management and environmental protection.[663] Generally, an integrated water system provides information on, *inter alia*, 'precipitation, runoff, water resources various uses of water; water quantity and quality; all the aquatic objects (rivers,

657 Open and Transparent Water Data Act, *supra* note 41, Chapter 1 (12401).

658 House Bill 651, *supra* note 42, Section 3, p. 2.

659 Open and Transparent Water Data Act, *supra* note 41, Chapter 2, Article 3 (12415)(a).

660 House Bill 651, *supra* note 42, Section 5(A)3.

661 *Id.*, Section 5(A)4.

662 P. Fitch et al., *'Integrated Groundwater Data Management'*, in A. J. Jakeman et al. (eds), *Integrated Groundwater Management: Concepts, Approaches and Challenges* (Dordrecht: Springer, 2016) 668.

663 A. M. de C. Moura, M. Victorino & A. Tanaka, *'Combining Mediator and Data Warehouse Technologies for Developing Environmental Decision Support Systems'*, in M. J. Egenhofer & D. M. Mark (eds), *Geographic Information Science: Second International Conference* (Dordrecht: Springer, 2002) 196.

lakes groundwater and the sea) and the interactions between them'.[664] It also provides information related to land-water interactions and water-biodiversity and ecosystem interactions, among others.[665]

> At the broader scale, national datasets exist for a large number of geospatial features of land, water, and air that are needed to fully understand variation among these ecosystems. However, such datasets originate from different sources and have different spatial and temporal resolutions. By taking an open-science perspective and by combining site-based ecosystem datasets and national geospatial datasets, science gains the ability to ask important research questions related to grand environmental challenges that operate at broad scales.[666]

Already, attempts have been made to develop freshwater GIS-supported information systems, including the 'collection, processing and visualization of ecological data specifically related to rivers'.[667] Integrating environmental data and knowledge from various scales (national, regional, global) became a reality because of technological and computing advances, especially BDA, which is transforming research in environmental science.[668] This led to the development of integrated modelling that combines parts of the hydrological cycle with human connections and the environment. This shift has affected data management and requires that 'data are not only well stored, but also well described, easily discoverable and accessible, and in consistent form for use

664 P. Serban & R. M. Damian, *'Romania'*, in J. Ganoulis, I. L. Murphy & M. Brilly (eds), *Transboundary Water Resources in the Balkans: Initiating a Sustainable Co-Operative Network* (Leiden: Kluwer Academic Publishers, 2000) 137.

665 V. V. Nikolic & S. P. Simonovic, *'Multi-method Modeling Framework for Support of Integrated Water Resources Management'*, 2: Environmental Processes (2015) 461–483; Y. N. Pokhrel et al., *'Recent Progresses in Incorporating Human Land – Water Management into Global Land Surface Models toward their Integration into Earth System Models'*, 3:4, WIRES Water (2016) 548–574; R. Cremades et al., *'Ten Principles to Integrate the Water-Energy-Land Nexus with Climate Services for Co-Producing Local and Regional Integrated Assessments'*, 693: Science of the Total Environment (2019) 133662.

666 P. A. Soranno et al., *'Building a Multi-scaled Geospatial Temporal Ecology Database from Disparate Data Sources: Fostering Open Science and Data Reuse'*, 4:28, GigaScience (2015) 1–15, 1.

667 H. Pundt et al., *'A GIS-Supported Freshwater Information System Including a Pen-Computer Component for Field Data Recording'*, in K. Kovar & H. P. Nachtnebel (eds), *Application of Geographic Information Systems in Hydrology and Water Resources Management* (Vienna: IAHS Publication No. 235, 1996) 703.

668 Soranno et al., *supra* note 667, at 2.

in the different models in an integrated modeling system'.[669] The use of new technologies in monitoring and computing such BDA have allowed the development of more sophisticated integrated modelling systems.[670]

> Characteristics of data integration include the ability to cross spatial scales from local to regional to global, utilization of common data formats to ensure interoperability between datasets, and establishing linkages between science and applications. Results of data integration create shared information for dissemination and training products, new assessment tools to meet collective needs, and decision support systems for analysis and forecasting. Integrated datasets create cross-sectoral links to improve water stewardship that is inclusive of human and ecological needs.[671]

There are many examples of integrated water and ecological data management.

> Groundwater modeling is increasingly being undertaken at larger scales and groundwater flow is being incorporated into earth system modeling – fully coupled biogeochemical climate models – reflecting the growing awareness of the importance of groundwater systems to society. Therefore, there is a growing need to share data across different jurisdictional and groundwater management areas.[672]

Despite these technological developments, other factors are equally relevant for the sustainable management of freshwater resources, including innovation in public policy to keep up with developments occurring in the technological field.[673] This is particularly important given the 'complex data-scape that demands streamlined data standards across scientific communities where data processing systems are fragmented due to multiple sources and methodologies,

---

669 Fitch et al., *supra* note 663, at 668; G. F. Laniak et al., *'Integrated Environmental Modeling: A Vision and Roadmap for the Future'*, 39 Environmental Modelling & Software (2013) 3–23.

670 Fitch et al., *supra* note 663.

671 M. Laituri & F. Sternlieb, *'Water Data Systems: Science, Practice, and Policy'*, 153:1 Journal of Contemporary Water Research & Education (2014) 1–3, 2.

672 Fitch et al., *supra* note 663, at 668.

673 W. Sarni, *'Democratized, Distributed and Digital: 2019 Will Be Transformative for Water'*, 3 January 2019, at https://www.greenbiz.com/article/democratized-distributed-and-digital-2019-will-be-transformative-water, last accessed 20 January 2020.

limited data sharing, and incomplete data coverage'.[674] In fact, data integration 'creates unique data needs and problems, such as how to interpret information derived from multiple sources, of variable quality, using different formats, and collected according to different protocols and procedures'.[675] Indeed, only a combination of science, practice, rules and policies encourages the adoption of innovative ways to ensure and strengthen water data sharing arrangements and agreements.[676] Therefore, there is a great focus on water data as a means for water cooperation and peace. Various initiatives have been established to that end, such as the Coalition for Water Data and Peace and the Global Observatory on Water and Peace.[677] The objective of such initiatives is to ensure 'easily accessible and reliable water data to inform policy- and decision-making to national governments in support of peace and sustainable development'.[678]

In the context of the Ramotswa aquifer, there is a need to integrate existing water and ecological data information from multiple databases and provide data on completed water transfers and exchanges. This would be one of the tasks of the integrated water data platform established for the aquifer, or existing ones such as RIMS which may be used instead. As mentioned above, RIMS already 'compile[s], house[s] and display[s] mappable data from the Ramotswa Aquifer'.[679] In fact, it is likely that RIMS will be used as the integrated water data platform. Partners in the BDA project, including IGRAC, are seeking to further expand 'RIMS as a shared data repository in which to capture, store and process data and information for the countries sharing the same water resource and make a recommendation on the long-term hosting of this repository'.[680]

4.4.3.3 *Developing Protocols and Standards for Data Sharing*

The integrated water data platform of the California Open Water Data Act has among its tasks the development of 'protocols for data sharing, documentation,

674 Laituri & Sternlieb, *supra* note 672, at 1.

675 P. Gottschalk & H. Solli-Saether, *E-Government Interoperability and Information Resource Integration: Frameworks for Aligned Development* (Hershey: IGI Global, 2009) 87.

676 Laituri & Sternlieb, *supra* note 672, at 1–3.

677 F. Münger et al., *'The Key Role of Water Management and Data for Peacebuilding'*, 2020, at https://public.wmo.int/en/resources/bulletin/key-role-of-water-management-and-data-peacebuilding, last accessed 20 January 2020.

678 World Meteorological Organization, *'Mobilization on Water Data and Peace'*, 27 November 2018, at https://hydrohub.wmo.int/en/news-events/coalition-water-data-and-peace, last accessed 14 June 2021.

679 IGRAC, *supra* note 652.

680 IGRAC, *supra* note 34.

quality control, public access, and promotion of open-source platforms and decision support tools related to water data and to submit to the Legislature a report on those protocols'.[681] The Act obliges the agency developing these protocols to prepare and submit reports describing them in collaboration with other state agencies including, *inter alia*, technology and open data experts and water data users.[682] Similarly, the New Mexico Water Data Act requires the development of 'common water data standards and best practices for data collection, sharing, transparency, documentation and quality control'[683] and the establishment of 'best practices to make water data open, discoverable, interoperable and integrated'.[684] The Act also requires that the 'water research undertaken with state funding shall comply with the common water data standards and best practices developed by the council'.[685]

States at the basin level have established several framework conventions based on which future agreements, protocols or arrangements addressing specific issues could be adopted. This has been the case for instance in Central Asia where the parties established the Agreement on Cooperation in Joint Management, Use and Protection of Water Resources of Interstate Sources (Almaty Agreement) in 1992.[686] The Almaty Agreement is considered as a framework convention. Related agreements include the Agreement on Joint Activities in Addressing the Aral Sea and the Zone Around the Sea Crisis, Improving the Environment and Ensuring the Social and Economic Development of the Aral Sea Region (1993),[687] the Agreement on the Use of Water and Energy Resources of the Syr Darya Basin (1998)[688] and the Framework Convention on Environmental Protection for Sustainable Development in Central Asia.[689] Likewise,

681 Open and Transparent Water Data Act, *supra* note 41, p. 1.

682 *Id.*, Chapter 2; Article 1 (12406) a.

683 House Bill 651, *supra* note 42, Section 5(A)2.

684 *Id.*, Section 5(A)3.

685 *Id.*, Section 5(B)3.

686 Agreement between the Republic of Kazakhstan, the Kyrgyz Republic, the Republic of Tajikistan, Turkmenistan and the Republic of Uzbekistan on Cooperation in the Field of Joint Management on Utilization and Protection of Water Resources from Interstate Sources, 1992, at http://www.icwc-aral.uz/statute1.htm, last accessed 14 June 2021.

687 Agreement on Joint Activities in Addressing the Aral Sea and the Zone Around the Sea Crisis, Improving the Environment, and Ensuring the Social and Economic Development of the Aral Sea Region, 1993.

688 Agreement between the Governments of the Republic of Kazakhstan, the Kyrgyz Republic, and the Republic of Uzbekistan on the Use of Water and Energy Resources of the Syr Darya Basin, 1998, at https://www.ce.utexas.edu/prof/mckinney/papers/aral/agreements/SyrDaryaAgr-Mar17-98.pdf, last accessed 14 June 2021.

689 I. A. Ibrahim, *'The Importance of International Water Law to the Successful Implementation of the Belt and Road Initiative: Evidence from Central Asia'*, in G. Martinico & X. Wu (eds),

China and Kazakhstan signed the Agreement between the Government of Kazakhstan and the Government of China on Cooperation in the Use and Protection of Transboundary Rivers in 2001, which is a framework convention.[690] Based on this agreement, numerous other agreements addressing specific matters related to water management were adopted. These include the

> Agreement for Emergency Notification of the Parties about Natural Disasters on Transboundary Rivers (inter-ministerial) (2005); Agreement on the Mutual Exchange of Hydrological and Hydro Chemical Information (Data) of Border Gauging Stations on Major Transboundary Rivers (inter-ministerial) (2006); Agreement on the Development of Scientific-Research Cooperation (inter-ministerial) (2006); Agreement on Cooperation in the Construction of Joint Waterworks 'Dostyk' (Khorgos River) (2010); Agreement on Water Quality Protection of Transboundary Rivers (2011); [and]Agreement on Cooperation on Environmental Protection (2011).[691]

In fact, numerous framework conventions have been adopted over the years at the regional and basin level, including the SADC Protocol.[692] Agreements at the basin level include the Mekong River Basin Agreement,[693] the Senegal

'A Legal Analysis of the Belt and Road Initiative: Towards a New Silk Road?' (Cham: Palgrave Macmillan, 2020) 159–160; Framework Convention for the Protection of the Environment for Sustainable Development in Central Asia, Ashkhabad, 22 November 2006, at https://leap.unep.org/sites/default/files/treaty/TRE-143806.pdf, last accessed 14 June 2021.

690 Ibrahim, *supra* note 690, at 153–158; Agreement between the Government of the Republic of Kazakhstan and the Government of the People's Republic of China on Cooperation in the Use and Protection of Transboundary Rivers, Astana, 12 September 2001, at http://www.cawater-info.net/library/eng/l/kazakhstan_china.pdf, last accessed 14 June 2021.

691 S. Ho, *'China's Transboundary River Policies towards Kazakhstan: Issue-Linkages and Incentives for Cooperation'*, 42:2 Water International (2017) 142–162, 150.

692 R. Tekateka, *'Transboundary Water Management Issues Under the NWA and Regional Collaboration, Policies and Conventions'*, in B. Schreiner & R. Hassan (eds), *Transforming Water Management in South Africa: Designing and Implementing a New Policy Framework* (Dordrecht: Springer, 2011) 260.

693 Agreement on the Cooperation for the Sustainable Development of the Mekong River Basin, 1995, at https://www.ecolex.org/details/treaty/agreement-on-the-cooperation-for-the-sustainable-development-of-the-mekong-river-basin-tre-001223/, last accessed 14 June 2021.

River Water Charter,[694] the Niger Basin Water Charter,[695] and the Water Treaty between Mexico and the US.[696] The EU has adopted several directives addressing water resources, including the Water Framework Directive,[697] Urban Wastewater Treatment Directive,[698] Drinking Water Directive,[699] Bathing Waters Directive and Nitrates Directive.[700] The SADC region also has witnessed the adoption of non-binding instruments following the adoption of the SADC Revised Protocol. These include, *inter alia*, the SADC Regional Water Policy,[701] the SADC Regional Water Strategy,[702] the SADC Regional Awareness

694 Charter of Waters of the Senegal River, 2002, https://iea.uoregon.edu/treaty-text/4462, last accessed 14 June 2021.

695 M. M. Mbengue & N. Odili, *'The Environmental Management of Water Resources: What Impact on the Characterization of Fresh Water in International Law?'*, in M. Tignino & C. Bréthaut (eds), *Research Handbook on Freshwater Law and International Relations* (Cheltenham: Edward Elgar Publishing, 2018) 85–94; La Charte de l'Eau du Bassin du Niger, 2008, https://www.riob.org/sites/default/files/IMG/pdf/Charte_de_l_Eau_fre-2.pdf.

696 A. Sánchez, *'1944 Water Treaty Between Mexico and the United States: Present Situation and Future Potential'*, 18:36 Frontera Norte (2006) 125–144; Treaty Between the United States of America and Mexico, Washington, DC, 3 February 1944 and Protocol, Washington, DC, 14 November 1944, at http://extwprlegs1.fao.org/docs/pdf/bi-51880.pdf, last accessed 14 June 2021.

697 European Union, Directive 2000/60/EC of the European Parliament and of the Council of 23 October 2000 establishing a framework for Community action in the field of water policy, at https://eur-lex.europa.eu/eli/dir/2000/60/oj, last accessed 14 June 2021.

698 European Union, Council Directive of 21 May 1991 concerning urban waste water treatment (91/271/EEC), at https://eur-lex.europa.eu/legal-content/EN/TXT/PDF/?uri=CELEX:31991L0271&from=EN, last accessed 14 June 2021.

699 European Union, Directive (EU) 2020/2184 of the European Parliament and of the Council of 16 December 2020 on the quality of water intended for human consumption (recast) (Text with EEA relevance), at https://eur-lex.europa.eu/legal-content/EN/TXT/PDF/?uri=CELEX:32020L2184&from=ES, last accessed 14 June 2021.

700 W. Hansen & N. Kranz, *EU Water Policy and Challenges for Regional and Local Authorities* (Capacity Building on the European Community's Environmental Policy; Ecologic Institute for International and European Environmental Policy, Berlin – Brussels; Background Paper for the Seminar on Water Management; April 2003) 2–6; European Union, Directive 2006/7/EC of the European Parliament and of the Council of 15 February 2006 concerning the management of bathing water quality and repealing Directive 76/160/EEC, at https://eur-lex.europa.eu/legal-content/EN/TXT/PDF/?uri=CELEX:32006L0007&from=EN, last accessed 14 June 2021; European Union, Council Directive of 12 December 1991 concerning the protection of waters against pollution caused by nitrates from agricultural sources (91/676/EEC).

701 SADC Regional Water Policy, *supra* note 305.

702 SADC Regional Water Strategy, *supra* note 305.

and Communication Strategy for the Water Sector,[703] the SADC Regional Strategic Action Plans,[704] the SADC Guidelines for Strengthening River Basin Organisations Environmental Management,[705] the SADC Guidelines for Strengthening River Basin Organisations Establishment and Development,[706] the SADC Guidelines for Strengthening River Basin Organisations Stakeholder Participation,[707] and the SADC Guidelines for Strengthening River Basin Organisations Funding.[708] At the basin level, the Water Treaty Between Mexico and the US of 1944 is considered a framework convention on which numerous additional commitments were added. Article 25 of the treaty provided a specific mechanism for the adoption of new binding commitments in the form of executive agreements. These agreements take the form of amendments to the treaty and have allowed the treaty to adapt to changing circumstances since 1944.[709]

In the context of the Ramotswa aquifer, Botswana and South Africa are seeking to adopt a protocol or a series of protocols on groundwater data sharing. Two shortcomings arise from this approach. First, a framework convention is a general convention addressing the main issues related to a specific basin. Based on such a convention, future agreements and protocols can be adopted addressing specific matters such as groundwater data sharing. Hence,

703 Southern African Development Community, *'Regional Awareness and Communication Strategy for the SADC Water Sector'*, May 2008, at https://www.sadc.int/files/2213/5293/3542/SADC_Communication_Strategy_for_Water_Sector_2008.pdf, last accessed 14 June 2021.

704 Southern African Development Community Secretariat, *'Regional Strategic Action Plan on Integrated Water Resources Development and Management Phase IV, RSAP IV'*, Gaborone, Botswana, 2016, at https://www.sadc.int/files/9914/6823/9107/SADC_Water_4th_Regional_Strategic_Action_Plan_English_version.pdf, last accessed 14 June 2021.

705 Southern African Development Community, *'Guidelines for Strengthening River Basin Organisations'*, 2010, at https://www.sadc.int/files/4013/5333/8260/SADC_guideline_environment.pdf, last accessed 14 June 2021.

706 Southern African Development Community, *'SADC Guidelines for Strengthening River Basin Organisations Establishment and Development'*, 2010, at https://www.sadc.int/documents-publications/show/1035, last accessed 14 June 2021.

707 Southern African Development Community, *'SADC Guidelines for Strengthening River Basin Organisations – Stakeholder Participation'*, 2010, at https://www.sadc.int/documents-publications/show/1037, last accessed 14 June 2021.

708 South African Development Community, *'Towards a Common Future, Water & Sanitation'*, at https://www.sadc.int/themes/infrastructure/water-sanitation/, last accessed 20 January 2020; Southern African Development Community, *'SADC Guidelines for Strengthening River Basin Organisations – Funding* (2010)*'*, at https://www.sadc.int/documents-publications/show/1036, last accessed 14 June 2021.

709 S. Mumme, *The 1944 U.S.-Mexico Water Treaty as a Constitutional Document* (Mexico Center, Rice University's Baker Institute for Public Policy, March 2019) 7–8.

if Botswana and South Africa proceed with the establishment of a series of protocols, it has to be clear that these mechanisms are not a framework convention and are unable to address other issues beyond their scope. It may be though that both parties consider the SADC Protocol as the framework convention based on which specific agreements, like a series of protocols on groundwater data sharing, could be adopted. But this approach needs to be expressly stated in these protocols. Second, both parties must keep in mind that the adoption of a series of protocols on groundwater data sharing is not sufficient given the constant development in data science and the fast progress of disruptive technologies like BDA. Hence, the parties will be obliged to adopt follow-up instruments related to groundwater data sharing. Therefore, it would be wise to include a mechanism or a procedure within these protocols detailing the ways the parties can adopt future protocols and non-binding documents on groundwater data sharing, whether amendments to these protocols are feasible, and the role of the integrated water data platform or another similar structure in this context.

4.4.3.4 *Financing the Operations through a 'Water Data Administration Fund' or a 'Water Data Account'*

Both the Open and Transparent Water Data Act and the Water Data Act include provisions related to the financing of the tasks and operations under each act. The Open and Transparent Water Data Act created a water data administration fund to be 'available, upon appropriation, to the department, the state board, or the Department of Fish and Wildlife for the collection, management, and improvement of water and ecological data'.[710] Under the Act, the department of finance is to 'develop a standardized agreement to allow for the voluntary donation to the fund by any person, educational institution, government entity, corporation or other business entity, or organization'.[711] A similar structure, a water data account, was created under the Water Data Act.[712] The Act also provides that the water data council 'shall develop guidelines to manage and prioritize the use of funds from the water data account to carry out the purposes of the Water Data Act, including contracting with entities to make water data and information open, interoperable and integrated'.[713]

Anticipating water scarcity in the near future, pressure is growing to improve water management using emerging technologies and innovative policies.

710 Open and Transparent Water Data Act, *supra* note 41, Chapter 3 (12420) a.

711 *Id.*, Chapter 3 (12420) b.

712 House Bill 651, *supra* note 42, Section 7(A).

713 *Id.*, Section 7(B).

Reaching this objective requires further finances for the water agenda, especially in developing countries and emerging economies, through various means including national budgets, international development assistance and commercial finance.[714] Financial investments related to water resources address various needs, including 'irrigation for food security, providing drinking water and sanitation services, and reducing pollution by promoting wastewater treatment services'.[715] Further, long-term investments are required in 'resilient water infrastructure, climate-smart agricultural systems, improved drainage, nature-based flood protection, etc'.[716] Yet, there is a significant financing gap between what is required to address water related management issues and what is being offered.[717] In the developing world, water and sanitation receive inadequate funding since governments are focused on addressing stressed economies, existing debt, and other socio-political problems.[718] 'When compared with other sectors, particularly the other major social sectors of education and health, sanitation and drinking-water receive a relatively low priority for both Official Development Assistance (ODA) and domestic allocations'.[719] This situation is further worsened when combined with weak government systems and lack of human resources.[720] Most recently, the COVID-19 pandemic has led to a slashing of budgets, including those related to improving water resources and water management.[721]

Financing is essential to reaching any water-related management sustainability goal. Institutions providing drinking water and sanitation services must

---

714 G. J. Alaerts, *'Financing for Water – Water for Financing: A Global Review of Policy and Practice'*, 11:3 Sustainability (2019) 821, 821.

715 K. Sachwani, *'Financing the Water Sector – An Alternate Approach'*, 26 March 2020, at https://www.2030wrg.org/financing-the-water-sector-an-alternate-approach/, last accessed 20 January 2020.

716 *Id.*

717 *Id.*

718 S. Annamraju, B. Calaguas & E. Gutierrez, *'Financing Water and Sanitation: Key Issues in Increasing Resources to the Sector'* (A WaterAid Briefing Paper, November 2001) 6–7.

719 United Nations Department of Economic and Social Affairs, *'International Decade for Action "Water for Life" 2005–2015'*, at https://www.un.org/waterforlifedecade/financing.shtml, last accessed 20 January 2020.

720 World Health Organization, *'Weak Systems and Funding Gaps Jeopardize Drinking-Water and Sanitation in the World's Poorest Countries'*, 28 August 2019, at https://www.who.int/news/item/28-08-2019-weak-systems-and-funding-gaps-jeopardize-drinking-water-and-sanitation-in-the-world%E2%80%99s-poorest-countries, last accessed 20 January 2020.

721 C. Kammeyer, *'The COVID Crisis is Slashing California's State Budget. What Does it Mean for Water Management?'*, 26 May 2020, at https://pacinst.org/the-covid-crisis-is-slashing-californias-state-budget-what-does-it-mean-for-water-management/, last accessed 20 January 2020.

be financially sustainable in order to continue providing these services. To this end, governments often establish financing mechanisms like pooled financing facilities, revolving funds, and urban infrastructure funds.[722] Efforts in recent years have increased to ensure water financing. Recommendations have been made to encourage further investment in the water sector.[723] Innovative financing mechanisms also have been suggested.[724] For instance, investment platforms are being considered to expand the private capital available for the water sector. This became possible due to the emergence of financial technologies whereby 'investment platforms serve as a marketplace, linking investors with investable assets'.[725] Innovative financial means are being tested and traditional means of financing the water sector are being questioned due to the emergence of new challenges such as climate change, which requires adaptation, resilience and flexibility.[726] Innovative financing for the water sector is developing in parallel with clean technologies[727] and other emerging technologies that can enhance water management and respond to the increasing demand for water. New technologies and business models are being used for the water sector.[728]

Despite the gaps in water financing and the efforts made to reduce that gap, it is appropriate that a protocol or protocols addressing groundwater data sharing between Botswana and South Africa include provisions for establishing a funding mechanism. Such a mechanism can take the form of water data administration fund or a water data account or any other form that Botswana and South Africa agree to establish. Financial sustainability would guarantee

722 Bureau of Economic Growth, Agriculture, and Trade, U.S. Agency for International Development, Bureau of Oceans, Environment, and Science and U.S. Department of State, *'Addressing Water Challenges in the Developing World: A Framework for Action'* (An Annex of the 2008 Report to Congress for the Senator Paul Simon Water for the Poor Act; March 2009) 6.

723 High Level Panel on Water, *'Water Infrastructure and Investment'*, https://sustainabledevelopment.un.org/content/documents/hlpwater/08-WaterInfrastInvest.pdf, last accessed 20 January 2020.

724 OECD, *Innovative Financing Mechanisms for the Water Sector* (Paris: OECD Publications, 2010).

725 J. Ikeda et al., *Innovations in Commercial Finance for the Water and Sanitation Sector: The Potential of Investment Platforms for Mobilizing Financing for Development at Scale* (Inter-American Development Bank, Discussion Paper Nº IDB-DP-00799, August 2020) 4.

726 OECD, *Managing Water for All an OECD Perspective on Pricing and Financing* (Paris: OECD Publications, 2009) 4.

727 R. Pernick & C. Wilder, *Summary: The Clean Tech Revolution: Review and Analysis of Pernick and Wilder's Book* (Businessnews Publishing, 2016).

728 World Economic Forum Water Initiative, *Water Security: The Water-Food-Energy-Climate Nexus* (Geneva: World Economic Forum, 2011) 173.

the collection, processing and sharing of data, and the benefits from emerging technologies like BDA. This would be an incremental process given that both countries are in dire need of funding and financial resources,[729] which is why the financial means for implementation of the protocol must be secured. Having regular financial support will also guarantee the functioning of the integrated water management platform, which can then focus on the realisation of tasks such as integrating water and ecological data information from multiple databases. This approach will not only help to ensure sufficient funding for groundwater data collection, sharing and processing, but also the dissemination of emerging technologies like BDA in other water basins. This is because technology can be disseminated through explicit policies and regulations, while having the necessary funding demonstrates their usefulness.[730]

Even though states, especially developing nations, have a hard time finding the resources to support transboundary water management, the advantages of using BDA to improve water resources governance far outweighs the disadvantages of not doing so. States will miss a great opportunity by not investing in BDA, especially if some of the states sharing the same water resource are deploying BDA, which will provide leverage given the asymmetry of information that will occur.[731] This is mainly because BDA shows 'great promise in many water related applications such as planning optimum water systems, detecting ecosystem changes through big remote sensing and geographical information system, forecasting/predicting/detecting natural and manmade calamities, scheduling irrigations, mitigating environmental pollution, studying climate change impacts, etc'.[732] These benefits are extremely important in the transboundary water context as they would allow policy-makers to draft strategies on the basis of reliable data and information that has been stored and processed correctly.[733] Thus states such as China are exploring the potential of BDA for transboundary water management. Chinese officials advocated

729 E. Botlhale, *'Restoring Fiscal Balances Post the Global Economic Crisis in Botswana'*, 40:8 International Journal of Public Administration (2017) 706–716; D. Rodrik, *'Understanding South Africa's Economic Puzzles'*, 16:4 Economics of Transitions (2008) 769–797.

730 United States, Congress, Senate, Committee on Environment and Public Works, Subcommittee on Water and Wildlife, *'EPA's Role in Promoting Water Use Efficiency'* (Hearing Before the Subcommittee on Water and Wildlife of the Committee on Environment and Public Works; United States Senate; One Hundred Eleventh Congress; First Session, 31 March 2008) 106.

731 Ibrahim, *supra* note 9, at 1140–1141.

732 Adamala, *supra* note 46, at 10.

733 Ibrahim, *supra* note 9, at 1141–1142.

for its use through an official paper entitled 'China's Water Diplomacy in the Era of Big Data'.[734]

5 Implications of Establishing an Open Data Regulation on IWL

5.1 *Addressing Data and Information Sharing in the Context of BDA and Other Emerging Disruptive Technologies in the General Framework of IWL*

In a previous piece of research, Ibrahim argued for the inclusion of a general provision related to disruptive technologies, including BDA, within international water agreements when states are negotiating such treaties. The objective of such a provision is to address the increasingly important role disruptive technologies are playing in the transboundary water context and avoid subsequent amendments that take into account these technologies. Such a provision does not have to expressly state the type of disruptive technology, but could be of a general nature to cover all existing digital technologies and future ones. In the first scenario examined by the author, the parties are negotiating a potential future international water agreement that would be a framework convention similar to the UNWC or the UNECE Water Convention.[735] Examples of basin framework conventions that were previously discussed include the SADC Water Protocol,[736] Mekong River Basin Agreement,[737] Senegal River Water Charter,[738] Niger Basin Water Charter,[739] and the Water Treaty between Mexico and the US.[740]

The focus on including new provisions within IWL supports further developing and improving this field, and the literature is full of studies seeking the progressive development of IWL.[741] For instance, Dinar argues that IWL is 'vague and general, providing states with no clear rules as to how they are to

734 H. Zhang & M. Li, *'China and Global Water Governance: New Developments'*, in H. Zhang & M. Li (eds), *China and Transboundary Water Politics in Asia* (Oxon: Routledge, 2017) 219–236.

735 Ibrahim, *supra* note 9, at 1146–1147.

736 Tekateka, *supra* note 693, at 260.

737 Mekong Agreement, *supra* note 694.

738 Senegal River Charter, *supra* note 695.

739 Mbengue & Odili, *supra* note 696, at 85–94; La Charte de l'Eau du Bassin du Niger, *supra* note 696.

740 Sánchez, *supra* note 697, at 125–144.

741 See generally, A. Rieu-Clarke, A. Allan & S. Hendry (eds), *Routledge Handbook of Water Law and Policy* (Abingdon: Routledge, 2017); S. C. McCaffrey, C. Leb & R. T. Denoon (eds), *Research Handbook on International Water Law* (Cheltenham: Edward Elgar Publishing,

solve property rights conflicts'.[742] Bourquain argues that IWL should 'extend its contents and supplement its regulatory framework with specific rules on the basic human need for water'.[743] Bernadini argues for further normative guidance addressing the implementation of the UNECE Water Convention concerning groundwater due to its distinguishing features.[744]

The second scenario that requires analysis is one where an existing framework convention did not include a provision addressing disruptive technologies. Despite the theoretical possibility of amending such conventions, this is actually extremely complicated if not impossible due to several factors. It is complicated to amend an international treaty that took years and great effort to be adopted and was the result of a delicate compromise between states. Additionally, one has to keep in mind that states are not usually enthusiastic about amending an agreement that they have agreed to and ratified. Hence, it is easier to adopt a new treaty than amend existing treaties. This is the reality of international law, and not only IWL, even though from a practical perspective amending an existing treaty to update it is reasonable.[745]

Another question that must be addressed is whether a distinct provision on the integration of new technologies is truly necessary or whether the framework character of existing agreements and their provisions are flexible enough to adopt additional protocols and procedures related to new technologies without having to amend these agreements. This is especially the case when it comes to water basins that have an agreement and integrated water data platform in place. This is the situation in the Zambezi watercourse shared between Angola, Botswana, Malawi, Mozambique, Namibia, Tanzania, Zambia and Zimbabwe.[746] These states adopted the Agreement on the Establishment of

---

2019); B. O. Magsig, *International Water Law and the Quest for Common Security* (Abingdon: Routledge, 2015).

742 S. Dinar, *International Water Treaties: Negotiation and Cooperation along Transboundary Rivers* (Abingdon: Routledge, 2008) 37.

743 K. Bourquain, *Freshwater Access from a Human Rights Perspective: A Challenge to International Water and Human Rights Law* (Leiden: Martinus Nijhoff Publishers, 2008) 51.

744 F. Bernardini, *'The Normative and Institutional Evolution of the Convention'*, in A. Tanzi et al. (eds), *The UNECE Convention on the Protection and Use of Transboundary Watercourses and International Lakes* (Leiden: Brill/Nijhoff, 2015) 38.

745 See generally, M. Hakimi, *'Why Should We Care About International Law?'*, 118:6, Michigan Law Review (2020) 1283–1306; E. A. Posner, *'Do States Have a Moral Obligation to Obey International Law?'*, 55:5 Stanford Law Review (2003) 1901–1919; S. E. Kreps & A. C. Arend, *'Why States Follow the Rules: Toward a Positional Theory of Adherence to International Legal Regimes'*, 16, Duke Journal of Comparative & International Law (2006) 331–414.

746 M. Eriksson et al., *'Challenges and Commonalities in Basin-Wide Water Management'*, 5: Aquatic Procedia (2015) 44–57, 50–51.

the Zambezi Watercourse Commission.[747] They also established the Zambezi Water Resources Information Systems, 'an interactive, web-based data and information system based on contemporary and historical spatial data, hydrological time series, earth observation information, knowledge products and other related information'.[748]

Existing international mechanisms tasked with overseeing the implementation of existing agreements could play a role in this regard. These mechanisms include, for instance, the United Nations Economic Commission for Europe (UNECE) Water Secretariat.[749] This organ is composed of numerous water experts tasked with guiding the states in the implementation of the UNECE Water Convention as well as the UNWC due to the absence of a specific organ dedicated to that convention.[750] The Secretariat is also tasked with conducting studies related to water governance topics, and establishing and following existing water projects having specific objectives. Its mains tasks include financing of transboundary water cooperation,[751] identifying the benefits of transboundary water cooperation,[752] applying the water-energy-food ecosystem nexus approach;[753] monitoring, assessment and information sharing in transbound-

747 Agreement on the Establishment of the Zambezi Watercourse Commission, 2004, at http://www.zambezicommission.org/sites/default/files/publication_downloads/zamcom_agreement.pdf, last accessed 14 June 2021.

748 ZAMCOM, *'Zambezi Water Resources Information Systems (ZAMWIS)'*, at http://www.zambezicommission.org/programmes-activities/zambezi-water-resources-information-systems-zamwis, last accessed 14 June 2021.

749 UNECE, *'Staff of the UNECE Secretariat Servicing the Convention'*, at https://unece.org/environment-policy/water/contacts/staff-unece-secretariat-servicing-convention, last accessed 20 January 2020.

750 UNECE, *'The Water Convention and the Protocol on Water and Health'*, at https://unece.org/environment-policy/water, last accessed 20 January 2020; UNECE, *'UN Watercourses Convention'*, at https://unece.org/environment-policy/water/un-watercourses-convention, last accessed 20 January 2020.

751 UNECE, *'Financing of Transboundary Water Cooperation'*, at https://unece.org/environment-policy/water/areas-work-convention/financing-transboundary-water-cooperation, last accessed 20 January 2020.

752 UNECE, *'Benefits of Transboundary Water Cooperation'*, at https://unece.org/environment-policy/water/areas-work-convention/benefits-transboundary-water-cooperation, last accessed 20 January 2020.

753 UNECE, *'Water-Food-Energy-Ecosystem Nexus'*, at https://unece.org/environment-policy/water/areas-work-convention/water-food-energy-ecosystem-nexus, last accessed 20 January 2020.

ary basins;[754] offering guidance on water and adaptation to climate change;[755] supporting efforts on water allocation in a transboundary context;[756] assessing the risk to water from industrial accidents;[757] managing transboundary groundwater;[758] and making recommendations on payment for ecosystem services in integrated water resources management.[759] The Secretariat currently is conducting projects in the Caucasus, Central Asia, Eastern Europe and South-Eastern Europe.[760] These objectives and projects are implemented through regular events and publications while working groups are established to tackle specific topics. An entity like the UNECE Water Secretariat could include a new task on its agenda related to disruptive technologies on the basis of which new projects and working groups could be established. In fact, this topic is already being addressed under the 'monitoring, assessment and information sharing' work stream mentioned above.[761] The Expert Group on Monitoring, Assessment and Data Exchange has discussed, among other things, the integration of new disruptive technologies in transboundary water resources management.[762]

754 UNECE, *'Monitoring, Assessment and Information Sharing in Transboundary Basins'*, at https://unece.org/environment-policy/water/monitoring-assessment-and-information-sharing-transboundary-basins, last accessed 20 January 2020.

755 UNECE, *'Water and Adaptation to Climate Change'*, at https://unece.org/environment-policy/water/areas-work-convention/water-and-adaptation-climate-change, last accessed 20 January 2020.

756 UNECE, *'Water Allocation in a Transboundary Context'*, at https://unece.org/environment-policy/water/areas-work-convention/water-allocation-transboundary-context, last accessed 20 January 2020.

757 UNECE, *'Water and Industrial Accidents'*, at https://unece.org/environment-policy/water/areas-work-convention/water-and-industrial-accidents, last accessed 20 January 2020.

758 UNECE, *'Management of Transboundary Groundwaters'*, at https://unece.org/environment-policy/water/areas-work-convention/management-transboundary-groundwaters, last accessed 20 January 2020.

759 UNECE, *'Water and Ecosystems'*, at https://unece.org/environment-policy/water/areas-work-convention/water-and-ecosystems, last accessed 20 January 2020.

760 UNECE, *'Projects in the Caucasus'*, at https://unece.org/environment-policy/water/areas-work-convention/projects-caucasus, last accessed 20 January 2020; UNECE, *'Projects in Central Asia'*, at https://unece.org/environment-policy/water/areas-work-convention/projects-central-asia, last accessed 20 January 2020; UNECE, *'Projects in Eastern Europe'*, at https://unece.org/environment-policy/water/areas-work-convention/projects-eastern-europe, last accessed 20 January 2020; UNECE, *'Projects in South-Eastern Europe'*, at https://unece.org/environment-policy/water/areas-work-convention/projects-south-eastern-europe, last accessed 20 January 2020.

761 UNECE, *'Monitoring, Assessment and Information Sharing'*, *supra* note 755.

762 UNECE, *'Water Convention's Future Directions on Monitoring and Data Exchange in Transboundary Basins Outlined Based on Experience and Needs of over 70 Countries'*, at https://unece.org/environment/news/water-conventions-future-directions-monitoring-and-data-exchange-transboundary, last accessed 14 June 2021.

Another suggestion by Ibrahim for addressing the gap in existing water conventions is the adoption of protocols or follow-up agreements to existing international water framework conventions. Several protocols have been adopted under the UNECE Water Convention. These include the Protocol on Water and Health, which aims to 'protect human health and wellbeing by better water management, including the protection of water ecosystems, and by preventing, controlling and reducing water-related diseases'.[763] Another protocol is the Civil Liability and Compensation for Damage Caused by the Transboundary Effects of Industrial Accidents on Transboundary Waters.[764] The UNECE also has adopted various standards, such as the commercial agricultural produce quality standards, and helps with their interpretation and promotes their practical application.[765] It also develops 'best practices and standards, including model contracts for specific infrastructure sectors and subsectors'.[766] The UNECE has established regulatory cooperation and standardisation policies that aim at 'promoting regulatory policies to protect the health and safety of consumers and workers, and preserve our natural environment, without creating unnecessary barriers to trade'.[767] Most recently, the UNECE adopted the 2014 Model Provisions on Transboundary Groundwaters, which provide 'specific non-binding guidance for the implementation of the Convention with regard to groundwater and facilitating the application of the principles of the Convention to transboundary groundwaters'.[768] An alternative that might be more appropriate would be asking the ILC to draft appropriate instruments, especially as such instruments must be voted on at the UN.[769]

Hence, there are various options and suggestions that could be adopted depending on the whether a framework water convention exists or whether

763 UNECE, *'About the Protocol on Water and Health'*, at https://unece.org/environment-policy/water/protocol-on-water-and-health/about-the-protocol/introduction, last accessed 20 January 2020.

764 UNECE, *'Protocol on Civil Liability'*, at https://unece.org/environment-policy/water/protocol-civil-liability, last accessed 20 January 2020.

765 UNECE, *'Agricultural Quality Standards'*, at https://unece.org/agricultural-quality-standards, last accessed 20 January 2020.

766 UNECE, *'Economic Cooperation and Integration'*, at https://unece.org/economic-cooperation-and-integration-6, last accessed 20 January 2020.

767 UNECE, *'Regulatory Cooperation and Standardization Policies'*, at https://unece.org/regulatory-cooperation-and-standardization-policies, last accessed 20 January 2020.

768 UNECE, *'Model Provisions on Transboundary Groundwaters'*, at https://unece.org/environment-policy/publications/model-provisions-transboundary-groundwaters, last accessed 20 January 2020.

769 See, for instance, A. Nollkaemper, *'The Contribution of the International Law Commission to International Water Law: Does It Reverse the Flight from Substance?'*, 27, Netherlands Yearbook of International Law (1996) 39–73.

the international community is in the process of adopting a framework water convention. Where the international community is seeking to establish a new water convention, a provision addressing disruptive technologies should be included. The most recent international water instrument to be adopted is the Draft Articles on the Law of Transboundary Aquifers.[770] It remains to be seen if this instrument will become binding and if amendments to include provisions on disruptive technologies are made before its adoption as a convention.[771] Where a framework water convention exists, there should be an international mechanism like the ILC or the UNECE Water Secretariat through its Expert Group on Monitoring, Assessment and Data Exchange to address the gap on disruptive technologies, or a process to adopt new protocols, standards or non-binding measures.

5.2 *Should IWL Replicate Provisions of the Transparent and Open Data Act and the Data Water Act?*

As discussed above, several provisions in the Open and Transparent Data Act and the Water Data Act should be replicated in the protocol on data sharing between South Africa and Botswana to address the use of disruptive technologies like BDA. However, South Africa and Botswana are not the only countries seeking to address transboundary water management through BDA. In fact, big data initiatives are financed by international donors such as USAID and include numerous institutions at the regional level like the Water Research Commission of South Africa. These initiatives cover countries sharing transboundary water resources in Southern Africa, not only the Ramotswa aquifer. The goal is to promote regional collaboration on water issues through the use of BDA and the Ramotswa aquifer is one of the many projects that are being implemented.[772]

770 Draft Articles, *supra* note 471.

771 G. Eckstein & F. Sindico, *'The Law of Transboundary Aquifers: Many Ways of Going Forward, but Only One Way of Standing Still'*, 23:1, Review of European, Comparative & International Environmental Law (2014) 32–42; S. C. McCaffrey, *'The International Law Commission Adopts Draft Articles on Transboundary Aquifers'*, 103: 2, American Journal of International Law (2009) 272–293.

772 Bocchino & Adkisson, *supra* note 29; International Groundwater Resources Assessment Centre, *supra* note 553; Globalwaters.org, *'Big Data for Water Security: Scalable Geospatiotemporal Data Integration & Systems'*, at https://www.globalwaters.org/events/swp/big-data-water-security-scalable-geospatiotemporal-data-integration-systems, last accessed 20 January 2020.

Nevertheless, the use of BDA for water resources management is not limited to Southern Africa as its use is being assessed in various fields globally for the purpose of enhancing water resources management.[773] Southern Africa is one example of several basins around the world that have established water information systems and basin data platforms using big data technologies.[774] This means that BDA and disruptive technologies in general are expected to be used for the management of water resources globally and in the transboundary water context.

The previous section addressed the ways BDA can be included within IWL, offering two scenarios and suggestions. The first scenario is the inclusion of a new provision related to disruptive technologies within future water agreements; the second scenario addresses situations where water agreements have already been adopted. It was suggested that existing international mechanisms such as the UNECE Water Secretariat and the adoption of protocols or follow-up agreements to existing international water framework conventions be used to tackle these scenarios. This section will examine the potential content of a groundwater data protocol(s) to be developed between South Africa and Botswana based on the above analysis.

A provision addressing BDAs and disruptive technologies within IWL ideally would be drafted as follows:

Article 'x'

1. When sharing water resources, states can resort to the use of disruptive technologies to gain further information and data related to the shared fresh water with the objective of enhancing transboundary water management.
2. The use of disruptive technologies for data collection and processing shall be conducted while complying with the principle of equitable and reasonable utilisation, the obligation not to cause significant harm and the principle of cooperation.
3. The collection and processing of data and information shall comply with the procedural provisions of this convention, mainly those related to the

773 See generally, E. Wongso et al., *'A Data-Driven Framework to Characterize State-Level Water Use in the United States'*, 56:9, Water Resources Research (2020) 1–17; L. Schmidt et al., *'Challenges in Applying Machine Learning Models for Hydrological Inference: A Case Study for Flooding Events Across Germany'*, 56:5, Water Resources Research (2020) 1–10; N. Raval & M. Kumar, *'An Overview of Big Data Analytics: A State-of-the Art Platform for Water Resources Management'*, in M. Kumar et al. (eds), *Resilience, Response, and Risk in Water Systems: Shifting Management and Natural Forcings Paradigms* (Dordrecht: Springer, 2020) 43–56.

774 Adamala, *supra* note 46.

regular exchange of data and information, notification of natural emergencies and those caused by human activity, and notification of planned measures.

4. Where the parties agree on the use of disruptive technologies collectively for data collection and processing, they are advised to comply with the following measures:
   (a) Develop an integrated water data platform to collect, share and utilise data and information for water management while coordinating state agencies and water authorities that collect, store or utilise water data or that are involved in the management of water and related resources.[775]
   (b) Integrate existing water and ecological data information from multiple databases, mainly existing water and ecological data from local, state, and federal agencies, to implement water laws, improve the management of the state's water resources, and bring greater transparency to water transfers and the market.[776]
   (c) Develop protocols and common water data standards for data sharing, documentation, quality control, and public access, and promote open-source platforms and decision support tools related to water data.[777]
   (d) Finance operations through a 'water data administration fund' or a 'water data account' that receives funds from state agencies as well as grants and aid from international donors, private, commercial and private philanthropic entities among others. The integrated water data platform will develop guidelines to manage and prioritise the use of funds to carry out the various tasks.[778]

This proposed Article includes the main content of the provision related to the use of disruptive technologies, including BDA, in IWL. There are other elements that could be included, but they are rather more detailed. These

775 This provision is based on a combination of having the integrated water data platform from the Open and Transparent Water Data Act and the explanation of the role of such a platform from the Water Data Act.

776 This provision is based upon Chapter 2 (Art. 1) 12405 of the Open and Transparent Water Data Act, which was rephrased and amended to be included here as a measure with the provision related to disruptive technology in international water law.

777 This provision is based upon Chapter 2 (Art. 1) 12406(a) of the Open and Transparent Water Data Act and on Section 5(A)2 of the Water Data Act.

778 This provision is based on a combination of two provisions within the Open and Transparent Water Data Act (Chapter 3, 12420(a)) and the Water Data Act (Section 6(B)). It is not clear if South Africa and Botswana would be interested in funding the operations; outside sources of funding may help partially in this regard.

include the tasks of the integrated water data platform, namely, '(1) identify key water data sets, information and tools needed to support water management and planning; (2) develop common best practices for data collection, sharing, transparency, documentation and quality control; (3) establish best practices to make water data open, discoverable, interoperable and integrated; and (4) identify and prioritize water data and information gaps and needs for further development'.[779] However, it is suggested here that these detailed tasks should be left out from IWL and international framework conventions (e.g., UNWC and UNECE Water Convention), which have the objective of adopting general provisions to guide states seeking to establish basin water treaties.[780] Such detailed tasks should be included and negotiated within basin water treaties, considering the context of the basin and all related factors, such as the technological capacity of each state.[781]

However, the term disruptive technologies must be defined within the convention. For instance, it could be defined as 'technology that can fundamentally change not only established technologies but also the rules and business models of a given market, and often business and society overall'.[782] Then, a non-exhaustive list of potential technologies should be mentioned including AI, the Internet of Things, blockchain technologies, and BDA.[783]

This suggestion concerning the provision related to disruptive technologies applies to the first scenario in which the international community is seeking to adopt a new water convention. As for the scenario where a framework water convention is already in place, an international mechanism such as the UNECE Water Secretariat could use the model provision proposed above. The proposed model provision could be applied to conduct studies, establish new standards, and engage in projects seeking to determine how state signatories to an existing water convention framework can use disruptive technologies despite the

779 These tasks are mentioned in Section 5(A) of the Water Data Act.

780 See generally, S. M. A. Salman, *'The Helsinki Rules, the UN Watercourses Convention and the Berlin Rules: Perspectives on International Water Law'*, 23:4 International Journal of Water Resources Development (2007) 625–640; A. M. Tanzi, *'The Inter-Relationship Between No Harm, Equitable and Reasonable Utilisation and Cooperation Under International Water Law'*, 20 International Environmental Agreements: Politics, Law and Economics (2020) 619–629.

781 See, for instance, C. A. Fox & C. Sneddon, *'Transboundary River Basin Agreements in the Mekong and Zambezi Basins: Enhancing Environmental Security or Securitizing the Environment?'*, 7, International Environmental Agreements: Politics, Law and Economics (2007) 237–261.

782 N. R. Harshadeep & W. Young, *'Disruptive Technologies for Improving Water Security in Large River Basins'*, 12(10) Water (2020) 2783, 2786.

783 Harris, *supra* note 10; Cag, *supra* note 10.

absence of such a provision from the existing conventions. Moreover, and as suggested above, follow-up agreements, protocols, and binding and nonbinding agreements to existing international water framework conventions could also be adopted where an international organ like the UNECE Water Secretariat can lead the process.

5.3 *Limitations of the Findings*

Some limitations need to be considered when assessing the findings of this monograph and any future research. First, this monograph was drafted at the time when stakeholders are negotiating and examining a prototype of transboundary groundwater data and information sharing protocols. Hence, the analysis and the findings must be considered in this context. Future studies need to be conducted based on the final version of any groundwater data sharing protocol or protocols adopted, and updated and amended accordingly. This is of utmost importance as the suggestion of establishing a protocol or a series of protocols at the basin level is likely to face difficulty in terms of implementation given the many challenges facing transboundary water management in general.[784] Additionally, specific challenges exist in the context of the Ramotswa aquifer. In this regard, the authors are very grateful to several stakeholders, particularly the Water Research Commission of South Africa and Winrock International, which provided reports concerning the implementation of BDA in the transboundary water management context of the Ramotswa aquifer shared between Botswana and South Africa.

The second limitation is the inability to determine whether Botswana and South Africa could implement the recommendations made here due to the financial commitment required. Currently, financial and technical support from international donors and agencies play a significant role in these countries. One will have to wait to see if these countries use BDA in the management of shared water resources in the long term and without such support. There is also a need to assess cases where BDA has been implemented in transboundary water management to confirm the findings of this monograph or even provide new findings.

The third limitation is related to the existence of very few regulatory frameworks that are innovative and address the data gaps resulting from the existence of various agencies and authorities collecting data. The monograph focuses on state-level frameworks in California and New Mexico. As such, the

784 Baranyai, *supra* note 525, at 53–68; M. Zeitoun, M. Goulden & D. Tickner, *'Current and Future Challenges Facing Transboundary River Basin Management'*, 4,5: WIRES Climate Change (2013) 331–349.

suggestions made here may vary in the future or more elements could be added in new regulations that provide innovative ways of addressing water data gaps and new technologies at the national or international levels.

Conclusion

Like any other global regulatory framework, IWL has developed over many decades. Existing conventions were adopted after years of negotiations, and compromises were made by stakeholders.[785] Even then, the adoption of water conventions suffered the same fate international treaties face, that is, the need to be updated. Yet, this usually does not happen once an international treaty is adopted.[786] IWL has also struggled with understanding the difference between surface water and groundwater because the (1) hidden nature of groundwater resources historically has affected its development as politicians and policy-makers initially ignored this treasure;[787] (2) lack of scientific understanding of groundwater in the past and currently affects the adoption of proper water regulations;[788] and (3) new developments because of scientific progress.[789] This led to the adoption of rules that are inadequate for simultaneously addressing surface water and groundwater and resulted in the adoption of a non-binding instrument solely addressing TBAs in 2008.[790] All these

785 Leb (2020), *supra* note 20, at 42–70; J. W. Dellapenna & J. Gupta, *'The Evolution of Global Water Law'*, in J. W. Dellapenna & J. Gupta (eds), *The Evolution of the Law and Politics of Water* (Dordrecht: Springer, 2009) 3–19.

786 See generally, A. Aust, *Modern Treaty Law and Practice* (3d ed., Cambridge: Cambridge University Press, 2013); U. Linderfalk, *On the Interpretation of Treaties: The Modern International Law as Expressed in the 1969 Vienna Convention on the Law of Treaties* (Dordrecht: Springer, 2007); O. A. Hathaway et al., *'The Treaty Power: Its History, Scope, and Limits'*, 98, Cornell Law Review (2013) 239–326.

787 G. E. Eckstein, *'Rethinking Transboundary Ground Water Resources Management: A Local Approach along the Mexico-U.S. Border'*, 25, The Georgetown International Environmental Law Review (2012) 95–128, 106; F. Daibes-Murad, *A New Legal Framework for Managing the World's Shared Groundwaters* (London: IWA Publishing, 2005) 12.

788 K. Mechlem, *'Groundwater Governance: The Role of Legal Frameworks at the Local and National Level – Established Practice and Emerging Trends'*, 8:8, Water (2016) 1–16.

789 A. Durán-Sánchez, J. Álvarez-García & M. de la Cruz del Río-Rama, *'Sustainable Water Resources Management: A Bibliometric Overview'*, 10:9, Water (2018) 1–19.

790 See generally, F. Sindico, *International Law and Transboundary Aquifers* (Cheltenham: Edward Elgar Publishing, 2020); Eckstein, *supra* note 637; K. Mechlem, *'International Groundwater Law: Towards Closing the Gaps?'*, 14:1, Yearbook of International Environmental Law (2003) 47–80.

factors add further complexity to any attempt to understand the way IWL will be impacted by the use of disruptive technologies.

The use of BDA for enhancing water governance in the national and transboundary contexts is only emerging where other disruptive technologies have already made an impact or are expected to do so in the near future.[791] The example analysed in this monograph related to the application of BDA to the Ramotswa aquifer shared between South Africa and Botswana, is one example among many transboundary basins in Southern Africa where the application of BDA for enhancing water management is being assessed. The funding and support provided by international donors such as USAID to projects related to the use of BDA in the transboundary water context in Southern Africa highlights the high expectations concerning the significant role BDA will play in water management.[792] In fact, countries like China have also expressed their interest in understanding the potential role BDA can play in transboundary water management.[793]

Assessing the potential for regulation of BDA and disruptive technologies, while considering the realities of transboundary water agreements and IWL, was not and is still not an easy task. This monograph offers an in-depth analysis of the interplay between BDA and water resources in the transboundary water context, an overview of the selected case study, and an assessment of the traditional data and information exchange provisions within IWL. Still, it is not clear exactly how the use of BDA in transboundary water management can be regulated. Some propositions were made to fill the legal vacuum by using certain provisions from international climate change law or international space law. However, other solutions may be more appropriate given the focus of these regulatory frameworks on water data.

Recent legal developments in the US concerning open water data are suitable for the regulation of the use of BDA in transboundary water management. The California Open and Transparent Water Data Act of 2016 and the New

791 R. Chalh et al., *'Big Data Open Platform for Water Resources Management', 2015 International Conference on Cloud Technologies and Applications (CloudTech)* (2015); Sun & Scanlon, *supra* note 86, at 1–29; Raval & Kumar, *supra* note 774, at 45.

792 Winrock International, *'Using Big Data to Ensure Water Security'*, at https://winrock.org/using-big-data-to-ensure-water-security/, last accessed 20 January 2020; Southern African Development Community, Transfrontier Conservation Areas, *'Big Data Analytics and Transboundary Water Collaboration: Call for Research Proposals'*, 18 May 2018, at https://tfcaportal.org/big-data-analytics-and-transboundary-water-collaboration-call-research-proposals, last accessed 20 January 2020; Big Data Analytics and Transboundary Water Collaboration for Southern Africa, https://devbigdata.sadc-gmi.org/, last accessed 20 January 2020.

793 Zhang & Li, *supra* note 735, at 219–236.

Mexico Water Data Act of 2019 offer innovative legal mechanisms as both states have an urgent need to address the gaps in water data management that affects water security.[794] Even though the acts were not intended to be applied at the national level, their innovative provisions should be applied to transboundary water management to address the use of BDA. As discussed above, these provisions have been extensively addressed in the monograph benefiting from the Ramotswa aquifer that was selected as a case study.

New topics are opened for discussion within IWL with the potential inclusion of certain provisions of the Open and Transparent Water Data Act and the Water Data Act within transboundary water agreements. This means that IWL also needs to address the use of BDA in transboundary water conventions and instruments. Various scenarios within IWL and the way BDA can be regulated according to each scenario were offered. In particular, a model provision on disruptive technologies to be adopted to address BDA was proposed. This provision combines various elements of IWL, mainly substantive provisions and various types of data and information exchange within this field, with replicated provisions of the Open and Transparent Water Data Act and the Water Data Act.

Bibliography

Adamala, S., '*An Overview of Big Data Applications in Water Resources Engineering*', 2:1, Machine Learning Research (2017) at 10–18.

Addison, J., '*An Overview of California's Water Challenges and Solutions*', 29 October 2018, at https://meetingoftheminds.org/an-overview-of-californias-water-challenges-and-solutions-28860, last accessed 14 June 2021.

Affelt, A., '*Big Data, Big Opportunity*', 21:2, Australian Law Librarian (2013) 78–85.

Agreement between the Governments of the Republic of Angola, the Republic of Botswana, and the Republic of Namibia on the Establishment of a Permanent Okavango River Basin Water Commission (OKACOM), Windhoek, 16 September 1994, http://www.fao.org/3/w7414b/w7414b0m.htm, last accessed 14 June 2021.

Agreement between the Government of the Republic of Kazakhstan and the Government of the People's Republic of China on Cooperation in the Use and Protection of Transboundary Rivers, Astana, 12 September 2001, at http://www.cawater-info.net/library/eng/l/kazakhstan_china.pdf, last accessed 14 June 2021.

Agreement between the Government of the Republic of South Africa, the Government of the Kingdom of Swaziland and the Government of the People's Republic of

794 Open and Transparent Water Data Act, *supra* note 41; House Bill 651, *supra* note 42.

Mozambique Relative to the Establishment of a Tripartite Permanent Technical Committee, Pretoria, 17 February 1983, at http://www.fao.org/3/w7414b/w7414b0h.htm, last accessed 14 June 2021.

Agreement Between the Governments of the Republic of Kazakhstan, the Kyrgyz Republic, and the Republic of Uzbekistan on the Use of Water and Energy Resources of the Syr Darya Basin, 1998, at https://www.ce.utexas.edu/prof/mckinney/papers/aral/agreements/SyrDaryaAgr-Mar17-98.pdf, last accessed 14 June 2021.

Agreement between the Republic of Kazakhstan, the Kyrgyz Republic, the Republic of Tajikistan, Turkmenistan and the Republic of Uzbekistan on Cooperation in the Field of Joint Management on Utilization and Protection of Water Resources from Interstate Sources, 1992, at http://www.icwc-aral.uz/statute1.htm, last accessed 14 June 2021.

Agreement on Joint Activities in Addressing the Aral Sea and the Zone Around the Sea Crisis, Improving the Environment, and Ensuring the Social and Economic Development of the Aral Sea Region, 1993.

Agreement on the Action Plan for the Environmentally Sound Management of the Common Zambezi River System, Harare, 28 May 1987, http://www.fao.org/3/w7414b/w7414b0j.htm, last accessed 14 June 2021.

Agreement on the Cooperation for the Sustainable Development of the Mekong River Basin, 1995, at https://www.ecolex.org/details/treaty/agreement-on-the-cooperation-for-the-sustainable-development-of-the-mekong-river-basin-tre-001223/, last accessed 14 June 2021.

Agreement on the Establishment of the Limpopo Watercourse Commission (2003), at https://iea.uoregon.edu/treaty-text/4453, last accessed 14 June 2021.

Agreement on the Establishment of the Zambezi Watercourse Commission, 2004, at http://www.zambezicommission.org/sites/default/files/publication_downloads/zamcom_agreement.pdf, last accessed 14 June 2021.

Agreement Relative to the Establishment of the Limpopo Basin Permanent Technical Committee, 1986, at https://iea.uoregon.edu/treaty-text/4452, last accessed 14 June 2021.

AI Myths, '*AI Can Be Objective/Unbiased*', at https://www.aimyths.org/ai-can-be-objective-or-unbiased, last accessed 14 June 2021.

Aladalah, M., Cheung, Y., & Lee, V. C. S., '*Towards a Model for Engaging Citizens via Gov2.0 to Meet Evolving Public Value*', in Information Resources Management Association (ed.), *Civic Engagement and Politics: Concepts, Methodologies, Tools, and Applications* (Hershey: IGI Global 2019) 276–294.

Alaerts, G. J., '*Financing for Water – Water for Financing: A Global Review of Policy and Practice*', 11:3 Sustainability (2019) 821.

Allan, J. A., & Miramuchi, N., '*Why Negotiate? Asymmetric Endowments, Asymmetric Power and the Invisible Nexus of Water, Trade and Power that Brings Apparent Water*

Security', in A. Earle et al. (eds), *Transboundary Water Management: Principles and Practice* (London: Earthscan, 2010) 13–26.

Allen, A. L., '*Protecting One's Own Privacy in a Big Data Economy*', 130: Harvard Law Review (2016) 71–78.

Andrews, S., et al., *Reinventing Business through Disruptive Technologies: Sector Trends and Investment Opportunities for Firms in Emerging Markets* (International Finance Corporation, World Bank, March 2019).

Annamraju, S., Calaguas, B., & Gutierrez, E., '*Financing Water and Sanitation: Key Issues in Increasing Resources to the Sector*' (A WaterAid Briefing Paper, November 2001).

Arslan, M., et al., '*A Review on Applications of Big Data for Disaster Management*' (The 13th International Conference on Signal Image Technology & Internet Based Systems, December 2017).

Aureli, A., et al., '*Education and Training for Transboundary Groundwater Management as an Instrument of Dialogue and Communication*', in C. J. G. Darnault (ed), *Overexploitation and Contamination of Shared Groundwater Resources* (Dordrecht: Springer, 2006) 2531.

Aust, A., *Modern Treaty Law and Practice* (3d ed., Cambridge: Cambridge University Press, 2013).

Baba, A., et al. (eds) *Climate Change and its Effects on Water Resources: Issues of National and Global Security* (Dordrecht: Springer, 2011).

Baranyai, G., *European Water Law and Hydropolitics: An Inquiry into the Resilience of Transboundary Water Governance in the European Union* (Dordrecht: Springer, 2020).

Barocas, S., & Selbst, A. D., '*Big Data's Disparate Impact*', 104:3, California Law Review (2016) 671–732.

Barrett, S., *Environment and Statecraft: The Strategy of Environmental Treaty-Making* (Oxford: Oxford University Press, 2005).

Basel Protocol on Liability and Compensation for Damage Resulting from Transboundary Movements of Hazardous Wastes and their Disposal Basel, 10 December 1999, at http://www.basel.int/Countries/StatusofRatifications/TheProtocol/tabid/1345/Default.aspx, last accessed 14 June 2021.

Beier, G., Kiefer, J., & Knopf, J., '*Potentials of Big Data for Corporate Environmental Management: A Case Study from the German Automotive Industry*', Journal of Industrial Ecology (2020) 1–14.

Berman, J. J., *Principles of Big Data: Preparing, Sharing, and Analyzing Complex Information* (Walthham: Morgan Kaufman, 2013).

Bernardini, F., '*The Normative and Institutional Evolution of the Convention*', in A. Tanzi et al. (eds), *The UNECE Convention on the Protection and Use of Transboundary Watercourses and International Lakes* (Leiden: Brill/Nijhoff, 2015) 32–43.

Biesbroek, R., Badloe, S., & Athanasiadis, I. N., '*Machine Learning for Research on Climate Change Adaptation Policy Integration: An Exploratory UK Case Study*', 20:85, Regional Environmental Change (2020) 1–13.

Big Data Analytics and Transboundary Water Collaboration for Southern Africa, https://devbigdata.sadc-gmi.org/, last accessed 20 January 2020.

Biswas, A. K., '*Management of Transboundary Waters: An Overview*', in O. Varis, C. Tortajada, & A. K. Biswas (eds), *Management of Transboundary Rivers and Lakes* (Dordrecht: Springer, 2008) 1–20.

Biswas, A. K., '*Preface*', in A. K. Biswas (eds), *Managing Transboundary Waters of Latin America* (Abingdon: Routledge, 2013) ix–x.

Bjornlund, H., et al., '*Institutional Innovation and Smart Water Management Technologies in Small-Scale Irrigation Schemes in Southern Africa*', 45:6, Water International (2020) 621–650.

Blodgett., D., et al., '*An Analysis of Water Data Systems to Inform the Open Water Data Initiative*', 52:4, Journal of the American Water Resources Association (2016) 845–858.

Bocchino, C., '*Exploring Big Data Solutions for Southern Africa (USAID from the American People)*', at https://www.swpwater.org/exploring-big-data-solutions-for-southern-africa/, last accessed 20 January 2020.

Bocchino, C., & Adkisson, K., '*Using Big Data Analytics for Transboundary Water Management*', 28 July 2020, at https://www.preventionweb.net/news/view/72968, last accessed 20 January 2020.

Borges de Carvalho, P. R., '*Transnational Space Law in the 21st Century: What Laws Govern Data in Outer Space?*', 3 October 2020, https://tclf.in/2020/10/03/transnational-space-law-in-the-21st-century-what-laws-govern-data-in-outer-space/, last accessed 14 June 2021.

Botlhale, E., '*Restoring Fiscal Balances Post the Global Economic Crisis in Botswana*', 40:8 International Journal of Public Administration (2017) 706–716.

Bourne, C. B., *International Water Law: Selected Writings of Professor Charles B. Bourne* (London: Kluwer Law International, 1997).

Bourquain, K., *Freshwater Access from a Human Rights Perspective: A Challenge to International Water and Human Rights Law* (Leiden: Martinus Nijhoff Publishers, 2008).

Boyd, W., '*Environmental Law, Big Data, and the Torrent of Singularities*', 64 UCLA Law Review Discourse (2016) 544–570.

Breggin, L. K., & Amsalem, J., *Big Data and Environmental Protection: An Initial Survey of Public and Private Initiatives* (Washington, DC: Environmental Law Institute, 2014).

Brown, A., '*Biased Algorithms Learn from Biased Data: 3 Kinds Biases Found In AI Datasets*', Forbes, 7 February 2020, at https://www.forbes.com/sites/cognitiveworld/2020/02/07/biased-algorithms/?sh=55bfdfe976fc, last accessed 14 June 2021.

Burchi, S., '*International and Domestic Water Law in Central Asia – Implementing International Law Obligations Regarding Transboundary Waters: The Role of Domestic Water Legislation*', 4:2, Central Asian Journal of Water Research (2018) 59–68.

Bureau of Economic Growth, Agriculture, and Trade, U.S. Agency for International Development, Bureau of Oceans, Environment, and Science, and U.S. Department of State, '*Addressing Water Challenges in the Developing World: A Framework for Action*' (An Annex of the 2008 Report to Congress for the Senator Paul Simon Water for the Poor Act; March 2009) 1–21.

Byrnes, N. '*Why We Should Expect Algorithms to Be Biased*', 24 June 2016, at https://www.technologyreview.com/2016/06/24/159118/why-we-should-expect-algorithms-to-be-biased/, last accessed 14 June 2021.

Cag, D., '*11 Amazing Examples of Disruptive Technology*', 4 September 2020, at https://richtopia.com/emerging-technologies/11-disruptive-technology-examples, last accessed 20 January 2020.

Cairns, S., Richthofen, A. V., & Stokols, A., *Disruptive Technology for Development* (World Bank Group (WBG); Future Cities Laboratory (FCL), 25–27 June 2018).

Caldarola, M. C., & Schrey, J., *Big Data and Law* (Oxford: Beck/Hart, 2020).

Calza, F., Parmentola, A., & Tutore, I., '*Big Data and Natural Environment. How Does Different Data Support Different Green Strategies?*', 2: Sustainable Futures (2020) 100029.

Cannataci, J., Falce, V., & O. Pollicino (eds), *Legal Challenges of Big Data* (Cheltenham: Edward Elgar Publishing, 2020).

Cantor, A., et al., *Data for Water Decision Making: Informing the Implementation of California's Open and Transparent Water Data Act through Research and Engagement* (Center for Law, Energy & the Environment, UC Berkeley School of Law, Berkeley, CA, January 2018).

Carabantes, M., '*Black-Box Artificial Intelligence: An Epistemological and Critical Analysis*', 35, AI & Society (2019) 309–317.

Carroll, M. W., '*Intellectual Property and Related Rights in Climate Data*', in J. D. Sarnoff (ed.), *Research Handbook on Intellectual Property and Climate Change* (Cheltenham: Edward Elgar Publishing, 2016) 384–398.

Cartagena Protocol on Biosafety to the Convention on Biological Diversity, Montreal, 29 January 2000, 2226 UNTS 208.

Case Concerning Pulp Mills on the River Uruguay (*Argentina v. Uruguay*), Judgment, ICJ Reports 2010, p. 14.

Chalh, R., et al., '*Big Data Open Platform for water Resources Management*', *2015 International Conference on Cloud Technologies and Applications* (*CloudTech*) (2015).

Chamberlain, K., '*Water Reckoning Looms in New Mexico's Future: "We're not Prepared for What's Ahead of Us"*', NM Political Report (19 September 2020), https://

nmpoliticalreport.com/2020/09/19/water-reckoning-looms-in-new-mexicos-future-were-not-prepared-for-whats-ahead-of-us/, last accessed 14 June 2021.

Charter of Waters of the Senegal River, 2002, https://iea.uoregon.edu/treaty-text/4462, last accessed 14 June 2021.

Chenoweth, J., *'Effective Multi-jurisdictional River Basin Management'*, 24:4, Water International (1999) 368–376.

Chenoweth, J. L., & Feitelson, E., *'Analysis of Factors Influencing Data and Information Exchange in International River Basins'*, 26:4, Water International (2001) 499–512.

Chiwewe, T., & Bocchino, C., *'AI Pilot to Address Transboundary Water Challenges in Southern Africa Launches'*, 11 November 2019, at https://www.ibm.com/blogs/research/2019/11/ai-pilot-to-address-transboundary-water-challenges/, last accessed 20 January 2020.

Christensen, C. M., Raynor, M. E., & McDonald, R., *'What Is Disruptive Innovation?'*, 2015, at https://hbr.org/2015/12/what-is-disruptive-innovation, last accessed 20 January 2020.

Christensen et al., C. M., *'Disruptive Innovation: An Intellectual History and Directions for Future Research'*, 55:7, Journal of Management Studies (2018) 1043–1078.

Cohen, S., *Understanding Environmental Policy* (New York: Columbia University Press, 2014).

Compagnucci, M. C., *Big Data, Databases and "Ownership" Rights in the Cloud* (Dordrecht: Springer, 2020).

Conca, K., Wu, F., & Mei., C., *'Global Regime Formation or Complex Institution Building? The Principled Content of International River Agreements'*, 50:2, International Studies Quarterly (2006) 263–285.

Conley, R., *'How Data Analysis is Disrupting the Legal Industry'*, 20 March 2019, at https://www.biggerlawfirm.com/how-data-analysis-is-disrupting-the-legal-industry/, last accessed 14 June 2021.

Convention on Access to Information, Public Participation in Decision-making and Access to Justice in Environmental Matters, Aarhus, 25 June 1998, Article 1, at https://unece.org/DAM/env/pp/documents/cep43e.pdf, last accessed 14 June 2021.

Convention on the Law of the Non-navigational Uses of International Watercourses, New York, 21 May 1997, https://legal.un.org/ilc/texts/instruments/english/conventions/8_3_1997.pdf, last accessed 14 June 2021.

Convention on the Protection and Use of Transboundary Watercourses and International Lakes, (Helsinki, 17 March 1992), at https://unece.org/fileadmin/DAM/env/water/pdf/watercon.pdf, last accessed 14 June 2021.

Cooley, H., & Gleick, P. H., *'Climate-proofing Transboundary Water Agreements'*, 56:4, Hydrological Sciences Journal (2011) 711–718.

Corrales, M. C., Fenwick, M., & Forgó, M., *New Technology, Big Data and the Law* (Dordrecht: Springer, 2017).

Council of Europe, Declaration by the Committee of Ministers on the manipulative capabilities of algorithmic processes (Adopted by the Committee of Ministers on 13 February 2019 at the 1337th meeting of the Ministers' Deputies). at https://search.coe.int/cm/pages/result_details.aspx?ObjectId=090000168092dd4b, last accessed 14 June 2021.

Council of Europe, Recommendation CM/Rec(2020)1 of the Committee of Ministers to Member States on the human rights impacts of algorithmic systems (Adopted by the Committee of Ministers on 8 April 2020 at the 1373rd meeting of the Ministers' Deputies), https://www.coe.int/en/web/freedom-expression/committee-of-ministers-adopted-texts/-/asset_publisher/aDXmrolovvsU/content/recommendation-cm-rec-2020-1-of-the-committee-of-ministers-to-member-states-on-the-human-rights-impacts-of-algorithmic-systems?_101_INSTANCE_aDXmrolovvsU_viewMode=view/, last accessed 14 June 2021.

Cremades, R., et al., '*Ten Principles to Integrate the Water-Energy-Land Nexus with Climate Services for Co-Producing Local and Regional Integrated Assessments*', 693: Science of the Total Environment (2019) 133662.

Daibes-Murad, F., *A New Legal Framework for Managing the World's Shared Groundwaters* (London: IWA Publishing, 2005).

Data.Europe.eu, '*What is Open Data*', at https://data.europa.eu/en/trening/what-open-data last accessed 14 June 2021.

Davis, T., '*NM Puts Focus on Better Water Data*', 25 January 2020, at https://www.abqjournal.com/1413327/nm-puts-focus-on-better-water-data.html, last accessed 20 January 2020.

de Chazournes, L. B., *Fresh Water in International Law* (Oxford: Oxford University Press, 2013).

Declaration by the Committee of Ministers on the manipulative capabilities of algorithmic processes (Adopted by the Committee of Ministers on 13 February 2019 at the 1337th meeting of the Ministers' Deputies).

Dellapenna, J. W., & Gupta, J., '*The Evolution of Global Water Law*', in J. W. Dellapenna & J. Gupta (eds), *The Evolution of the Law and Politics of Water* (Dordrecht: Springer, 2009) 3–19.

Dellappenna, J. W., & Loures, F. R., '*Filling Gaps: A Protocol to Govern Groundwater Resources of Relevance to International Law*', in F. R. Loures & A. Rieu-Clarke (eds), *The UN Watercourses Convention in Force: Strengthening International Law for Transboundary Water Management* (Abingdon: Routledge, 2013) 263–269.

Deng, M., & Di, L., '*Building Open Environments to Meet Big Data Challenges in Earth Sciences*', in H. A. Karimi (ed.), *Big Data: Techniques and Technologies in Geoinformatics* (Boca Raton: CRC, 2014) 69–90.

Devins, C., et al., '*The Law and Big Data*', 27:2, Cornell Journal of Law and Public Policy (2017) 357–413.

Dinar, S., *International Water Treaties: Negotiation and Cooperation along Transboundary Rivers* (Abingdon: Routledge, 2008).

Dinar, A., et al, *Bridges Over Water: Understanding Transboundary Water Conflict, Negotiation and Cooperation* (Singapore: World Scientific Publishing, 2013).

Dinar, S., & Dinar, A., *International Water Scarcity and Variability: Managing Resource Use Across Political Boundaries* (Oakland: University of California Press, 2017).

Dinar, A., & Tsur, Y., '*Introduction and Conclusion*', in A. Dinar & Y. Tsur (eds), *Management of Transboundary Water Resources Under Scarcity: A Multidisciplinary Approach* (Singapore: World Scientific Publishing, 2017).

Drieschova, A., Fischhendler, I., & Giordano, M., '*The Role of Uncertainties in the Design of International Water Treaties: An Historical Perspective*', 105 Climatic Change (2011) 387–408.

Dublin Statement on Water and Sustainable Development, 1992, at http://www.cawater-info.net/bk/water_law/pdf/dublin_statement.pdf, last accessed 14 June 2021.

Durán-Sánchez, A., Álvarez-García, J., & de la Cruz del Río-Rama, M., '*Sustainable Water Resources Management: A Bibliometric Overview*', 10:9, Water (2018) 1–19.

Earle, A., et al., *Indigenous and Institutional Profile: Limpopo River Basin* (International Water Management Institute, IWMI Working Paper 112, 2006).

Ebers, M., & Navas, S. (eds), *Algorithms and Law* (Cambridge: Cambridge University Press, 2020).

Eckstein, G., & Eckstein, Y., '*A Hydrogeological Approach to Transboundary Ground Water Resources and International Law*', 19:2, American University International Law Review (2003) 201–258.

Eckstein, G. E., '*Rethinking Transboundary Ground Water Resources Management: A Local Approach along the Mexico-U.S. Border*', 25 The Georgetown International Environmental Law Review (2012) 95–128.

Eckstein, G., & Sindico, F., '*The Law of Transboundary Aquifers: Many Ways of Going Forward, but Only One Way of Standing Still*', 23:1, Review of European, Comparative & International Environmental Law (2014) 32–42.

Eckstein, G., *The International Law of Transboundary Groundwater Resources* (Abingdon: Routledge, 2017).

Emanuilov, I., '*From Space Big Data to Big Space Brother: Do States Have a Right to Privacy? (Part I)*', 23 July 2019, https://www.law.kuleuven.be/citip/blog/from-space-big-data-to-big-space-brother-do-states-have-a-right-to-privacy-part-i/, last accessed 14 June 2021.

Eriksson, M., et al., '*Challenges and Commonalities in Basin-Wide Water Management*', 5: Aquatic Procedia (2015) 44–57.

Espinoza, M. I., & Aronczyk, M., '*Big Data for Climate Action or Climate Action for Big Data?*', 8:1, Big Data & Society (2021) 1–15.

European Space Agency, '*Conference on Big Data from Space – BiDS'17*', 28–30 November 2017, at https://earth.esa.int/web/guest/events/all-events/-/article/conference-on-big-data-from-space-bids-17, last accessed 14 June 2021.

European Union, Council Directive of 21 May 1991 concerning urban waste water treatment (91/271/EEC).

European Union, Council Directive of 12 December 1991 Concerning the Protection of Waters against Pollution Caused by Nitrates from Agricultural Sources (91/676/EEC).

European Union, Directive 2006/7/EC of the European Parliament and of the Council of 15 February 2006 concerning the management of bathing water quality and repealing Directive 76/160/EEC, at https://eur-lex.europa.eu/legal-content/EN/TXT/PDF/?uri=CELEX:32006L0007&from=EN, last accessed 14 June 2021.

European Union, Directive (EU) 2020/2184 of the European Parliament and of the Council of 16 December 2020 on the quality of water intended for human consumption (recast) (Text with EEA relevance), at https://eur-lex.europa.eu/legal-content/EN/TXT/PDF/?uri=CELEX:32020L2184&from=ES, last accessed 14 June 2021.

European Union, Directive 2000/60/EC of the European Parliament and of the Council of 23 October 2000 establishing a framework for Community action in the field of water policy, at https://eur-lex.europa.eu/eli/dir/2000/60/oj, last accessed 14 June 2021.

Faghmous, J. H., & Kumar, V., '*A Big Data Guide to Understanding Climate Change: The Case for Theory-Guided Data Science*', 2:3, Big Data (2014) 155–163.

Fahey, S., '*The Democratization of Big Data*', 7, Journal of National Security Law & Policy (2014) 325–331.

Farmer, G. T., & Cook, J., *Climate Change Science: A Modern Synthesis* (Dordrecht: Springer, 2013).

Fitch, P., et al., '*Integrated Groundwater Data Management*', in A. J. Jakeman et al. (eds), *Integrated Groundwater Management: Concepts, Approaches and Challenges* (Dordrecht: Springer, 2016) 667–692.

Food and Agricultural Organization of the United Nations, '*FAOLEX Database, Botswana – Country Profiles*', http://www.fao.org/faolex/country-profiles/general-profile/en/?iso3=BWA, last accessed 20 January 2020.

Food and Agricultural Organization of the United Nations, '*FAOLEX Database, South Africa – Country Profiles*', http://www.fao.org/faolex/country-profiles/general-profile/en/?iso3=ZAF, last accessed 20 January 2020.

Ford, J. D., et al., '*Opinion: Big Data has Big Potential for Applications to Climate Change Adaptation*', 113:39, PNAS (2016) 10729–10732.

Fox, C. A., & Sneddon, C., '*Transboundary River Basin Agreements in the Mekong and Zambezi Basins: Enhancing Environmental Security or Securitizing the Environment?*', 7, International Environmental Agreements: Politics, Law and Economics (2007) 237–261.

Framework Convention for the Protection of the Environment for Sustainable Development in Central Asia, Ashkhabad, 22 November 2006, at https://leap.unep.org/sites/default/files/treaty/TRE-143806.pdf, last accessed 14 June 2021.

Frenken, K. (ed.), *Irrigation in Africa in Figures: AQUASTAT Survey* (Rome: Food and Agriculture Organization of the United Nations, FAO Water Reports 29, 2005).

Gaffoor, Z., et al., *Big Data Analytics and Modelling: Localising Transboundary Data Sets in Southern Africa: A Case Study Approach: Deliverable 1: Project Scoping and Overview Report* (Report to the Water Research Commission; WRC Project No 2878).

Gaffoor, Z., et al., *Big Data Analytics and Modelling: Localising Transboundary Data Sets in Southern Africa: A Case Study Approach* (Report to the Water Research Commission; WRC Report No. TT 843/20; February 2021).

Gaffoor, Z., et al., *Big Data Analytics and Modelling: Localising Transboundary Data Sets in Southern Africa: A Case Study Approach Deliverable 5: A Comparative Tool for Inventory Datasets* (Report to the Water Research Commission, February 2020).

Gaffoor, Z., et al., *Big Data Analytics and Modelling: Localising Transboundary Data Sets in Southern Africa: A Case Study Approach: Deliverable 3: Policy Brief on Modeling and Data Analytical Tools for Downscaling in a Transboundary Water Management Context* (University of the Western Cape & CSIR, November 2019).

Gaffoor, Z., et al., '*Big Data Analytics and Its Role to Support Groundwater Management in the Southern African Development Community*', 12:10, Water (2020) 1–28.

Gallaher, S., & Heikkila, T., '*Challenges and Opportunities for Collecting and Sharing Data on Water Governance Institutions*', 153:1, Journal of Contemporary Water Research & Education (2014) 66–78.

Garrett, B. L., '*Big Data and Due Process*', 99, Cornell Law Review Online (2014) 101–110.

Gemmell, A., et al., '*Big Data Analytics and Transboundary Water Collaboration: Theme 1: Consolidation of Data and Application of Big Data Tools to Enhance National and Transboundary Data Sets in Southern Africa that Support Decision-Making for Security of Water; Resources*' (Deliverable 1: Inception Report 4; Version 1.1; UMVOTO Africa (Pty) Ltd, 28 March 2019).

Gerlak, A. K., Lautze, J., & Giordano, M., '*Water Resources Data and Information Exchange in Transboundary Water Treaties*', 11 International Environmental Agreements: Politics, Law and Economics (2011) 179–199.

Gerlak, A. K., Lautze, J., & Giordarno, M., '*Greater Exchange, Greater Ambiguity: Water Resources Data and Information Exchange in Transboundary Water Treaties*', in

R. Q. Grafton et al. (eds), *Global Water: Issues and Insights* (Canberra: Australian National University, 2014) 57–63.

Ghotkar, M., & Rokde, P., '*Big Data: How it is Generated and its Importance*', IOSR Journal of Computer Engineering (2016) 1–5.

Giebler, H., & Merkel, W., '*Freedom and Equality in Democracies: There is No Trade-off!*', 22 February 2018, at https://socialeurope.eu/freedom-equality-democracies-no-trade-off, last accessed 14 June 2021.

Giordano, M., et al., '*A Review of the Evolution and State of Transboundary Freshwater Treaties*', 14, International Environmental Agreements: Politics, Law and Economics (2014) 245–264.

Global Campaign for Free Expression, '*Statement on the Right to Communicate by Article 19*', February 2003, at https://www.article19.org/data/files/pdfs/publications/right-to-communicate.pdf, last accessed 14 June 2021.

Global Database, '*Big Data vs Open Data: What's the Difference?*', at https://uk.globaldatabase.com/article/big-data-vs-open-data-what-s-the-difference, last accessed 14 June 2021.

Globalwaters.org, '*Big Data for Water Security: Scalable Geospatiotemporal Data Integration & Systems*', at https://www.globalwaters.org/events/swp/big-data-water-security-scalable-geospatiotemporal-data-integration-systems, last accessed 20 January 2020.

Gomo, M., & Vermeulen, D., '*A Transboundary Aquifer of Potential Concern in Southern Africa*', 19:6, Water Policy (2017) 1160–1171.

Gottschalk, P., & Solli-Saether, H., *E-Government Interoperability and Information Resource Integration: Frameworks for Aligned Development* (Hershey: IGI Global, 2009).

Government of Canada, '*Protocol for Safe Drinking Water in First Nations Communities*', at https://www.sac-isc.gc.ca/eng/1100100034913/1533666029471, last accessed 20 January 2020.

Government of Canada, '*Protocol for Centralised Drinking Water Systems in First Nations Communities*', at https://www.sac-isc.gc.ca/eng/1100100034998/1533666593873, last accessed 20 January 2020.

Grafanaki, S., '*Autonomy Challenges in the Age of Big Data*', 27:4, Fordham Intellectual Property, Media & Entertainment Law Journal (2017) 803–868.

Greggio, E., & Stewart, E., '*How Can Online Data Platforms Improve Management of Water, Sanitation and Hygiene Services?*', 9 February 2019, at https://washmatters.wateraid.org/blog/how-can-online-data-platforms-improve-management-of-water-sanitation-and-hygiene-services, last accessed 20 January 2020.

Grigg, N. S., '*Smart Water Management: Can It Improve Accessibility and Affordability of Water for Everyone?*', 45:6, Water International (2020) 608–620.

Groundwater Management Institute, *SADC Framework for Groundwater Data Collection and Management* (April 2019).

Guo, H. D., Zhang, L., & Zhu, L. W., '*Earth Observation Big Data for Climate Change Research*', 6:2, Advances in Climate Change Research (2015) 108–117.

Guru 99, '*What is BIG DATA? Introduction, Types, Characteristics, Example*', at https://www.guru99.com/what-is-big-data.html#1, last accessed 14 June 2021.

Hafner, M., Tagliapietra, S., & de Strasser, L., *Energy in Africa: Challenges and Opportunities* (Dordrecht: Springer, 2018).

Hakimi, M., '*Why Should We Care About International Law?*', 118:6, Michigan Law Review (2020) 1283–1306.

Hansen, W., & Kranz, N., *EU Water Policy and Challenges for Regional and Local Authorities* (Capacity Building on the European Community's Environmental Policy; Ecologic Institute for International and European Environmental Policy, Berlin – Brussels; Background Paper for the Seminar on Water Management; April 2003).

Harris, E., '*9 Amazing Examples of Disruptive Technology (Inspired by the WTIA)*', at https://www.resultist.com/blog/9-amazing-examples-of-disruptive-technology-inspired-by-the-wtia, last accessed 20 January 2020.

Harris, R., & Baumann, I., '*Open Data Policies and Satellite Earth Observation*', 32, Space Policy (2015) 44–53.

Harshadeep, N. R., & Young, W., '*Disruptive Technologies for Improving Water Security in Large River Basins*', 12(10) Water (2020) 2783.

Hartley, K., & Kuecker, G., '*The Moral Hazards of Smart Water Management*', 45:6 Water International (2020) 693–701.

Hassani, H., Huang, X., & Silva, E., '*Big Data and Climate Change*', 3:1, Big Data and Cognitive Computing (2019) 1–12.

Hassanien, A. E., *Machine Learning and Big Data Analytics Paradigms: Analysis* (Dordrecht: Springer, 2021).

Hathaway, O. A., et al., '*The Treaty Power: Its History, Scope, and Limits*', 98, Cornell Law Review (2013) 239–326.

Helsinki Rules on the Uses of the Waters of International Rivers Helsinki, August 1966, at https://www.internationalwaterlaw.org/documents/intldocs/ILA/ILA-HelsinkiRules1966-as_amended.pdf, last accessed 14 June 2021.

Heyns, P. S. V. H., Patrick, M. J., & Turton, A. R., '*Transboundary Water Resource Management in Southern Africa: Meeting the Challenge of Joint Planning and Management in the Orange River Basin*', 24:3 International Journal of Water Resources Development (2008) 371–383.

High Level Panel on Water, '*Water Infrastructure and Investment*', https://sustainabledevelopment.un.org/content/documents/hlpwater/08-WaterInfrastInvest.pdf, last accessed 20 January 2020.

Hildebrandt M., '*Algorithmic Regulation and the Rule of Law*', 376: Philosophical Transactions of the Royal Society A (2018) 1–11.

Hirsch, D. D., & King, J. H., '*Big Data Sustainability: An Environmental Management Systems Analogy*', 72:3 Washington and Lee Law Review Online (2016) 406–419.

Ho, S., '*China's Transboundary River Policies towards Kazakhstan: Issue-Linkages and Incentives for Cooperation*', 42:2 Water International (2017) 142–162.

Huang, T., '*A Web of Data Analytics Services*', in P. Soille, S. Loekken & S. Albani (eds), *Proceedings of the 2019 Conference on Big Data from Space (BiDS'19):Turning Data into Insights* (Munich: Joint Research Centre, 19–21 February 2019).

Ibrahim, I. A., '*Legal Implications of the Use of Big Data in the Transboundary Water Context*', 34, Water Resources Management (2020) 1139–1153.

Ibrahim, I. A., '*Water Governance in the Mekong after the Watercourses Convention 35th Ratification: Multilateral or Bilateral Approach?*', 36:1, International Journal of Water Resources Development (2020) 200–220.

Ibrahim, I. A., '*The Importance of International Water Law to the Successful Implementation of the Belt and Road Initiative: Evidence from Central Asia*', in G. Martinico & X. Wu, (eds), '*A Legal Analysis of the Belt and Road Initiative: Towards a New Silk Road?*' (Cham: Palgrave Macmillan, 2020) 145–169.

Ikeda, J., et al., *Innovations in Commercial Finance for the Water and Sanitation Sector: The Potential of Investment Platforms for Mobilizing Financing for Development at Scale* (Inter-American Development Bank, Discussion Paper Nº IDB-DP-00799, August 2020).

Information Resources Management Association (eds), *Disruptive Technology: Concepts, Methodologies, Tools, and Applications* (Hershey: IGI Global, 2020).

Institute of International Law, Resolution on the Pollution of Rivers and Lakes and International Law, Athens, 12 September 1979, at https://www.internationalwaterlaw.org/documents/intldocs/IIL/IIL-Resolution_of_Athens.pdf, last accessed 14 June 2021.

International Groundwater Resources Assessment Center, '*Big Data for Groundwater Management*', at https://www.un-igrac.org/special-project/big-data-groundwater-management, last accessed 20 January 2020.

International Groundwater Resources Assessment Centre, '*GGRETA*', at https://www.un-igrac.org/special-project/ggreta, last accessed 20 January 2020.

International Groundwater Resources Assessment Centre, '*RAMOTSWA*', at https://www.un-igrac.org/special-project/ramotswa, last accessed 20 January 2020.

International Groundwater Resources Assessment Centre, '*Stampriet Aquifer*', at https://www.un-igrac.org/case-study/stampriet-aquifer, last accessed 20 January 2020.

International Groundwater Resources Assessment Centre, '*UMVOTO*', at https://www.un-igrac.org/donor-partner/umvoto, last accessed 20 January 2020.

International Law Association, Rules on the Water Pollution in an International Drainage Basin, Montreal, 1982, at https://www.internationalwaterlaw.org/documents/intldocs/ILA/ILA-Rules_on_the_Water_Pollution_in_an_International_Drainage_Basin-Montreal1982.pdf, last accessed 14 June 2021.

International Law Commission, Resolution on Confined Transboundary Groundwater, Adopted by the Commission at its forty-sixth session, in 1994, and submitted to the General Assembly as a part of the Commission's report covering the work of that session on the topic Law of the non-navigational uses of international watercourses.

International Legal Commission, Draft Articles on the Law of Transboundary Aquifers (2008), at https://legal.un.org/ilc/texts/instruments/english/draft_articles/8_5_2008.pdf, 14 June 2021.

Interview with Jonathan Lautze, Research Group Leader: Integrated Management of Basins and Aquifers, 10 June 2021, at https://www.iwmi.cgiar.org/about/staff-list/jonathan-lautze/, last accessed 14 June 2021.

Islam, S., & Susskind, L. E., *Water Diplomacy: A Negotiated Approach to Managing Complex Water Networks* (Abingdon: Routledge, 2013).

Jacobs, I. M., & Nienaber, S., '*Waters Without Borders: Transboundary Water Governance and the Role of the 'Transdisciplinary Individual' in Southern Africa*', 37:5, Water SA (2011) 665–678.

Jafroudi, M., '*Enhancing Climate Resilience of Transboundary Water Allocation Agreements: The Impact of Shortening the Agreement's Lifetime on Cooperation Stability*', 18, International Environmental Agreements: Politics, Law and Economics (2018) 707–722.

Johns, F., '*The Turn to Data Analytics and International Law*', 3:4, ESIL Reflections (2014) 1–7.

Johns, F., & Grolman, L., *Big Data and International Law* (Oxford: Oxford University Press, 2019).

Jones, P. A., '*Compliance Mechanisms of International Water Agreements*', 25:4 Water International (2000) 554–564.

Just, R. E., & Netanyahu, S., '*Preface*', in R. E. Just & S. Netanyahu (eds), *Conflict and Cooperation on Trans-Boundary Water Resources* (Dordrecht: Springer, 1998).

Kammeyer, C., '*The COVID Crisis is Slashing California's State Budget. What Does it Mean for Water Management?*', 26 May 2020, at https://pacinst.org/the-covid-crisis-is-slashing-californias-state-budget-what-does-it-mean-for-water-management/, last accessed 20 January 2020.

Keeso, A., '*Big Data and Environmental Sustainability: A Conversation Starter*' (Smith School Working Paper Series No 14-04, December 2014).

Kh, R. '*Can Big Data Help Save The Environment?*', at https://www.smartdatacollective.com/can-big-data-help-save-environment/, last accessed 14 June 2021.

Khudayberganov, Y., '*Security and Water Resources Management Problems and Experience in the Amudarya Basin*', in C. Madramootoo & V. Dukhovny (eds), *Water and Food Security in Central Asia* (Dordrecht: Springer, 2011) 59–67.

Kibaroglu, A., '*An Analysis of Turkey's Water Diplomacy and its Evolving Position vis-à-vis International Water Law*', in P. Wouters, H. Chen & J. E. Nickum (eds), *Transboundary Water Cooperation: Principles, Practice and Prospects for China and its Neighbors* (Abingdon: Routledge, 2018) 131–143.

Kilgour, M., & Dinar, A., '*Flexible Water Sharing Within an International River Basin*', 18, Environmental and Resource Economics (2001) 43–60.

Kirkovska, A., '*Big Data and Its Impact in the Space Sector, One Bit at a Time: Why is Big Data Important for Space Exploration?*', 14 September 2018, at https://medium.com/spacedecentral/big-data-and-its-impact-in-the-space-sector-one-bit-at-a-time-1e2d378ad4cc, last accessed 14 June 2021.

Kitchin, R., '*Big Data, New Epistemologies and Paradigm Shifts*', Big Data & Society (2014) 1–12.

Kitchin, R., Lauriault, T. P., & McArdle, G., '*Smart Cities and the Politics of Urban Data*', in S. Marvin, A. Luque-Ayala & C. McFarlane (eds), *Smart Urbanism: Utopian Vision or False Dawn?* (Abingdon: Routledge, 2016) 16–33.

Knüppe, K., '*The Challenges Facing Sustainable and Adaptive Groundwater Management in South Africa*', 37:1, Water SA (2011) 67–79.

Kosmala, M. et al., '*Assessing Data Quality in Citizen Science*', 14:10, Frontiers in Ecology and the Environment (2016) 551–560.

Kotze, K., '*South Africa's Energy Conundrum*', 8 April 2019, at https://globalriskinsights.com/2019/04/south-africas-energy-conundrum/, last accessed 14 June 2021.

Kreps, S. E., & Arend, A. C., '*Why States Follow the Rules: Toward a Positional Theory of Adherence to International Legal Regimes*', 16, Duke Journal of Comparative & International Law (2006) 331–414.

Kuehl, H. F., '*UPDATE: A Basic Guide to International Environmental Legal Research*', May/June 2017, at https://www.nyulawglobal.org/globalex/International_Environmental_Legal_Research1.html, last accessed 14 June 2021.

Kuisma, S., et al., '*The Report that Sparked this Special Issue*', 45:6, Water International (2020) 520–525.

Kyoto Protocol to the United Nations Framework Convention on Climate Change, Kyoto, 11 December 1997, 2303 UNTS 162.

La Charte de l'Eau du Bassin du Niger, 2008, at https://www.riob.org/sites/default/files/IMG/pdf/Charte_de_l_Eau_fre-2.pdf, last accessed 14 June 2021.

Lalturi, M., & Sternlieb, F., '*Water Data Systems: Science, Practice, and Policy*', 153:1 Journal of Contemporary Water Research & Education (2014) 1–3.

Lajaunie, C., Schafer, B., & Mazzega, P., '*Big Data Enters Environmental Law*', 8:3, Transnational Environmental Law (2019) 523–545.

Laniak, G. F., et al., '*Integrated Environmental Modeling: A Vision and Roadmap for the Future*', 39 Environmental Modelling & Software (2013) 3–23.

Lautze, J., & Giordano, M., '*Transboundary Water Law in Africa: Development, Nature, and Geography*', 45:4, Natural Resources Journal (2005) 1053–1087.

Lautze, J., et al., *Joint Strategic Action Plan for the Ramotswa Transboundary Aquifer Area – Roadmap* (SAP Roadmap Report, December 2016).

Lautze, J., et al., *Draft Joint Strategic Action Plan for the Ramotswa Transboundary Aquifer Area* (IWMI; DWA – Botswana; DWS – South Africa, March 2018).

Lautze, J., et al., '*Joint Strategic Action Plan for the Ramotswa Transboundary Aquifer Area*' (Integrated Water Management Institute, May 2019).

Leb, C., *Cooperation in the Law of Transboundary Water Resources* (Cambridge: Cambridge University Press, 2013).

Leb, C., '*General Obligation to Cooperate and Regular Exchange of Data and Information (Articles 8 and 9)*', in L. B. de Chazournes et al. (eds), *The UN Convention on the Law of the Non-navigational Uses of International Watercourses: A Commentary* (Oxford: Oxford University Press, 2018) 123–140.

Leb, C., '*Data Innovations for Transboundary Freshwater Resources Management: Are Obligations Related to Information Exchange Still Needed?*', 4:4, International Water Law (2020) 3–78.

Lee, N. T., Resnick, P., & Barton, G., '*Algorithmic Bias Detection and Mitigation: Best Practices and Policies to Reduce Consumer Harms*', 22 May2019, at https://www.brookings.edu/research/algorithmic-bias-detection-and-mitigation-best-practices-and-policies-to-reduce-consumer-harms/, last accessed 14 June 2021.

Lerman, J., '*Big Data and Its Exclusions*', 66, Stanford Law Review Online (2013) 55–63.

Leslie, D., et al., *Artificial Intelligence, Human Rights, Democracy, and the Rule of Law: A Primer* (The Council of Europe, 2021).

Levy, K. E. C., '*Relational Big Data*', 66, Stanford Law Review Online (2013) 73–79.

Limpopo River Awareness Kit, '*Governance: Southern African Development Community, Instruments of the Sector*', at http://www.limpopo.riverawarenesskit.org/LIMPOPORAK_COM/EN/GOVERNANCE/SADC/INSTRUMENTS_OF_THE_SECTOR.HTM, last accessed 20 January 2020.

Limpopo River Awareness Kit, '*Governance: Southern African Development Community, River Basin Organisations*', at http://www.limpopo.riverawarenesskit.org/LIMPOPORAK_COM/EN/GOVERNANCE/SADC/RIVER_BASIN_ORGANISATIONS.HTM, last accessed 20 January 2020.

Limpopo River Awareness Kit, '*Governance: Southern African Development Community, SADC Action Plan*', at http://www.limpopo.riverawarenesskit.org/LIMPOPORAK

_COM/EN/GOVERNANCE/SADC/SADC_ACTION_PLAN.HTM, last accessed 20 January 2020.

Limpopo River Awareness Kit, '*Governance: Southern African Development Community, SADC Guidelines*', at http://www.limpopo.riverawarenesskit.org/LIMPOPORAK_COM/EN/GOVERNANCE/SADC/GUIDELINES_FOR_STRENGTHENING_RB.HTM, last accessed 20 January 2020.

Limpopo River Awareness Kit, '*Governance: Southern African Development Community, SADC Protocol*', at http://www.limpopo.riverawarenesskit.org/LIMPOPORAK_COM/EN/GOVERNANCE/SADC/SADC_WATER_PROTOCOL.HTM, last accessed 20 January 2020.

Limpopo River Awareness Kit, '*Governance: Southern African Development Community, SADC Water Division*', at http://www.limpopo.riverawarenesskit.org/LIMPOPORAK_COM/EN/GOVERNANCE/SADC/SADC_WATER_DIVISION.HTM, last accessed 20 January 2020.

Limpopo River Awareness Kit, '*Governance: Southern African Development Community, SADC Water Policy and Strategy*', at http://www.limpopo.riverawarenesskit.org/LIMPOPORAK_COM/EN/GOVERNANCE/SADC/SADC_WATER_POLICY_AND_STRATEGY.HTM, last accessed 20 January 2020.

Limpopo River Awareness Kit, '*Governance: Southern African Development Community, SADC Water Sector*', at http://www.limpopo.riverawarenesskit.org/LIMPOPORAK_COM/EN/GOVERNANCE/SADC/SADC_WATER_SECTOR.HTM, last accessed 20 January 2020.

Limpopo River Awareness Kit, '*Governance: Water Governance in the Limpopo Basin, History of LIMCOM*', at http://www.limpopo.riverawarenesskit.org/LIMPOPORAK_COM/EN/GOVERNANCE/WATER_GOVERNANCE_IN_THE_LIMPOPO/LIMCOM.HTM, last accessed 20 January 2020.

Limpopo River Awareness Kit, '*Governance: Water Governance in the Limpopo Basin, LIMCOM Objectives and Structure*', at http://www.limpopo.riverawarenesskit.org/LIMPOPORAK_COM/EN/GOVERNANCE/WATER_GOVERNANCE_IN_THE_LIMPOPO/OBJECTIVES_AND_STRUCTURE.HTM, last accessed 20 January 2020.

Limpopo River Awareness Kit, '*Governance; Water Governance in the Limpopo Basin, National Policies & Laws*', at http://www.limpopo.riverawarenesskit.org/LIMPOPORAK_COM/EN/GOVERNANCE/WATER_GOVERNANCE_IN_THE_LIMPOPO/NATIONAL_POLICIES_AND_LAWS/BOTSWANA.HTM, last accessed 20 January 2020.

Limpopo River Awareness Kit, '*Governance, Water Governance in the Limpopo Basin, National Policies & Laws, Botswana*', at http://www.limpopo.riverawarenesskit.org/LIMPOPORAK_COM/EN/GOVERNANCE/WATER_GOVERNANCE_IN_THE

_LIMPOPO/NATIONAL_POLICIES_AND_LAWS/BOTSWANA.HTM, last accessed 14 June 2021.

Limpopo River Awareness Kit, '*Governance, Water Governance in the Limpopo Basin, National Policies & Laws, Mozambique*', at http://www.limpopo.riverawarenesskit.org/LIMPOPORAK_COM/EN/GOVERNANCE/WATER_GOVERNANCE_IN_THE_LIMPOPO/NATIONAL_POLICIES_AND_LAWS/MOZAMBIQUE.HTM, last accessed 14 June 2021.

Limpopo River Awareness Kit, '*Governance, Water Governance in the Limpopo Basin, National Policies & Laws, South Africa*', at, http://www.limpopo.riverawarenesskit.org/LIMPOPORAK_COM/EN/GOVERNANCE/WATER_GOVERNANCE_IN_THE_LIMPOPO/NATIONAL_POLICIES_AND_LAWS/SOUTH_AFRICA.HTM, last accessed 14 June 2021.

Limpopo River Awareness Kit, '*Governance, Water Governance in the Limpopo Basin, National Policies & Laws, Zimbabwe*', at http://www.limpopo.riverawarenesskit.org/LIMPOPORAK_COM/EN/GOVERNANCE/WATER_GOVERNANCE_IN_THE_LIMPOPO/NATIONAL_POLICIES_AND_LAWS/ZIMBABWE.HTM, last accessed 14 June 2021.

Linderfalk, U., *On the Interpretation of Treaties: The Modern International Law as Expressed in the 1969 Vienna Convention on the Law of Treaties* (Dordrecht: Springer, 2007).

Ling, T. C., '*Disruptive Innovation and the Natural Resource Revolution*', 7 June 2017, at https://www.lexology.com/library/detail.aspx?g=a8034b69-3c1d-4bb3-9ccb-950f947ff7e2, last accessed 20 January 2020.

Lokers, R., et al., '*Analysis of Big Data Technologies for Use in Agro-Environmental Science*', 84 Environmental Modelling & Software (2016) 494–504.

Lucivero, F., '*Big Data, Big Waste? A Reflection on the Environmental Sustainability of Big Data Initiatives*', 26, Social and Engineering Ethics (2020) 1009–1030.

Lyall, F., '*Climate Change and Space Law*', in R. G. Rayfuse & S. V. Scott (eds), *International Law in the Era of Climate Change* (Cheltenham: Edward Elgar Publishing, 2012) 175–189.

Mabhaudhi, T., et al., '*Southern Africa's Water – Energy Nexus: Towards Regional Integration and Development*', 8:6, Water (2016) 1–21.

Mabiza, C. C., *Integrated Water Resources Management, Institutions and Livelihoods under Stress: Bottom-Up Perspectives from Zimbabwe* (Dissertation submitted in fulfilment of the requirements of the Board for Doctorates of Deft University of Technology and of the Academic Board of the UNESCO-IHE Institute for Water Education for the degree of DOCTOR; CRC Press, 2013).

Magombeyi, M., et al., *Agricultural Water Management Solutions for Smallholder Farmers in the Ramotswa Transboundary Aquifer Area* (Integrated Water Management Institute, December 2018).

Magsig, B. O., *International Water Law and the Quest for Common Security* (Abingdon: Routledge, 2015).

Mah, A., '*Environmental Justice in the Age of Big Data: Challenging Toxic Blind Spots of Voice, Speed, and Expertise*', 3:2 Environmental Sociology (2017) 122–133.

Maidment, D. R., '*Open Water Data in Space and Time*', 52:4, Journal of the American Water Resources Association (2016) 816–824.

Mäihäniemi, B., *Competition Law and Big Data: Imposing Access to Information in Digital Markets* (Cheltenham: Edward Elgar Publishing, 2020).

Mak, V., Tai, E. T., T., & Berlee, A. (eds) *Research Handbook in Data Science and Law* (Cheltenham: Edward Elgar Publishing, 2018).

Mak, V., *Legal Pluralism in European Contract Law* (Oxford: Oxford University Press, 2020).

Malzbender, D., & Earle, A., *Water Resources of the SADC: Demands, Dependencies and Governance Responses* (African Centre for Water Research, 2007).

Mantelero, A., '*AI and Big Data: A Blueprint for a Human Rights, Social and Ethical Impact Assessment*', 34:4, Computer Law & Security Review (2018) 754–772.

Manungufala, T., & Dini, J., '*Transboundary Cooperation*', in L. Filho et al. (eds), *Clean Water and Sanitation* (Dordrecht: Springer, 2022).

Manyika, J., Silberg, J., & Presten, B., '*What Do We Do About the Biases in AI?*', 25 October 2019, at https://hbr.org/2019/10/what-do-we-do-about-the-biases-in-ai, last accessed 14 June 2021.

Marr, B., '*A Brief History of Big Data Everyone Should Read*', 25 February 2015, https://www.weforum.org/agenda/2015/02/a-brief-history-of-big-data-everyone-should-read/, last accessed 14 June 2021.

Mayer-Schönberger, V., & Cukier, K., *Big Data: A Revolution That Will Transform How We Live, Work, and Think* (Boston: Houghton Mifflin Harcourt, 2013).

Mbengue, M. M., & Odili, N., '*The Environmental Management of Water Resources: What Impact on the Characterization of Fresh Water in International Law?*', in M. Tignino & C. Bréthaut (eds), *Research Handbook on Freshwater Law and International Relations* (Cheltenham: Edward Elgar Publishing, 2018) 68–95.

McCaffrey, S. C., Leb, C., & Denoon, R. T. (eds), *Research Handbook on International Water Law* (Cheltenham: Edward Elgar Publishing, 2019).

McCaffrey, S. C., '*The International Law Commission Adopts Draft Articles on Transboundary Aquifers*', 103: 2, American Journal of International Law (2009) 272–293.

McFall-Johnsen, M., '*New Mexico Faces Extreme Water Scarcity on Par with the United Arab Emirates. Experts Warn More "Day Zeros" are Looming*', 7 August 2019, https://www.businessinsider.com/new-mexico-faces-extreme-water-stress-2019-8, last accessed 14 June 2021.

McGill, B. M., et al., '*Complex Interactions between Climate Change, Sanitation, and Groundwater Quality: A Case Study from Ramotswa, Botswana*', 27, Hydrogeology Journal (2019) 997–1015.

Mechlem, K., '*International Groundwater Law: Towards Closing the Gaps?*', 14:1, Yearbook of International Environmental Law (2003) 47–80.

Mechlem, K., '*Groundwater Governance: The Role of Legal Frameworks at the Local and National Level – Established Practice and Emerging Trends*', 8:8, Water (2016) 1–16.

Mekong River Commission for Sustainable Development, '*Procedures for Data and Information Exchange and Sharing*', 2001, at https://www.mrcmekong.org/assets/Publications/policies/Procedures-Data-Info-Exchange-n-Sharing.pdf, last accessed 14 June 2021.

Michigan Tech, '*Eight Ways Big Data Affects Your Personal Life*', 30 April 2020, https://onlinedegrees.mtu.edu/news/ways-big-data-affects-your-personal-life, last accessed 14 June 2021.

Milosevic, Z., et al., '*Real-Time Analytics*', in R. Buyya, R. N. Calheiros & A. V. Dastjerdi (eds), *Big Data: Principles and Paradigms* (Cambridge: Morgan Kaufman, 2015).

Mirumachi, N., *Transboundary Water Politics in the Developing World* (Abingdon: Routledge, 2015).

Misuraca, G., Mureddu, F., & Osimo, D., '*Policy-Making 2.0: Unleashing the Power of Big Data for Public Governance*', in M. Gascó-Hernández (ed.), *Open Government: Opportunities and Challenges for Public Governance* (Dordrecht: Springer, 2014) 171–188.

Mitchell, S. M., & Zawahri, N. A., '*The Effectiveness of Treaty Design in Addressing Water Disputes*', 52:2 Journal of Peace Research (2015) 187–200.

Mohamed, A. E., '*Comparing Africa's Shared River Basins – The Limpopo, Orange, Juba and Shabelle Basins*', 2:7 Universal Journal of Geoscience (2014) 200–211.

Moniz, P. F., et al., '*A GIS-Based Solution for Urban Water Management*', 45:6, Water International (2020) 660–677.

Moran, T. et al., *Evaluating the Use of Data Platform for Water Management Decisions* (Final Report submitted to the S. D. Bechtel, Jr. Foundation, 9 August 2019, revised 10 January 2020).

Moran, T., et al., *Evaluating the Use of Data Platform for Water Management Decisions: Supplemental Material* (Water in the West; Stanford Digital Repository, submitted 9 August 2019, revised 10 January 2020).

Moran, T., et al., '*Evaluating the Use of Data Platforms for Water Management Decisions: Key Findings and Recommendations*', 4 June 2020, at https://purl.stanford.edu/cb612zf3515, last accessed 20 January 2020.

Moran, T., et al., '*Evaluating the Use of Data Platforms for Water Management Decisions*', 8 June 2020, at https://waterinthewest.stanford.edu/publications/evaluating-use-data-platforms-water-management-decisions, last accessed 20 January 2020.

Montreal Protocol on Substances that Deplete the Ozone Layer, Montreal, Montreal, 16 September 1987, 1522 UNTS 29.

Moura, A. M. de C., Victorino, M., & Tanaka, A., '*Combining Mediator and Data Warehouse Technologies for Developing Environmental Decision Support Systems*', in M. J. Egenhofer & D. M. Mark (eds), *Geographic Information Science: Second International Conference* (Dordrecht: Springer, 2002) 196–208.

Moynihan, R., & Magsig, B. O., '*Prevention and Mitigation of Harmful Conditions and Emergency Situations (Articles 27 and 28)*', in L. B. de Chazournes et al. (eds), *The UN Convention on the Law of the Non-navigational Uses of International Watercourses: A Commentary* (Oxford: Oxford University Press, 2018) 277–299.

Mubako, S. T., & Mintz-Habib, N., '*Climate Change Adaptation and Water in Semi-Arid Regions: A Case Study of the Limpopo Basin, Southern Africa*', in D. Stucker & E. Lopez-Gunn (eds), *Adaptation to Climate Change through Water Resources Management: Capacity, Equity and Sustainability* (Abingdon: Routledge, 2015) 197–219.

Mukuyu, P., et al., '*The Devil's in the Details: Data Exchange in Transboundary Waters*', 45 (7/8) Water International (2020) 884–900.

Mumme, S., *The 1944 U.S.-Mexico Water Treaty as a Constitutional Document* (Mexico Center, Rice University's Baker Institute for Public Policy, March 2019).

Münger, F., et al., '*The Key Role of Water Management and Data for Peacebuilding*', 2020, at https://public.wmo.int/en/resources/bulletin/key-role-of-water-management-and-data-peacebuilding, last accessed 20 January 2020.

Myatt, M., '*Currents: Get to Know 6 Programs Driving Open Water Data*', 9 July 2019, at https://waterfdn.org/get-to-know-6-programs-driving-open-water-data/, last accessed 20 January 2020.

National Advisory Council for Environmental Policy and Technology, *Information to Action: Strengthening EPA Citizen Science Partnerships for Environmental Protection* (EPA 220-R-18-001, April 2018).

National Water Act, South Africa, 1998, at http://www.limpopo.riverawarenesskit.org/LIMPOPORAK_COM/_SYSTEM/DMSSTORAGE/3461EN/RSA_NATIONALWATERACT_1998.PDF, last accessed 14 June 2021.

Naff, T., '*Information, Water, and Conflict: Exploring the Linkages in the Middle East*', 22:1 Water International (1997) 16–28.

Ndlhovu, L., et al., *Imagining Solutions for Extracting Further Value from Existing Datasets on Surface and Groundwater Resources in Southern Africa: Deliverable 2 – Collection of Existing Surface and Groundwater Analytical Data and Conducting Preliminary Data Analytics* (Water Research Commission, July 2019).

Nijsten, G. J., et al., '*Transboundary Aquifers of Africa: Review of the Current State of Knowledge and Progress Towards Sustainable Development and Management*', 20, Journal of Hydrology: Regional Studies (2018) 21–34.

Nikolic, V. V., & Simonovic, S. P., '*Multi-method Modeling Framework for Support of Integrated Water Resources Management*', 2: Environmental Processes (2015) 461–483.

Nollkaemper, A., '*The Contribution of the International Law Commission to International Water Law: Does It Reverse the Flight from Substance?*', 27, Netherlands Yearbook of International Law (1996) 39–73.

Nuapia, Y., et al., *Imagining Solutions for Extracting Further Value from Existing Datasets on Surface and Groundwater Resources in Southern Africa: Deliverable 1 – Project Approach and Workplan* (Water Research Commission, Project No. K5/2881, February 2019).

Nuapia, Y., et al., *Imagining Solutions for Extracting Further Value from Existing Datasets on Surface and Groundwater Resources in Southern Africa: Deliverable 3 – Citizen Science and Advanced Data Analytics* (Water Research Commission, Project No. K5/2881, October 2019).

Odili, N. C., *Shared Water Resources in West Africa: Relevance and Application of the UN Watercourses and the UNECE Water Convention* (Leiden: Brill, 2018).

Olendorf, R., & Wang, Y., '*Big Data in Libraries*', in S. C. Suh & T. Anthony (eds), *Big Data and Visual Analytics* (Dordrecht: Springer, 2017) 191–202.

Open Knowledge Foundation, '*What is Open?*', at https://okfn.org/opendata/, last accessed 20 January 2020.

Organisation for Economic Co-operation and Development (OECD), *Environmental Management in Eastern Europe, Caucasus and Central Asia* (Paris: OECD Publishing, 2005).

Organisation for Economic Co-operation and Development, *Managing Water for All an OECD Perspective on Pricing and Financing* (Paris: OECD Publications, 2009).

Organisation for Economic Co-operation and Development, *Innovative Financing Mechanisms for the Water Sector* (Paris: OECD Publications, 2010).

Organisation for Economic Co-operation and Development, *International Regulatory Co-operation Addressing Global Challenges* (Paris: OECD Publishing, 2013).

Organisation for Economic Co-operation and Development, '*Women Make Up Most of the Health Sector Workers But They Are Under-Represented in High-Skilled Jobs*', at https://www.oecd.org/gender/data/women-make-up-most-of-the-health-sector-workers-but-they-are-under-represented-in-high-skilled-jobs.htm, last accessed 14 June 2021.

Paisley, R. K., & Henshaw, T. W., '*"If You Can't Measure It, You Can't Manage It": Transboundary Waters, Good Governance And Data & Information Sharing & Exchange*', 24:1, Indiana International & Comparative Law Review (2014) 203–248.

Paisley, R. K., & Curlier, M., '*Creating Basin Mechanisms in Southern Africa*', in S. C. McCaffrey, C. Leb & R. T. Denoon (eds), *Research Handbook on International Water Law* (Cheltenham: Edward Elgar Publishing, 2019) 341–360.

Parhami, B., '*Energy Implications of Big Data*', in S. Sakr & A. Y. Zomaya (eds), *Encyclopaedia of Big Data Technologies* (Dordrecht: Springer, 2019).

Paskus, L., '*Bill Would Shine a Light on State's Water Situation*', 1 March 2019, at https://nmpoliticalreport.com/2019/03/01/bill-would-shine-a-light-on-states-water-situation/, last accessed 20 January 2020.

Pedregal, B., et al., '*Information and Knowledge for Water Governance in the Networked Society*', 8:2, Water Alternatives (2015) 1–19.

Pellegrin, T., '*Economics of Big Data: A Value Perspective on State of the Art and Future Trends*', in R. Akerkar (ed.), *Big Data Computing* (Boca Raton: CRC Press, 2014) 343–372.

Pernick, R., & C. Wilder, *Summary: The Clean Tech Revolution: Review and Analysis of Pernick and Wilder's Book* (Businessnews Publishing, 2016).

Peruginelli, G., & Faro, S., *Knowledge of the Law in the Big Data Age* (Amersterdam: IOS Press, 2019).

Petersen-Perlman, J. D., Veilleux, J. C., & Wolf, A. T., '*International Water Conflict and Cooperation: Challenges and Opportunities*', 42:2 Water International (2017) 105–120.

Petrie, B., et al., *Risk, Vulnerability & Resilience in the Limpopo River Basin: Climate Change, Water and Biodiversity – A Synthesis* (For the USAI D Southern Africa "Resilience in the Limpopo River Basin" (RESILIM) Program, One World Sustainable Investments, Cape Town, South Africa, 2014).

Pietersen, K., Kanyerere, T., & Wanangwa, G. J., *Big Data Analytics and Modelling: Localising Transboundary Data Sets in Southern Africa: A Case Study Approach. Deliverable 2a: Workshop with Key Stakeholders to Understand the Status Quo* (Report to the Water Research Commission, WRC Project 2878, September 2019).

Plengsaeng, B., Wehn, U., & van der Zaag, P., '*Data-Sharing Bottlenecks in Transboundary Integrated Water Resources Management: A Case Study of the Mekong River Commission's Procedures for Data Sharing in the Thai Context*', 39:7, Water International (2014) 933–951.

Pokhrel, Y. N., et al., '*Recent Progresses in Incorporating Human Land – Water Management into Global Land Surface Models toward their Integration into Earth System Models*', 3:4, WIREs Water (2016) 548–574.

Posner, E. A., '*Do States Have a Moral Obligation to Obey International Law?*', 55:5 Stanford Law Review (2003) 1901–1919.

Protocol on Shared Watercourse Systems in the Southern African Development Community (SADC) Region, Johannesburg, 28 August 1995, http://www.fao.org/3/w7414b/w7414b0n.htm, last accessed 14 June 2021.

Puig, S., Pauwelyn, J., & Alschner, W., '*The Data-Driven Future of International Law*', at https://www.ejiltalk.org/the-data-driven-future-of-international-law/, last accessed 20 January 2020.

Pundt, H., et al., '*A GIS-Supported Freshwater Information System Including a Pen-Computer Component for Field Data Recording*', in K. Kovar & H. P. Nachtnebel (eds), *Application of Geographic Information Systems in Hydrology and Water Resources Management* (Vienna: IAHS Publication No. 235, 1996).

Raval, N., & Kumar, M., '*An Overview of Big Data Analytics: A State-of-the-Art Platform for Water Resources Management*', in M. Kumar et al. (eds), *Resilience, Response, and Risk in Water Systems: Shifting Management and Natural Forcings Paradigms* (Dordrecht: Springer, 2020) 43–56.

Regional Agreement on Access to Information, Public Participation and Justice in Environmental Matters in Latin America and the Caribbean, Escazú, Costa Rica, 4 March 2018, at https://treaties.un.org/doc/Treaties/2018/03/20180312%2003-04%20PM/CTC-XXVII-18.pdf, last accessed 14 June 2021.

Republic of Mozambique, Act No. 16/91 Regulating Water Resources Belonging to the Public Domain, https://www.ecolex.org/details/legislation/act-no-1691-regulating-water-resources-belonging-to-the-public-domain-lex-faoc003125/, last accessed 14 June 2021.

Revised Protocol on Shared Watercourses in the Southern African Development Community, 7 August 2000, at https://www.sadc.int/files/3413/6698/6218/Revised_Protocol_on_Shared_Watercourses_-_2000_-_English.pdf, last accessed 14 June 2021.

Riahi, Y., & Riahi, S., '*Big Data and Big Data Analytics: Concepts, Types and Technologies*', 5:9 International Journal of Research and Engineering (2018) 524–528.

Rieu-Clarke, A., et al., *Transboundary Water Governance and Climate Change Adaptation: International Law, Policy Guidelines and Best Practice Application* (Paris: United Nations Educational, Scientific and Cultural Organization, 2015).

Rieu-Clarke, A., Allan, A., & Hendry, S., (eds), *Routledge Handbook of Water Law and Policy* (Abingdon: Routledge, 2017).

Ramotswa Information Management System (RIMS), '*Ramotswa Information Management System*', at https://www.un-igrac.org/sites/default/files/resources/files/RIMS%20final%20version.pdf, last accessed 14 June 2021.

Rodrik, D., '*Understanding South Africa's Economic Puzzles*', 16:4 Economics of Transitions (2008) 769–797.

Rubinfeld, D. L., & Gal, M. S., '*Access Barriers to Big Data*', 59, Arizona Law Review (2017) 339–381.

Sachwani, K., '*Financing the Water Sector – An Alternate Approach*', 26 March 2020, at https://www.2030wrg.org/financing-the-water-sector-an-alternate-approach/, last accessed 20 January 2020.

SADC-GMI, IGRAC, IGS, *SADC Framework for Groundwater Data Collection and Management* (SADC-GMI Report, Bloemfontein, South Africa, 2019).

SADC-GMI, *Framework for Institutionalising Groundwater Management in the SADC Region* (SADC GMI Report, Bloemfontein, South Africa, 2019).

Salman, S. M. A., '*Legal Regime for Use and Protection of International Watercourses in the Southern African Region: Evolution and Context*', 41:4, Natural Resources Journal (2001) 981–1022.

Salman, S. M. A., '*Introductory Note to SADC: Revised Protocol on Shared Watercourses in the Southern African Development Community*', 40:2, International Legal Materials (2001) 317–319.

Salman, S. M. A., '*Shared Watercourses in the Southern African Development Community: Challenges and Opportunities*', 6:1, Water Policy (2004) 25–38.

Salman, S. M. A., '*The Helsinki Rules, the UN Watercourses Convention and the Berlin Rules: Perspectives on International Water Law*', 23:4 International Journal of Water Resources Development (2007) 625–640.

Salman, S. M. A., '*The Grand Ethiopian Renaissance Dam: The Road to the Declaration of Principles and the Khartoum Document*', 41:4, Water International (2016) 512–527.

Salman, S. M. A., '*Notification Concerning Planned Measures on Shared Watercourses: Synergies between the Watercourses Convention and the World Bank Policies and Practice*' (Leiden: Brill, 2019).

Salman, S. M. A., '*Equitable and Reasonable Utilization and the Obligation Against Causing Significant Harm – Are they Reconcilable?*', 115, American Journal of International Law (2021) 183–188.

Sánchez, A., '*1944 Water Treaty Between Mexico and the United States: Present Situation and Future Potential*', 18:36 Frontera Norte (2006) 125–144.

Sarfaty, G., '*Can Big Data Revolutionize International Human Rights Law?*', 39:1, University of Pennsylvania Journal of International Law (2017) 73–101.

Sarker, Md. N. I., et al., '*Disaster Resilience through Big Data: Way to Environmental Sustainability*', 51 International Journal of Disaster Risk Reduction (2020).

Sarni, W., '*Democratized, Distributed and Digital: 2019 Will Be Transformative for Water*', 3 January 2019, at https://www.greenbiz.com/article/democratized-distributed-and-digital-2019-will-be-transformative-water, last accessed 20 January 2020.

Schillinger, J., et al., '*Water in War: Understanding the Impacts of Armed Conflict on Water Resources and their Management*', 7:6, WIREs Water (2020) 1–19.

Schmeier, S., '*International Water Law Principles in Negotiations and Water Diplomacy*', 115, American Journal of International Law (2021) 173–177.

Schmidt, L., et al., '*Challenges in Applying Machine Learning Models for Hydrological Inference: A Case Study for Flooding Events Across Germany*', 56:5, Water Resources Research (2020) 1–10.

Schumann, A., *Using Outcome Indicators to Improve Policies: Methods, Design Strategies and Implementation* (Paris: OECD Regional Development Working Papers 2016/02).

Sebestyén, V., Czvetkó, T., & Abonyi, J., '*The Applicability of Big Data in Climate Change Research: The Importance of System of Systems Thinking*', 9, Frontiers in Environmental Science (2021) 1–26.

Serban, P., & Damian, R. M., '*Romania*', in J. Ganoulis, I. L. Murphy & M. Brilly (eds), *Transboundary Water Resources in the Balkans: Initiating a Sustainable Co-Operative Network* (Leiden: Kluwer Academic Publishers, 2000) 137–152.

Sieber, R. E., & Johnson, P. A., '*Civic Open Data at a Crossroads: Dominant Models and Current Challenges*', 32:3, Government Information Quarterly (2015) 308–315.

Sindico, F., & Pateiro, L. M., '*The Interplay between the UN Watercourses Convention and the Law on Transboundary Aquifers (Article 2)*', in L. B. de Chazournes et al. (eds), *The UN Convention on the Law of the Non-navigational Uses of International Watercourses: A Commentary* (Oxford: Oxford University Press, 2018) 383–408.

Sindico, F., *International Law and Transboundary Aquifers* (Cheltenham: Edward Elgar Publishing, 2020).

Sivinski, G., Okuliar, A., & Kjolbye, L., '*Is Big Data a Big Deal? A Competition Law Approach to Big Data*', 13:2/3 European Competition Journal (2017) 199–227.

Soille, P., Loekken, S., & Albani, S., '*Preface*', in P. Soille, S. Loekken & S. Albani (eds), *Proceedings of the 2019 Conference on Big Data from Space (BiDS'19): Turning Data into Insights* (Munich: Joint Research Centre, 19–21 February 2019).

Soranno, P. A., et al., '*Building a Multi-scaled Geospatial Temporal Ecology Database from Disparate Data Sources: Fostering Open Science and Data Reuse*', 4:28, Giga Science (2015) 1–15.

Southern African Development Community, '*Guidelines for Strengthening River Basin Organisations*', 2010, at https://www.sadc.int/files/4013/5333/8260/SADC_guideline_environment.pdf, last accessed 14 June 2021.

Southern African Development Community, '*Regional Awareness and Communication Strategy for the SADC Water Sector*', May 2008, at https://www.sadc.int/files/2213/5293/3542/SADC_Communication_Strategy_for_Water_Sector_2008.pdf, last accessed 14 June 2021.

Southern African Development Community, '*Regional Water Strategy' Final Draft*, June 2006, at https://www.sadc.int/files/2513/5293/3539/Regional_Water_Strategy.pdf, last accessed 14 June 2021.

Southern African Development Community, '*Regional Water Policy*', August 2005, at https://www.sadc.int/files/1913/5292/8376/Regional_Water_Policy.pdf, last accessed 14 June 2021.

Southern African Development Community, '*SADC Guidelines for Strengthening River Basin Organisations Establishment and Development*', 2010, at https://www.sadc.int/documents-publications/show/1035, last accessed 14 June 2021.

Southern African Development Community, '*SADC Guidelines for Strengthening River Basin Organisations – Funding (2010)*', at https://www.sadc.int/documents-publications/show/1036, last accessed 14 June 2021.

Southern African Development Community, '*SADC Guidelines for Strengthening River Basin Organisations – Stakeholder Participation*', 2010, at https://www.sadc.int/documents-publications/show/1037, last accessed 14 June 2021.

Southern African Development Community, *Southern African Vision for Water Life and Environment in the 21st Century* (2009).

Southern African Development Community, '*Towards a Common Future, Water & Sanitation*', at https://www.sadc.int/themes/infrastructure/water-sanitation/, last accessed 20 January 2020.

Southern African Development Community Secretariat, *Regional Strategic Action Plan on Integrated Water Resources Development and Management Phase IV* (2016).

Southern African Development Community Secretariat, '*Regional Strategic Action Plan on Integrated Water Resources Development and Management Phase IV, RSAP IV*', Gaborone, Botswana, 2016, at https://www.sadc.int/files/9914/6823/9107/SADC_Water_4th_Regional_Strategic_Action_Plan_English_version.pdf, last accessed 14 June 2021.

Southern African Development Community, Transfrontier Conservation Areas, '*Big Data Analytics and Transboundary Water Collaboration: Call for Research Proposals*', 18 May 2018, at https://tfcaportal.org/big-data-analytics-and-transboundary-water-collaboration-call-research-proposals, last accessed 20 January 2020.

State of California, Assembly Bill No. 1755; Chapter 506: An act to add Part 4.9 (commencing with Section 12400) to Division 6 of the Water Code, relating to water data. [Approved by Governor September 23, 2016. Filed with Secretary of State September 23, 2016.] Legislative Counsel's Digest. AB 1755, Dodd. The Open and Transparent Water Data Act.

State of New Mexico, House Bill 651; 54th Legislature, First Session, 2019; Introduced by Melanie A. Stansbury and Gail Armstrong and Antoinette Sedillo Lopez.

Sterckx, A., Vargas, C. R., & Gemmell, A., *Big Data Analytics and Transboundary Water Collaboration: Theme 1: Consolidation of Data and Application of Big Data Tools to Enhance National and Transboundary Data Sets in Southern Africa that Support Decision-Making for Security of Water Resources – Deliverable 4: Groundwater Data Sharing Protocol* (UMVOTO Africa (Pty) Ltd, K5 Number: 2880, 18 December 2019).

Sterckx, A., Vargas, C. R., & Gemmell, A., *Big Data Analytics and Transboundary Water Collaboration, Theme 1: Consolidation of Data and Application of Big Data Tools to Enhance National and Transboundary Data Sets in Southern Africa that Support Decision-Making for Security of Water Resources – Deliverable 3: Quality Control System Report* (IGRAC & Umvoto, 29 November 2019).

Sterckx, A., *State of Groundwater Data Collection and Data Management in SADC Member States* (Capacity Building for Groundwater Data Collection and Management in SADC Member States (SADC-GWdataCoM project), Final Report, 31 January 2019).

Stefoudi, D., '*Space Big Data: Big Data Troubles in the Final Frontier*', 16 June 2017, at https://leidenlawblog.nl/articles/space-big-data-big-data-troubles-in-the-final-frontier, last accessed 14 June 2021.

Sun, Y., & Scanlon, B. R., '*How Can Big Data and Machine Learning Benefit Environment and Water Management: A Survey of Methods, Applications, and Future Directions*', 14(7), Environmental Research Letters (2019) 1–29.

Swatuk, L. A., '*Water Conflict and Cooperation in Southern Africa*', 2:3, WIREs Water (2015) 215–230.

Systematic, '*Water Companies Develop Joint Data Platform*', 20 April 2020, at https://systematic.com/about/news/2020/water-informatics-platform/, last accessed 20 January 2020.

Tabuchi, J. P., Blanchet, B., & Rocher, V., '*Integrated Smart Water Management of the Sanitation System of the Greater Paris Region*', 45:6, Water International (2020) 574–603.

Tan, J., & Osborne, B., '*Analysis of Big Data from Space*', XLII:2/W7, The International Archives of the Photogrammetry, Remote Sensing and Spatial Information Sciences (2017) 1367–1371.

Tanzi, A. M., '*The Inter-Relationship Between No Harm, Equitable and Reasonable Utilisation and Cooperation Under International Water Law*', 20 International Environmental Agreements: Politics, Law and Economics (2020) 619–629.

Tayia, A., '*Transboundary Water Conflict Resolution Mechanisms: Substitutes or Complements*', 11:7, Water (2019) 1337.

Tekateka, R., '*Transboundary Water Management Issues Under the NWA and Regional Collaboration, Policies and Conventions*', in B. Schreiner & R. Hassan (eds), *Transforming Water Management in South Africa: Designing and Implementing a New Policy Framework* (Dordrecht: Springer, 2011) 253–270.

'*The 3rd World Water Forum Ministerial Declaration: Message from the Lake Biwa and Yodo River Basin*', 23 March 2003, at https://www.mofa.go.jp/policy/environment/wwf/declaration.html, last accessed 14 June 2021.

The Agency for Digital Italy, '*Artificial Intelligence at the Service of Citizens*', at https://ia.italia.it/assets/whitepaper.pdf, last accessed 14 June 2021.

The Christensen Institute, '*Disruptive Innovation*', at https://www.christenseninstitute.org/disruptive-innovations/, last accessed 20 January 2020.

Thu, H. N., & Wehn, U., '*Data Sharing in International Transboundary Contexts: The Vietnamese Perspective on Data Sharing in the Lower Mekong Basin*', 536, Journal of Hydrology (2016) 351–364.

Timmerman, J. G., & Langaas, S., '*Water Information: What Is It Good For? The Use of Information in Transboundary Water Management*', 5:4, Regional Environmental Change (2005) 177–187.

Treaty on Principles Governing the Activities of States in the Exploration and Use of Outer Space, including the Moon and Other Celestial Bodies, New York, 27 January 1967, in force 10 October 1967, at https://www.unoosa.org/oosa/en/ourwork/spacelaw/treaties/introouterspacetreaty.html, last accessed 14 June 2021.

Treaty on the Development and Utilisation of the Water Resources of the Komati River Basin Between the Government of the Kingdom of Swaziland and the Government of the Republic of South Africa, 13 March 1992, at http://www.fao.org/3/w7414b/w7414b14.htm, last accessed 14 June 2021.

Treaty Between the United States of America and Mexico, Washington, DC, 3 February 1944 and Protocol, Washington, DC, 14 November 1944, at http://extwprlegs1.fao.org/docs/pdf/bi-51880.pdf, last accessed 14 June 2021.

Truby, J., '*Governing Artificial Intelligence to Benefit the UN Sustainable Development Goals*', 28:4, Sustainable Development (2020) 946–959.

Truby, J., & Brown, R., '*Human Digital Thought Clones: The Holy Grail of Artificial Intelligence for Big Data*', 30:2 Information & Communications Technology Law (2021) 140–168.

Truby, J., Brown, R. D., & Dahdal, A., '*Banking on AI: Mandating a Proactive Approach to AI Regulation in the Financial Sector*', 14:2, Law and Financial Markets Review (2020) 110–120.

Tsui, J., '*Using Big Data Technology for Environmental Protection*', 25 March 2020, at https://eponline.com/articles/2020/03/25/using-big-data-technology-for-environmental-protection.aspx, last accessed 14 June 2021.

Turton, A. R., Patrick, M. J., and Julien, F., '*Transboundary Water Resources in Southern Africa: Conflict or Cooperation?*', 49:3, Development (2006) 22–31.

Turton, A., '*The Southern African Hydropolitical Complex*', in O. Varis, C. Tortajada & A. K. Biswas et al. (eds), *Management of Transboundary Rivers and Lakes* (Dordrecht: Springer, 2008) 21–79.

Uhlir, P. F., & Schröder, P., '*Open Data for Global Science*', 6, Data Science Journal (2007) 36–53.

UNLEASH, '*The Open Water Data Index*', at https://unleash.org/solutions/open-water-data-index/, last accessed 20 January 2020.

United Nations, '*Big Data for Sustainable Development*', at https://www.un.org/en/sections/issues-depth/big-data-sustainable-development/ last accessed 20 January 2020.

United Nations, Climate Change, '*Climate Change Data Using Satellites, AI and Big Data: A Multi-Stakeholder Perspective*', 1 December 2020, at https://unfccc.int/about-us/partnerships/climate-change-data-using-satellites-ai-and-big-data-a-multi-stakeholder-perspective, last accessed 14 June 2021.

United Nations, Climate Change, '*Data for Climate Invites Researchers to Catalyze Data-Driven Climate Solutions*', 14 March 2017, at https://unfccc.int/news/data-climate-invites-researchers-catalyze-data-driven-climate-solutions, last accessed 14 June 2021.

United Nations, Department of Economic and Social Affairs, '*E-Government*', https://publicadministration.un.org/egovkb/en-us/about/unegovdd-framework, last accessed 14 June 2021.

United Nations Department of Economic and Social Affairs, '*International Decade for Action "Water for Life" 2005–2015*', at https://www.un.org/waterforlifedecade/financing.shtml, last accessed 20 January 2020.

United Nations Economic Commission for Europe, '*Protocol on Water and Health*', January 2014, at http://www.unece.org/index.php?id=35086#:~:text=The%20UNECE%20%E2%80%93%20WHO%2FEurope%20Protocol,and%20reducing%20water%2Drelated%20diseases, last accessed 20 January 2020.

United Nations Economic Commission for Europe, '*Protocol on Civil Liability and Compensation for Damage*', at https://www.unece.org/env/civil-liability/welcome.html, last accessed 20 January 2020.

United Nations Economic Commission for Europe, '*Staff of the UNECE Secretariat Servicing the Convention*', at https://unece.org/environment-policy/water/contacts/staff-unece-secretariat-servicing-convention, last accessed 20 January 2020.

United Nations Economic Commission for Europe, '*The Water Convention and the Protocol on Water and Health*', at https://unece.org/environment-policy/water, last accessed 20 January 2020.

United Nations Economic Commission for Europe, '*UN Watercourses Convention*', at https://unece.org/environment-policy/water/un-watercourses-convention, last accessed 20 January 2020.

United Nations Economic Commission for Europe, '*Financing of Transboundary Water Cooperation*', at https://unece.org/environment-policy/water/areas-work-convention/financing-transboundary-water-cooperation, last accessed 20 January 2020.

United Nations Economic Commission for Europe, '*Benefits of Transboundary Water Cooperation*', at https://unece.org/environment-policy/water/areas-work-convention/benefits-transboundary-water-cooperation, last accessed 20 January 2020.

United Nations Economic Commission for Europe, '*Water-Food-Energy-Ecosystem Nexus*', at https://unece.org/environment-policy/water/areas-work-convention/water-food-energy-ecosystem-nexus, last accessed 20 January 2020.

United Nations Economic Commission for Europe, '*Monitoring, Assessment and Information Sharing in Transboundary Basins*', at https://unece.org/environment-policy/water/monitoring-assessment-and-information-sharing-transboundary-basins, last accessed 20 January 2020.

United Nations Economic Commission for Europe, '*Water and Adaptation to Climate Change*', at https://unece.org/environment-policy/water/areas-work-convention/water-and-adaptation-climate-change, last accessed 20 January 2020.

United Nations Economic Commission for Europe, '*Water Allocation in a Transboundary Context*', at https://unece.org/environment-policy/water/areas-work-convention/water-allocation-transboundary-context, last accessed 20 January 2020.

United Nations Economic Commission for Europe, '*Water and Industrial Accidents*', at https://unece.org/environment-policy/water/areas-work-convention/water-and-industrial-accidents, last accessed 20 January 2020.

United Nations Economic Commission for Europe, '*Management of Transboundary Groundwaters*', at https://unece.org/environment-policy/water/areas-work-convention/management-transboundary-groundwaters, last accessed 20 January 2020.

United Nations Economic Commission for Europe, '*Water and Ecosystems*', at https://unece.org/environment-policy/water/areas-work-convention/water-and-ecosystems, last accessed 20 January 2020.

United Nations Economic Commission for Europe, '*Projects in the Caucasus*', at https://unece.org/environment-policy/water/areas-work-convention/projects-caucasus, last accessed 20 January 2020.

United Nations Economic Commission for Europe, '*Projects in Central Asia*', at https://unece.org/environment-policy/water/areas-work-convention/projects-central-asia, last accessed 20 January 2020.

United Nations Economic Commission for Europe, '*Projects in Eastern Europe*', at https://unece.org/environment-policy/water/areas-work-convention/projects-eastern-europe, last accessed 20 January 2020.

United Nations Economic Commission for Europe, '*Projects in South-Eastern Europe*', at https://unece.org/environment-policy/water/areas-work-convention/projects-south-eastern-europe, last accessed 20 January 2020.

United Nations Economic Commission for Europe, '*About the Protocol on Water and Health*', at https://unece.org/environment-policy/water/protocol-on-water-and-health/about-the-protocol/introduction, last accessed 20 January 2020.

United Nations Economic Commission for Europe, '*Protocol on Civil Liability*', at https://unece.org/environment-policy/water/protocol-civil-liability, last accessed 20 January 2020.

United Nations Economic Commission for Europe, '*Agricultural Quality Standards*', at https://unece.org/agricultural-quality-standards, last accessed 20 January 2020.

United Nations Economic Commission for Europe, '*Economic Cooperation and Integration*', at https://unece.org/economic-cooperation-and-integration-6, last accessed 20 January 2020.

United Nations Economic Commission for Europe, '*Regulatory Cooperation and Standardization Policies*', at https://unece.org/regulatory-cooperation-and-standardization-policies, last accessed 20 January 2020.

United Nations Economic Commission for Europe, '*Model Provisions on Transboundary Groundwaters*', at https://unece.org/environment-policy/publications/model-provisions-transboundary-groundwaters, last accessed 20 January 2020.

United Nations Economic Commission for Europe, '*Water Convention's Future Directions on Monitoring and Data Exchange in Transboundary Basins Outlined Based on Experience and Needs of over 70 Countries*', at https://unece.org/environment/news/water-conventions-future-directions-monitoring-and-data-exchange-transboundary, last accessed 14 June 2021.

United Nations Economic Commission for Europe (UNECE), Decision on International Co-operation on Shared Water Resources, (ECE/ENVWA/2) November 1982, Article 13, at https://unece.org/environment-policy/publications/ece-decision-international-co-operation-shared-water-resources, last accessed 14 June 2021.

United Nations Educational, Scientific and Cultural Organization, *Water and Climate Dialogue: Adapting to Climate Change: Why We Need Broader and 'Out-of-the-Box' Approaches* (UNESCO World Water Assessment Programme, 2011).

United Nations Environment Programme, Draft Principles of Conduct for the Guidance of States in the Conservation and Harmonious Exploitation of Natural Resources Shared by Two or More States: Report of the Intergovernmental Working Group of Experts on Natural Resources shared by two or more states on the work of its 3rd session held in Nairobi from 10 to 21 January 1977, UN Doc UNEP/GC/101, 25 February 1977.

United Nations Forum on Forests, *An Overview of International Law: Working Draft* (Ad hoc expert group on Consideration with a View to Recommending the Parameters of a Mandate for Developing a Legal Framework on All Types of Forests, New York, 7–10, September 2004, Background Document No. 3).

United Nations Framework Convention on Climate Change, New York, 9 May 1992, 1771 UNTS 107.

United Nations Framework Convention on Climate Change, '*Internship Assignment, Sustainable Development Mechanisms (SDM) Programme Regulatory Implementation Unit*', at https://unfccc.int/secretariat/employment/UserManagement/FileStorage/PN82J3XY5SBKE6HVGOUAWQIR7LT109, last accessed 14 June 2021.

United Nations Framework Convention on Climate Change, '*Internship Assignment, Sustainable Development Mechanisms (SDM) Programme Blockchain – Regulatory Development Unit (RDU)*', https://unfccc.int/secretariat/employment/UserManagement/FileStorage/PR3ADBS05MF2N47CYQZXWJIUK86E1L, last accessed 14 June 2021.

United Nations General Assembly, *Report of the United Nations Conference on Environment and Development (Rio De Janeiro, 3–14 June 1992)*, Annex I: Rio Declaration on Environment and Development, 12 August 1992, at https://www.un.org/esa/dsd/agenda21/Agenda%2021.pdf, last accessed 14 June 2021.

United Nations General Assembly, Resolution 41/65 Principles relating to remote sensing of the earth from outer space, adopted 3 December 1986.

United Nations Global Pulse, '*Big Data Climate Challenge, Climate Summit*', 2014, at https://www.unglobalpulse.org/challenges-hackathons/big-data-climate-challenge-2014/, last accessed 14 June 2021.

Universal Declaration of Human Rights, 10 December 1948 (General Assembly resolution 217 A(III)), at https://www.un.org/en/about-us/universal-declaration-of-human-rights, last accessed 20 January 2020.

United States, Congress, Senate, Committee on Environment and Public Works, Subcommittee on Water and Wildlife, '*EPA's Role in Promoting Water Use Efficiency*' (Hearing Before the Subcommittee on Water and Wildlife of the Committee on Environment and Public Works; United States Senate; One Hundred Eleventh Congress; First Session, 31 March 2008).

Villarreal, F. G., et al., '*SWM Technology for Efficient Water Management in Universities: The Case of PUMAGUA, UNAM, Mexico City*', 45:6, Water International (2020) 526–551.

Virtual Workshop, '*Advancing Protocols on Transboundary Groundwater Data Sharing in the Ramotswa Transboundary Aquifer Area (RTBAA)*', 20–21 January 2021.

Ward, F. A., '*Forging Sustainable Transboundary Water-Sharing Agreements: Barriers and Opportunities*', 15:3, Water Policy (2013) 386–417.

Water Education Foundation, '*California Water Issues Overview*', at https://www.watereducation.org/aquapedia/california-water-issues-overview, last accessed 14 June 2021.

Weiss, A., *Big Data Shocks: An Introduction to Big Data for Librarians and Information Professionals* (London: Rowman & Littlefield Publishing Group, 2018).

Widmer, T., '*How the Census Changed America*', 1 May 2019, at https://www.newyorker.com/culture/culture-desk/how-the-census-changed-america, last accessed 14 June 2021.

Williams, J., '*Stagnant Rivers: Transboundary Water Security in South and Southeast Asia*', 10:12, Water (2018) 1819.

Williams, S., '*More Than Data: Working with Big Data for Civics*', 11:1, I/S: A Journal of Law and Policy (2015) 181–199.

Winrock International, '*Using Big Data to Ensure Water Security*', at https://winrock.org/using-big-data-to-ensure-water-security/, last accessed 20 January 2020.

Woetzel, J. et al., '*How Technology is Reshaping Supply and Demand for Natural Resources*', 15 February 2017, at https://www.mckinsey.com/business-functions/

sustainability/our-insights/how-technology-is-reshaping-supply-and-demand-for-natural-resources, last accessed 20 January 2020.

Wongso, E., et al., '*A Data-Driven Framework to Characterize State-Level Water Use in the United States*', 56:9, Water Resources Research (2020) 1–17.

Wooden, A., '*Space Data: The Final Analytics Frontier*', https://www.intel.co.uk/content/www/uk/en/it-management/cloud-analytic-hub/big-data-from-satellites.html, last accessed 14 June 2021.

World Bank, '*Open Data Essentials*', at http://opendatatoolkit.worldbank.org/en/essentials.html, last accessed 14 June 2021.

World Bank, '*Botswana: Issues and Options in the Energy Sector*', 2010, at http://documents.worldbank.org/curated/en/396731468742179889/Botswana-Issues-and-options-in-the-energy-sector, last accessed 14 June 2021.

World Bank, *Water Resources Management* (Policy Paper, 1993).

World Bank Group, *Data for Better Lives* (Washington, DC: World Development Report, International Bank for Reconstruction and Development/World Bank, 2021).

World Economic Forum Water Initiative, *Water Security: The Water-Food-Energy-Climate Nexus* (Geneva: World Economic Forum, 2011).

World Health Organization, '*Weak Systems and Funding Gaps Jeopardize Drinking-Water and Sanitation in the World's Poorest Countries*', 28 August 2019, at https://www.who.int/news/item/28-08-2019-weak-systems-and-funding-gaps-jeopardize-drinking-water-and-sanitation-in-the-world%E2%80%99s-poorest-countries, last accessed 20 January 2020.

World Meteorological Organization, '*Mobilization on Water Data and Peace*', 27 November 2018, at https://hydrohub.wmo.int/en/news-events/coalition-water-data-and-peace, last accessed 14 June 2021.

World Resources Institute, '*Data Platforms*', at https://www.wri.org/resources/data-platforms, last accessed 20 January 2020.

Xu, J., & Zhang, H., '*Environmental Activism and Big Data: Building Green Social Capital in China*', 12: 8, Sustainability (2020) 3386.

ZAMCOM, '*Zambezi Water Resources Information Systems (ZAMWIS)*', at http://www.zambezicommission.org/programmes-activities/zambezi-water-resources-information-systems-zamwis, last accessed 14 June 2021.

Završnik, A. (ed.), *Big Data, Crime and Social Control* (Abingdon: Routledge, 2018).

Zeitoun, M., Goulden, M., & Tickner, D., '*Current and Future Challenges Facing Transboundary River Basin Management*', 4,5: WIREs Climate Change (2013) 331–349.

Zhang, H., & Li, M., '*China and Global Water Governance: New Developments*', in H. Zhang & M. Li (eds), *China and Transboundary Water Politics in Asia* (Oxon: Routledge, 2017) 219–236.

Zhu, T., & Ringler, C., '*Climate Change Impacts on Water Availability and Use in the Limpopo River Basin*', 4:1, Water (2012) 63–84.

Zhu, T., & Ringler, C., *Climate Change Implications for Water Resources in the Limpopo River Basin* (IFPRI Discussion Paper 0096, April 2010).

Ziganshina, D., '*Procedural System of Transboundary Water Cooperation in the Aral Sea Basin*', in A. Kibaroglu et al. (eds), *Water Law and Cooperation in the Euphrates-Tigris Region: A Comparative and Interdisciplinary Approach* (Leiden: Brill/Nijhoff, 2013) 279–302.

www.ingramcontent.com/pod-product-compliance
Lightning Source LLC
Chambersburg PA
CBHW031326230926
51848CB00001B/104
9789004507616